I Believe in The Holy Spirit

I Believe in The Holy Spirit

by

MICHAEL GREEN

HODDER AND STOUGHTON
LONDON SYDNEY AUCKLAND TORONTO

To the students of St. John's College, Nottingham, who have taught me more of what it means to live in the Spirit.

Preface

THIS BOOK IS THE first in a new series entitled *I Believe*. The aim of the series, which is being published by Hodders in England and Eerdmans in the U.S.A., is to take a fresh look at controversial areas of the Christian faith. The books are being written by Christian scholars who have one foot firmly placed in the Bible, and the other foot equally firmly placed in the contemporary scene. Each writer will seek to give an overall biblical interpretation of his subject, but to do so in such a way as to be of practical value to modern Christians who may be perplexed by controversy over some area of the subject. Thus in this particular book, whilst trying to present as fully and clearly as space and my understanding allow, the teaching of the Scriptures about the Holy Spirit, I should have been failing to meet the aim of the series if I had not had a good deal to say about the controversial issues of the baptism, the gifts, and the fullness of the Holy Spirit.

An international, trans-cultural, and interconfessional team of writers have been commissioned to take part in this series. They are men who are scholars in their own right, but have agreed to forgo, to a large extent, that apparatus of scholarship, the endless quotation of other writers and the dreary mileage of footnote, which tends to confuse and discourage the general reader. For the general reader is very much in mind in this series. We want it to be of service to thoughtful Christians who desire to know what the biblical material has to say on controverted issues of the day. Therefore the style adopted is comparatively light, though the content of the series is, I hope, of some weight. But it seems to me quite unnecessary for scholars to use abstruse technical jargon, on the one hand, and to parade in footnotes all the secondary sources they have consulted, on the other. What is important is that the author should so know his way round his chosen subject that he would be prepared, if challenged, to support his statements in the book by recourse to the appropriate literature of the subject.

I have chosen to write on the Holy Spirit myself for this

reason. During the past fifteen years I have had the privilege of living in a Christian community where the charismatic question has been a very live issue, and where "charismatic" and "non-charismatic" Christians have lived together in a high degree of mutual love and trust. It cannot be denied that the charismatic movement has in places brought division and suspicion. It is my conviction, and my experience, that this need not be so, and that the Spirit of unity would have it otherwise. I therefore offer this book in the hope that it may embody a healing and a catholic perspective on this most exciting and disturbing movement of our times.

I want to thank Edward England of Hodders for his warm and constant encouragement over the whole series. He, Professor G. W. H. Lampe, and the Revd. D. C. K. Watson, Vicar of St. Cuthbert's, York, have all read the manuscript and made many most helpful corrections and suggestions. And as all three are particularly busy men I want to put on record my deep gratitude to them. Thanks, too, are due to the Governors of St. John's College, Nottingham, for allowing me a sabbatical term in the summer of 1973, and to the Vice-Principal, the Revd. J. W. Charley and the rest of the staff team here who generously did my work for me in my absence. In addition, I want to thank the many Christians of different outlooks and affiliations who have taught me by their lives and lips, and some dynamic congregations who have shown me by their church fellowships, a little more of what life in the Spirit can mean. But most of all, thank God for making his Holy Spirit available to us!

PENTECOST, 1974

MICHAEL GREEN,
ST. JOHN'S COLLEGE,
NOTTINGHAM

Contents

Contents

CHAPTER I

The Holy Spirit

The Spirit: unknown—or domesticated?

THE CHRISTIAN CHURCH has always had a good many professing members who know about as much about the Holy Spirit in their experience as those disciples at Ephesus who were asked by Paul, "Did you receive the Holy Spirit when you believed?" and replied, "No, we have never even heard that there is a Holy Spirit" (Acts 19: 2). Of course, this group at Ephesus must have heard something about the Holy Spirit if they listened at all attentively to John the Baptist, but they did not realise that the promised Spirit was available for them; that he could make a difference to their lives. Many churchmen of all denominations have been in the same state. They have heard in a vague way about the Holy Spirit, but have either put it all down to typical ecclesiastical in-talk, or assumed that it was not intended for ordinary folk like themselves. For all practical purposes, the Holy Spirit could be discounted. Christianity was a matter of churchgoing, of soldiering on and trying to do one's best, and of believing in the existence of God and the historical life and death of Jesus (even if his deity and his resurrection were not to be taken too seriously).

On the other hand, there have always been people in the Christian Church who were very sure about the Holy Spirit. It was simple. He was the divine backer of their particular emphasis in theology and practice. A good deal has been written in recent years about Primitive Catholicism, the tendency apparent even within the New Testament period itself to domesticate the Holy Spirit, to make him the perquisite of the Church, at the beck and call of baptising priest or ordaining bishop. The man who is validly baptised or rightly instituted into office in the Church is assured that he has the Holy Spirit. It is not only Catholic Christendom which has been guilty of seeking to domesticate the Holy Spirit in this way. Protestants have been no less anxious to do so, for the Holy Spirit is a disturbing influence. Let him therefore be paid lip service, but for all practical purposes be shut up in the Bible where he can do no harm. Let his presence attend the confessional statement of our particular brand of Protestantism. Let the bizarre and miraculous elements which the New Testament documents narrate about his activity be relegated to those far-off apostolic days: it would be very embarrassing and doctrinally untidy if the Holy Spirit were to speak to men today, or to enable miracles to be performed and men to speak in tongues not their own. The Bible, accordingly, is the safest place for the Spirit. That is where he belongs; not in the hurly-burly of real life.

The Spirit: in the human spirit—and in other faiths?

There was at least this to be said for the main line Catholic and Protestant positions. They were comprehensible and clear, if narrow and restrictive. However, since the growth of biblical criticism in the last two centuries, and the revolt against authoritarianism in the past thirty years, there has been a marked tendency to seek the Holy Spirit in other quarters. Since we can no longer be shackled by the authoritarianism of a discredited Bible and a crumbling Papacy, it is to the human spirit that we must look for inspiration. To begin with, liberal theologians thought of the Holy Spirit of God as speaking to contemporary man through those elements in Bible or Church tradition which accorded best with their own enlightened insights. Pope and Bible were dethroned, to make way for the Professor of Theology. But unfortunately he did not last very long, and his views were soon considered out of date or positively erroneous by his successors. Why, then, should it be assumed that the Holy Spirit was particularly active in professors? Surely this was a hang-over from the scholasticism of an infallible Bible and the authoritarianism of an ecclesiastical teaching office? Perhaps it would be better to seek the contemporary witness of the Spirit in ecumenical discussions, where all could contribute their special insight and the Holy Spirit would, doubtless, be found along with the majority of the votes at the end of the day? I have been to enough ecclesiastical congresses which have claimed that the voice of the Holy Spirit lay behind the votes of the big battalions to be sickened by it. It was not a habit of the Holy Spirit in biblical times to be identified with the views of the majority!

Often we are invited to take a broader view of the whole scene: let us suppose that we find the Holy Spirit at work in Buddhism and Communism, in humanism and atheism. Is it to the Holy Spirit, then, that I must assign Buddhism's denial of the possibility of forgiveness, or Communism's cavalier attitude to truth and human life, or the self-satisfied man-centredness of much contemporary humanism? This broad interpretation of the person and work of the Holy Spirit is somewhat confusing, to say the least. The whole subject bristles with problems.

The charismatic Spirit?

Is it surprising that against a background as inchoate as this a new and virile movement should have arisen, central to whose belief is the power and reality of the Holy Spirit? At the beginning of this century there were no Pentecostals. Now the number must be about 20 million, drawn from almost every nation on earth, and almost every denomination too. The characteristic emphases of this movement can be seen from glancing at some of the book titles published on the subject in recent years. It is, first and foremost *The Haven of the Masses*, a movement of the people; neither dominated by its ministry, nor dependent on foreign indoctrination. *They speak with other tongues*, which is embarrassing and distasteful to many non-members of the Pentecostal scene. The claim that they and they alone have *The Baptism with the Holy Spirit*, in contrast to water baptism which marks the rest of Christendom, and the conversion which figures as largely in Evangelical theology as does confirmation in Catholic. *As at the Beginning* the gifts of Pentecost have been renewed to a parched Church, and *It can happen to Anybody*. For the church of God's frozen people this is the *Pathway to Power;* individual and church alike are *Gathered for Power. The Third Force* has come into the Christian spectrum, and it is a force to be reckoned with. Healings, exorcisms, tongues, prophecy are merely the spectacular tip of the iceberg, the heart of which is a living, loving, believing Christian fellowship.

What, then, in the face of these many and conflicting voices, is the Christian to make of the Holy Spirit? Where shall we begin? It is important to remember that we are mere men, talking about God. And it is not possible for us to know anything at all about him unless he is generous enough to disclose himself. Another book in this series is tackling the question of revelation; suffice it to say at this point that without revelation we cannot say anything about the Lord who is Spirit. St. Paul makes this very clear. "What person can know a man's thoughts", he asks, "except the spirit of the man which is in him? So also no one comprehends the thoughts of God except the Spirit of God" (1 Corinthians 2: 11). In other words, it takes God to reveal God. And Paul claims that God has done so, through the Spirit interpreting spiritual truths to men who possess the Spirit. Accordingly, the purpose of this book is to examine what the Scriptures, particularly in the fuller light afforded by the New Testament, have to teach about the Holy Spirit, and to relate their message to our own situation.

Theologians often distinguish between God as he is in himself, and God as he has revealed himself to us. It seems to me to be both useless and presumptuous to attempt to pierce the incognito of the essential Godhead. It is quite enough for me to try to grasp the way in which God has disclosed himself to us. And without too much distortion, you could say that it is a drama in three acts.

Act One: on from Eden

Act One is a long one. It lasts from the beginning of the world's history until the coming of Jesus Christ. It comprises the whole history of the people of Israel until the coming of the Messiah. The Law, the Prophets and the Writings (the three divisions of the Old Testament Scriptures) combine to teach one basic lesson. It was this. There is one God, and no runners up. That is the lesson Abraham learnt in polytheistic Ur of the Chaldees. It had to be learnt time and again by his descendents throughout the succeeding twenty centuries. Yahweh, the God of Israel, was the only deity. The other gods of the heathen were idols (literally "nothings" in Hebrew). The downtrodden captives in Egypt at the time of the Exodus came to realise that Yahweh, the only self-existent one (Exodus 3: 14), was a mighty deliverer who could be trusted. The Mosaic Law underlines the fact that their whole social, religious and daily life must be governed by loyalty to that one God who brought them out of the land of Egypt, out of the house of bondage. They forgot the message times without number. The Old Testament records them running after false gods, the gods of the nations round about them, whenever opportunity offered. An Elijah has to drag them back from the worship of the heathen fertility gods introduced by Jezebel. A Hosea has to recall them to Yahweh, their first love, when they have gone and committed adultery, like Hosea's own wife, with some other "Lord" on whom they have lavished their worship and devotion. Jeremiah and Isaiah never tire of reminding the people that there is one God who can save his people, and that all other refuges are in vain. At last the lesson got home, and in the last two centuries before Christ, the Jewish people gave signal proof of their loyalty to the one God. Under the Maccabeans they withstood the attempts of Antiochus to overcome their country and shatter their religion. Later, under Roman occupation, they maintained with unbreakable courage their strict monotheism; so much so that the Roman governor did not even dare to bring his standards into Jerusalem lest the medallions on them depicting the emperor should be thought to infringe the Second Commandment. Roman coinage struck in Palestine carried no image of the emperor. Indeed, when Pilate produced a coin which had an augur's staff on its obverse, it could well have cost him his job; for an augur's staff smelt of pagan religion, and that could not be tolerated in Judea. Finally, as everyone knows, Jewish faith in the one God who alone was fit to govern Israel led to the Great Revolt of A.D. 66–70. It culminated in the capture of Jerusalem, and the destruction of that temple whose empty Holy of Holies eloquently proclaimed the greatness of God whose name was too holy to mention and whose nature was too inscrutable to copy by any image. Act One was complete. Israel knew beyond a shadow of doubt that there was one God, the Creator of the whole world, who had disclosed himself in a special way to their nation.

Act Two: on from Bethlehem

But this one who could not be named with impunity, who could not be copied without distortion, still remained very much beyond our ken. In Act Two God comes in person to make himself known. After years of scrutinising Jesus of Nazareth, of listening to his teaching, of watching his character, of observing his miracles, after witnessing that shameful death and experiencing that glorious resurrection, the men who had known him best were sure of it. This man had brought God into focus.

"God, who spoke of old in many and varied ways to our

fathers through the prophets, has in these last days spoken to
us in a Son. Him he has appointed the heir of all things.
Through him he created the worlds. He reflects the glory of
God, and bears the very stamp of his nature, upholding the
universe by the word of his power."

"In him dwells all the fulness of the godhead in bodily
form."

"He is the image of the invisible God, the firstborn of all
creation; for in him all things were created, in heaven and on
earth . . . all things were created in him and for him. His is
the priority over everything, and in him all things hold
together."

"No man has ever seen God; the only Son, himself God,
who is in the bosom of the Father, he has made him known."

In words like these Paul, John and the writer of the Epistle
to the Hebrews struggle to express the unheard-of claim, that
they themselves would have deemed blasphemous but for the
irrefragable evidence of the life, death and resurrection of
Jesus, that God had indeed visited and redeemed his people.
The one it was unlawful to name had taken the name of
"Emmanuel" ("God with us") and "Jesus" ("God saves").
He had done just that; lived with them, and saved them from
a doom and and a captivity worse than that which gripped
their forefathers in Pharaoh's Egypt. They could no longer
plead ignorance of God. He had become one of them, their
contemporary. In Jesus all of God that could take on human
expression had been expressed. God, they had come to see, was
Christlike. Act Two was complete. The one true God was not
only over them as their Creator. He was alongside them, to
reveal himself to them in human terms, and to rescue them
from the self-induced estrangement into which they had fallen.

Act Three: on from Pentecost

Act Three began at Pentecost, and it has not ended. Nor will
it end until the completion of God's purposes for this world at
the return of Christ. God the Creator, the God who had come
alongside men in Jesus, now made himself available to come
within their very personalities. It is inconceivable that anyone
sat down to think out any doctrine so intrinsically improbable
as the Trinity. It was forced upon them by experience.
Convinced as they were of the unity and uniqueness of God,
the disciples became confident that he was present in Jesus.
After Pentecost, they became assured that their experience of

God's activity in their midst and in their mission was nothing less than the continued work and presence of Jesus among them. Accordingly, they did not shrink from speaking indifferently of "the Spirit of God" and "the Spirit of Jesus" or "the Spirit of Christ". Jesus of Nazareth was now the prism through which the various shafts of light in the Old Testament about the Spirit became luminous and in focus to them.

An analogy such as I have just drawn in this three act drama of salvation, can be dangerously misleading. It could lead to what the theologians have called "Modalism", as though God disclosed himself in these three successive modes or forms—forms which do not correspond to any differences in his own nature, but are merely adopted for our benefit. I do not think that this will do. The ministry of Jesus provides sufficient refutation. On the one hand he is conceived and baptised by the Holy Spirit, and promises the gift of that Spirit to his followers after his death. On the other hand, he clearly looks to God as his Father, and into this Father's hand he commits his spirit when he dies. There is, in other words, a double overlap in the ministry of Jesus, which prevents us from assuming that Father, Son and Spirit are three moulds into which the Deity pours himself at different periods in the history of salvation.

Despite the dangers, however, this three act drama can provide a useful provisional approach to our understanding of the person and work of the Holy Spirit, and is perhaps worth investigating in greater detail. So in the next chapter I shall look at the main strands of teaching in the Old Testament about the Holy Spirit, in the light of fuller perspective brought about by Jesus, the supreme bearer of the Spirit.

The Spirit in the Old Testament

Spirit of God

THE WORD USED for the Spirit of God in both Hebrew and Greek is highly significant. *Ruach* in Hebrew and *Pneuma* in Greek have the three main meanings of "wind", "breath" and "spirit". The Spirit of God is his life-giving breath without which man remains spiritually inert. It is his mysterious wind, which man cannot get under his own tidy control: as Nicodemus was reminded by Jesus, "The wind (*pneuma*) blows where it will, and you hear its sound but you do not know where it comes from or where it is going. So it is with every one who is born of the Spirit (*pneuma*)" (John 3: 8). As well as being mysterious the wind is powerful: it was by a mighty wind that God assuaged the waters of the Flood (Genesis 8: 1), and by a wind that he caused the waters to recede before Israel at the Exodus (Exodus 14: 21). Those twin notions of power and mystery mark much of the teaching of Old and New Testaments alike when they treat of the Spirit of God.

This brings us up short at the outset of our study. The Spirit of God in the Bible is no natural quality of man. It is no hidden recess within our bodies. For one thing, the Hebrews did not divide man up into spirit, mind and body as we tend to do: they thought of him as a single entity, an animated body, a living person. For another, they had a perfectly good word to describe our human vitality, the quality that marks off a living person from a dead one: and that was *nephesh*. Only comparatively rarely is this word brought into contact with *ruach*, though we cannot expect, and do not find complete consistency. It is true that *ruach* is used of man's spirit in a number of ways. It is used in the story of the Flood, for instance, to denote "the breath of life" (Genesis 6: 17) which God gives — and takes back again. It is used to denote full vitality, real spirited living;

contrast the deflation of the Queen of Sheba when she saw all Solomon's treasure—"there was no more *ruach* left in her" (1 Kings 10: 5). It comes to mean the seat of the emotions, intellect, and will—particularly often applied to the governing impulse in a man's life (e.g. Proverbs 25: 28, Psalm 32: 2, Numbers 14: 24). Occasionally, therefore, a man's *ruach* "spirit" seems to be equated with his *nephesh*, his "life", but this is by no means the normal usage. *Ruach* and *nephesh* can be thought of as each having their own circle of meaning. Occasionally the circumferences of those circles intersect, but the main content of each is clear. *Nephesh* is natural; it belongs to man. *Ruach* is supernatural: it belongs to God. Though *ruach* may be found in man, it is always so to speak, on loan, and not a possession; a resident alien, not a native.

And just as the Spirit cannot be equated with any property in man, equally it cannot be regarded as the stuff of which the world is made, the comprehensive life principle which integrates the universe, as the Stoics maintained—a view which, through pagan philosophical influence, crept into the intertestamental books of the Apocrypha. No, the Old Testament insists that this powerful, mysterious Spirit belongs to God, and to God alone. It is essentially the personal God, Yahweh, in action. It is therefore to the teaching of the Old Testament about the Spirit of the Lord, the *ruach adonai* that we shall be looking in order to get the background for the Christian doctrine of the Holy Spirit.

Invading Spirit

Perhaps the first thing that strikes us as we come to the Old Testament is the tremendous emphasis on the Spirit of God as a violent, invading force. It is like the wind that hurtled across the desert or whistled through the cedars or rushed down the wadis. "The grass withers, the flower fades when the *ruach adonai* blows upon it. Surely the people is grass", cried Isaiah (40: 7), and that is typical. There is a whole host of places where we are told that God's action is like the wind, strong, boisterous, uncontrollable. He sends the wind. He controls it. He causes it to cease.

In speaking of the "Spirit of the Lord" the Old Testament writers significantly retain this emphasis on God's violent invasion from outside our experience, disturbing and mysterious like the wind. It is their way of stressing that the Beyond has come into our midst, and we can neither organise nor domesticate him. This comes out very strongly in the Book of Judges. The oppressed people of Israel cry to the Lord to send them deliverance. His response is to "raise up a deliverer for the people, Othniel. The Spirit of the Lord came upon him; he judged Israel; he went out to war; and his hand prevailed." (Judges 3: 9, 10). Again, Gideon was a very ordinary man until "the Spirit of the Lord took possession of him" (Judges 6: 34). Then he became instrumental in a signal deliverance for his country. It was most noticeable in the case of that fabulous strong man, Samson. It was when "the Spirit of the Lord came mightily upon him", that "he tore a lion asunder as one tears a kid" (Judges 14: 6). This strength which enabled him to do so much for his country against the Philistine overlords was not his own. He was sharply reminded of that when he disobeyed God at Delilah's instigation, and woke up to find that "the Lord had left him" (Judges 16: 20). Sometimes the violent power of the Spirit is seen in almost physical terms, as when the Spirit of the Lord entered into Ezekiel and set him on his feet, or lifted him up, or brought him out into the valley (Ezekiel 2: 2, 3: 12, 37: 1).

I believe we have to take this aspect of the Spirit very seriously today. We have grown used to expecting the Spirit of God to speak in a gentle whisper, not a roaring wind. We have sought him in the promptings of our hearts or the resolutions of our committees. We are in danger of forgetting that it is God we are talking about: the God who created us, the God who sustains us and has sovereign rights over us. This God can and does break in to human life, and sometimes he does it through the violent, the unexpected, the alien. It was this same Spirit that drove Jesus off into the desert to be tempted after his baptism, that pioneered the mission of the early Church often in the most bizarre, unexpected and "unorthodox" ways; that gripped a man like Philip, removed him from a flourishing evangelistic campaign in Samaria and drove him into the desert—because there was one man who needed his help. When that help was given "the Spirit of the Lord caught up Philip", just like Ezekiel long before him, and "Philip was found at Azotus, and passing on he preached the gospel" (Acts 8: 26, 39, 40). I met a girl the other day who awoke to find herself gripped by the Spirit of God at 2 a.m. She was a cripple, and at once her hip was cured—a hip, incidentally, that had defied the efforts of the country's best doctors—and she found herself praising God in tongues. Now she is doing a remarkably useful piece of Christian service.

I think of another man, devious, self centred, arrogant, who went to criticise a charismatic meeting, but found himself seized with unaccountable trembling, tears, and a deep meeting with God, the God of the unexpected. The wind of God certainly blew on that man, Christian though he already was; he has not become a paragon of virtue overnight, but the manifest change in his disposition and attitudes cannot be denied. Perhaps this surrender to the invading power of God's Spirit, this willingness for him to take us and break us and use us, is one of the prime lessons which the charismatic movement throughout the Churches is teaching us at the present time. Some years ago Bishop Joe Fison expressed it well in his book about the Spirit, *Fire upon the Earth* (p. 9):

> Of course, this uprush of the primitive, the elemental and the unconscious, this "possession" by the Spirit, is not the be-all and end-all of the biblical evidence for the doctrine of the Holy Spirit. But it is the startingpoint of this doctrine, and only if we are prepared to start where the Bible starts are we likely to know in experience anything of the higher reaches of the Spirit's work. We cannot jump the queue.

Spirit of Prophecy

Closely allied to this emphasis on the "otherness" of the Spirit of God is the stress throughout the Old Testament on his inspiration of prophecy. It is one of the major themes of Scripture. This God who is beyond us and invades our world does not do so in order to terrify, but to communicate. The wind or Spirit of the Lord is indeed power, but it is morally defined power, designed to communicate the will of God and bring his creation into conformity with it. That is why, I think, there is a frequent link in the Bible between "the Spirit of the Lord" and "the Word of the Lord". The breath of God and the message of God cannot be divorced. Time and again, therefore, in the parallelism of Hebrew poetry *dabar* (word) and *ruach* (spirit) go hand in hand. Thus

> By the word of the Lord were the heavens made and all the host of them by the breath of his mouth (Psalm 33: 6).

or

> The Spirit of the Lord speaks by me, his word is upon my tongue (2 Samuel 23: 2).

When Saul disobeys God, and is rejected as king over Israel, we read, "You have rejected the word of the Lord", and consequently, in judgment, "the Spirit of the Lord departed from Saul" (1 Samuel 15: 26, 16: 14). John Taylor, in his moving and perceptive book *The Go-Between God*, has pointed out the importance of this link between the Spirit with all his undifferentiated power, and the Word, with all its particularity of meaning. By distinguishing too sharply between the divine Word and the divine Spirit the Church has lost a most important biblical perspective. Certainly that link is strong and clear in the Old Testament Scriptures. When the Spirit comes upon a man, he communicates some message from God. This message may take strange, mysterious forms. It may come through dreams, as when Joseph was able to recall and interpret Pharaoh's dreams through the Spirit of God within him (Genesis 41: 38f). It may come through visions. Men like Abraham (Genesis 15: 1), Jacob (Genesis 46: 2), Ezekiel (1: 1) and Daniel (1: 17, 4: 5, 7: 7) grasped something of the purposes of God in a vision. It may come through dance: when the Spirit of the Lord came upon King Saul he danced like a dervish. But even this medium was no mere excitement, as God broke in from the beyond and seized him: there was communication. He not only prophesied, but he became in some unspecified sense "a different man" (1 Samuel 10: 7–13). The later prophets laid less emphasis on ecstasy; Amos protests that he is no prophet in the ecstatic sense, such as were to be found in attendance at the sanctuaries of his day. "I am no prophet, nor a prophet's son; I am a herdsman, and the Lord took me from following the flock." Nevertheless he is quite clear that God has inspired his message. "The Lord said to me, 'Go, prophesy to my people, Israel'. Now therefore, hear the word of the Lord . . ." (Amos 7: 14–16). It is not ecstasy that marks prophecy, but meeting with God, so that God speaks through the prophet. Amos himself puts the matter with telling simplicity:

The lion has roared: who will not fear?
The Lord has spoken: who can but prophesy?

(Amos 3:8)

An early prophet like David claims that when he delivers his oracles no less than "the Spirit of the Lord speaks" (2 Samuel 23: 2). In the eighth century B.C. Hosea describes the prophet as supremely "the man of the Spirit" (9:7), and

Micah spells it out more fully with his claim, over against the false prophets who get no word from God:

> But as for me, I am filled with power,
> With the Spirit of the Lord,
> And with justice and might,
> To declare to Jacob his transgression
> And to Israel his sin.
>
> (Micah 3: 8)

Isaiah of Babylon, in a later age, knows that his message is true, because "The Lord God has sent me and his Spirit" (48: 16). Zechariah, after the Return from Babylon, has no doubt that it is through the Spirit of the Lord that God has sent "the law and the words" through the prophets (Zechariah 7: 12).

The point does not need labouring. When a man prophesies, it is because the Spirit of the Lord comes upon him and communicates a message through him. But there are several aspects of this prophetic Spirit that are specially important, and they are taken up in the New Testament.

Spirit and Servant

The Spirit of the Lord was promised to the Servant of Yahweh.

> Behold, my servant, whom I uphold,
> My chosen, in whom my soul delights,
> I have put my Spirit upon him,
> He will bring forth justice to the nations.
>
> (Isaiah 42: 1)

Just as the will of God cannot be known without the revelation of the Spirit, so the service of God cannot be carried through without the equipment of that same Spirit. It is only through God's revelation that we can know him. It is only through his power that we can serve him. Isaiah 61: 1 takes up this theme, and the prophet cries:

> The Spirit of the Lord God is upon me
> Because the Lord has anointed me
> To bring good tidings to the afflicted;

He has sent me to bind up the brokenhearted,
To proclaim liberty to the captives,
And the opening of prison to those who are bound;
To proclaim the year of the Lord's favour . . .

These prophetic visions of the Spirit coming upon the Servant
of Yahweh and upon his anointed prophet were specifically
claimed by Jesus. The first comes at his baptism, the second
at the first sermon he preached (Mark 1: 11, Luke 4: 18).
It is not easy to exaggerate their significance. As *the* prophet
Jesus could say with authority, "Amen, amen I say unto you",
and claim to speak final truth about God, "We speak of what
we know, and bear witness of what we have seen" (John 3: 11).
As *the* Servant of Yahweh, Jesus treads the path of suffering
and obedience right the way to Calvary: so much so that Peter
could describe his suffering and death in terms culled from the
famous prophecy of the Suffering Servant in Isaiah:

He committed no sin; no guile was found on his lips.
When he was reviled, he did not revile in return;
When he suffered he did not threaten
But trusted to him who judges justly.
He himself bore our sins in his body on the tree,
That we might die to sin and live to righteousness.
By his wounds you have been healed.
(1 Peter 2: 22ff)

Spirit and King

There is another area in which Jesus strikingly fulfilled one
of the main strands of Old Testament teaching about the Spirit.
God had given his Spirit to his anointed king in order to equip
him for his leadership of the people. Saul is the classic example.
Samuel anoints him king: he is promised, and receives, the
power of the Spirit of God upon him (1 Samuel 10: 1, 6).
Subsequently he disobeys God disastrously, and has to be set
aside as king in favour of David. Samuel anoints David, and
we read that "the Spirit of the Lord came mightily (literally
'leaped') upon David from that day forward" (1 Samuel 16:13).
What happened to Saul, then? "The Spirit of the Lord
departed from Saul", and from now on we read that an evil or
distressed *ruach elohim* troubled him. The Spirit of the Lord,
the *ruach adonai* passes to David to equip him for his princely
service. The profane word *elohim* (which need not necessarily

refer to Yahweh) is now used to describe Saul's fits of mania and ecstasy.

Unfortunately the kings of Israel were a pretty disappointing lot, and most of them showed little sign of the presence of the Lord the Spirit in their lives and reigns. However the link was not lost, and the hope grew in Israel that one day God would raise up a prince of the Davidic line for whom the Spirit would be no passing enduement, to be bestowed and withdrawn as he joined his predecessors in disobedience. Instead, the Spirit of the Lord would rest and remain on such a man. Hence the idyllic dream of Isaiah 11: 1ff:

There shall come forth a shoot from the stump of Jesse,
And a branch shall grow out of his roots.
And the Spirit of the Lord shall rest upon him,
The Spirit of wisdom and understanding,
The Spirit of counsel and might,
The Spirit of knowledge and the fear of the Lord.

This hope lived on in Judaism. In the intertestamental days we read of the Messiah, "God will make him mighty in the Holy Spirit" (*Psalms of Solomon* 17:37), and in the Targum or Commentary on Isaiah 42: 1, the Servant is seen as the Messiah, and God says of him, "I will cause my Holy Spirit to rest on him". It is therefore extremely significant that we read of Jesus in the New Testament that the Spirit descends and remains on him (John 1: 32) and that God did not give his Spirit by measure or sparingly to him (John 3: 24). In Jesus we have the final embodiment of God's ideal ruler, and he is fully equipped with an unwithdrawn endowment of the Holy Spirit.

Spirit and People

There was a further dimension to this prophetic hope. On the whole, you had to be someone rather special in Old Testament days to have the Spirit of God. A prophet, a national leader, a king, perhaps some specially wise man (Proverbs 1: 23) or artistic person (Exodus 31: 3) — in which case you would be beautifying the Lord's Tent of Meeting, or enunciating the Lord's wisdom. But the Spirit of God was not for every Tom, Dick and Harry. To be sure, there were promises in a very general sense that "My Spirit abides with you: fear not" (Haggai 2: 5), but this was an assurance to the people as a whole, not a promise to the individual. The gift of God's Spirit was on the whole to special people for special tasks. It was not generally available, nor was it necessarily permanent. Many a godly Jew must have felt what a wonderful thing it would be if Moses' longing could be fulfilled, "Would that all the Lord's people were prophets, that the Lord would put his Spirit upon them" (Numbers 11: 29): and that is just what the prophets were led by God to foretell for the last days.

And it shall come to pass afterwards,
That I will pour out my Spirit upon all flesh;
Your sons and your daughters shall prophesy,
Your old men shall dream dreams,
And your young men shall see visions.
Even upon the menservants and maidservants
In those days I will pour out my Spirit.
(Joel 2: 28ff)

He did precisely that, on the Day of Pentecost; and the gift has never been withdrawn. We shall be looking at this point more closely later, but for the moment it is sufficient to point out that the gift of the Spirit at Pentecost to all believers without distinction fulfilled one further hope of the prophets of old. Men like Jeremiah and Ezekiel looked for the day when God would forge a new covenant, or agreement, with men. The problem about the existing one was this. Although it all sprang from God's initiative, it was nevertheless very much a two-sided affair. "If you will obey my voice", said God to the Israelites after the Exodus, "and keep my covenant, you shall be my own possession among all peoples" (Exodus 19: 5). But there lay the rub. They could not and did not keep his covenant. They were constantly breaking their side of it. And though God remained faithful to his side of the agreement, and looked after his people wonderfully down the centuries, it was not very satisfactory as a covenant. It kept getting spoiled. Jeremiah longed for the day when God would, so to speak, underwrite both sides of the covenant. He would not only keep his side of the bargain, but enable Israel to keep hers, by putting his Spirit within her people. Listen to his vision:

The days are coming, says the Lord,
When I will make a new covenant with the house of Israel . . .
Not like the covenant which I made when I took them by
    the hand

To bring them out of the land of Egypt—my covenant which
they broke
Although I was a husband to them, says the Lord.
But this is the covenant that I will make with the house of
Israel
After those days, says the Lord:
I will put my law within them and I will write it upon their
hearts;
And I will be their God and they shall be my people.
And they shall no longer each man teach his neighbour and
his brother
Saying "Know the Lord",
For they shall all know me, from the least to the greatest,
says the Lord;
For I will forgive their iniquity, and I will remember their
sin no more.

(Jeremiah 31: 31ff)

A new covenant, involving a complete pardon, a personal
knowledge of the Lord, and the will of God no longer external
to them on tablets of stone, but written inwardly on their hearts.
A new covenant indeed! Ezekiel speaks in much the same
strain, and specifically attributes this change to the Spirit of
God:

I will sprinkle clean water upon you, and you shall be clean
from all your uncleannesses, and from all your idols I will
cleanse you. A new heart will I give you, and a new Spirit
will I put within you; and I will take out of your flesh the
heart of stone, and give you a heart of flesh. And I will put
my Spirit within you, and cause you to walk in my statutes.

(Ezekiel 36: 25ff)

That is what was wanted. A new Spirit, God's own Spirit
within man, which would warm his heart to want to go God's
way, and enable his will to keep it. Such was the hope for the
last days, and this was the hope that the Christians had seen
fulfilled since the resurrection and ascension of Jesus. Hebrews
8: 7ff and 10: 15ff work it out in detail.
Such was the prophetic hope, not only for the Suffering Servant or the Messiah of Israel but for the whole people of God.
Of course, it could not come without national repentance and
renewal on a grand scale. Ezekiel was bold enough to long for
this too, and God gave him the marvellous vision of the valley

of the dry bones (chapter 37) as an assurance that the longed-
for day would indeed come. God's *ruach*, his breath, could
infuse new life into dry bones; God's *ruach*, his Spirit, could
bring the people of Israel out of their graves, and give them life.

Creator Spirit?

There are three further surprises for us as we look at the Old
Testament teaching about the Spirit of God. In the first place,
he is hardly ever connected with creation. This is all the more
significant when one thinks of the nature mysticism that was
so common in every variety of ancient paganism. There was
no hint of it in the religion of Israel, which maintained such a
clear emphasis on the otherness, the transcendence of the
Creator God. Indeed, in the Old Testament, language about
the Spirit is restricted almost exclusively to the area of relationship between God and *man*.

Despite this, whole theologies have been erected on the
theme of the Creator Spirit. It is moving to think of the Spirit
of God being involved in the continuous and on-going process
of creation. It is fascinating to follow John Taylor's poetic
imagination in attributing to the Spirit of God the "inner
awareness of the unattained", "the stimulation of initiative and
choice", and the "principle of sacrifice" inherent in the creative
development of our world (*The Go-Between God*, chapter 2).
But the roots for all this in the Old Testament are rather shaky.

Professor Moule has seized on the fact that only in four
places in the whole of the Old Testament does the Spirit seem
to be associated with creation of the physical world—and even
these four are patient of another interpretation. Genesis 1: 2, 5,
"the Spirit of God was moving over the face of the waters"
may indicate a creative function for the Spirit, but may equally
describe the chaos referred to in the earlier part of that verse,
"the earth was without form and void, and darkness was upon
the face of the waters": and "a *ruach adonai*, a mighty hurricane
from God, was moving over the expanse of the unruly waters"
may be a better translation. Psalm 104: 30: "When thou
sendest forth thy Spirit they are created, and thou renewest
the face of the ground" refers to the animal creation, and may
mean not so much that the Spirit created them, but, as in
Genesis 2: 7, that God breathes his life into the already
moulded form of animals and man. In other words Psalm 104:
30 may speak of the energising rather than the creative work of
the Spirit, and thus fall into line with the rest of the Old

Testament teaching on *ruach* as "breath". Psalm 33: 6 is no more certain. To be sure "By the word of the Lord were the heavens made, and all their host by the breath (*ruach*) of his mouth" could mean that the *ruach*, the Spirit, created the heavens. But more probably, in the light of the parallel with "word" in the first half of the verse, *ruach* means God's *fiat*. His word is creative. When he says "Let there be light", light ensues. The last hint of a Creator Spirit in the Old Testament is in Job 33: 4, but once again this is ambiguous. It may mean "The Spirit of God has made me", but in view of the parallel "and the breath of the Almighty gives me life" it is just as likely to mean that the Spirit is the animating principle of life.

Professor Moule may not be right in the interpretation he gives to these four verses. The Old Testament *may* give these few hints of a Creator Spirit, and certainly this thought is found in the intertestamental period—where the parallelism between Wisdom, Word and Spirit is important—but the paucity of instances that can be adduced, and the plausibility of taking them in another sense, does make one very cautious of building up a great doctrine of co-operating with the Holy Spirit in his on-going work of creation. The Spirit of God breathes his life into man; he revives the dry bones; he infuses vitality into inert matter, but the evidence that he is involved in the work of creating the world is very slim indeed in the Old Testament and non-existent in the New. We would be wise not to build too high a building on such a flimsy foundation.

Holy Spirit?

The second surprise concerns the rarity of any mention in the Old Testament of the *Holy* Spirit. Pagan Greek literature does not have the phrase at all, and only twice do we find it in the Old Testament. In Isaiah 63: 10, 11 we read that the people on whom God had set his love "rebelled and grieved his Holy Spirit", although he had put his Holy Spirit in the midst of them when he rescued them from Egypt. In Psalm 51: 11 the writer prays to God in penitence,

> Create in me a clean heart O God, and put a new and right spirit within me
> Cast me not away from thy presence, and take not thy Holy Spirit from me.

In both cases the writers are very conscious of the moral and

ethical aspect of God's *ruach*. The nation of Isaiah 63 had
grieved this Holy One to whom they were dedicated. The
individual of Psalm 51 had done the same. The holiness of the
Spirit of the Lord stands in sharp contrast to the unholiness of
his fallible servants, and perhaps this is why the Spirit is here
called Holy. In the New Testament, of course, it is the normal
name for the Spirit. The reason for this may be because God
was increasingly called "the Holy One" (there was a slightly
increasing tendency in intertestamental writings and the Dead
Sea Scrolls to speak of "the Holy Spirit") but might just be due
to the character of Jesus. The one in whom the Spirit had a
permanent dwelling amazed men by the sinlessness of his life.
Such was the character produced in human life by the Spirit
of Yahweh once he was given full control. Such, therefore,
should be the character in the followers of Jesus, called as they
were to be "holy" or "separated to God" as his special
possession (1 Peter 1: 15f, 2: 9). As we have seen, Ezekiel and
Jeremiah expected God to change men in the days of the New
Covenant by putting his Spirit within them, so that they
should walk in his ways and keep his commandments: after
Pentecost the Holy Spirit begins to produce holiness in God's
people. This does not mean separation from sinners, in a sense
of isolation and self-satisfaction like the monks of Qumran;
instead, it means involvement with needy, fallen, spoiled
humanity, following the example and endued with the Spirit
of him who was a friend of tax gatherers and sinners.

Personalised Spirit?

The final surprise is that in the Old Testament the Spirit
does not appear as a divine being. He is rather seen as God's
personal presence and intervention. The point is well made in
a verse like Isaiah 31: 3.

The Egyptians are men, and not God;
and their horses are flesh and not spirit.

In those words, Isaiah is not contrasting flesh and spirit in
the way we might, as the exterior and the interior of the same
being. No. He is grouping flesh and men together, and God
and Spirit together. The Spirit is on God's side of reality;
quite different from our side. And when the Spirit of the Lord
is present with men, it means the gracious and personal
intervention of God himself. As we saw just now in that

passage in Isaiah 63, the Spirit is the personal expression of God himself, and can be grieved: he is holy, not only the divine power but the moral character of God: he is God in action for the benefit of his people — notice how the Spirit is equated with the "arm" of Yahweh, that is to say his saving activity. The Spirit is no less than the personal, moral, active power of the Lord God, and for the further revelation of his nature we must await Act Two, the coming of Jesus, to which we shall turn in the next chapter.

CHAPTER 3

The Spirit of Jesus

EACH IN HIS own way, the four evangelists make it abundantly
plain that a new era has dawned with the coming of Jesus of
Nazareth. It is the long-awaited era of the messianic kingdom,
the age characterised by the availability of the Spirit of God.
And Jesus is the Messiah, by virtue of his unprecedented
endowment with the Spirit of God. He is both the unique
bearer of the Spirit, and the unique dispenser of that Spirit
to the disciples; moreover, for ever afterwards the Spirit
remains stamped with his character.

1. *Jesus is the unique Man of the Spirit*

St. Mark on the Baptism of Jesus

Mark was in all probability the earliest evangelist. He knew
the power and the reality of the Holy Spirit in the church of
his day, when he wrote in the 60s of the first century. But he
went to great pains to exclude all mention of the Spirit as
available for believers from his Gospel, with one notable exception. Why was this? Surely because he wished to make it abundantly plain that it is Jesus, and Jesus only, who is the man of
the Spirit. Not until his death and resurrection could that same
Spirit become readily available for his followers.

Accordingly, he begins his Gospel with the story of the
baptism of Jesus. The crowds who flocked to listen to John's
preaching of repentance were baptised by him in the Jordan
in penitent expectation of the age of fulfilment which he
proclaimed. But when Jesus was baptised, Mark makes it plain
that the age of fulfilment *has already dawned*. A voice was heard
from heaven. Now there had been a great shortage of messages
from heaven for a very long time. The writings of the rabbis
repeatedly maintain that the Holy Spirit departed from Israel

32

after the last of the prophets, Haggai, Zechariah and Malachi (e.g. *T. Sota* 13: 2). What is more, the Spirit of God, and the *shekinah*, or glory of God, were not to be found in the Second Temple (*b. Yoma* 21 b). Men cherished a tremendous sense of nostalgia for the departed glories of the previous Temple, and for the Spirit of Yahweh which used in Old Testament days to be displayed in mighty deliverers and inspired prophets. Nostalgia, yes, and expectation, as men awaited the promises of Ezekiel and Jeremiah, of Joel and Isaiah about deliverance, an anointed king, and a renewal of the Spirit in the days of fulfilment. Well, says Mark, in effect: those days of fulfilment have arrived. In John the Baptist's ministry you find the fulfilment of the prophecies made long ago that a messenger would come to prepare the way of the Lord. That is precisely what the Baptist was doing. And Mark immediately introduces Jesus on to the scene: the messenger has indeed prepared the way of the Lord. Daring words those, for in the prophet Malachi they clearly referred to Yahweh himself. Mark is quietly claiming that in Jesus we have to do with none other than Yahweh, who had come to our world in the man Jesus. As if that is not enough, he makes two other shattering claims.

The first is that the age-long silence is ended. God has spoken again. The heavens are no longer brazen and unyielding. The rabbis believed that when the Holy Spirit was withdrawn from Israel at the end of the prophetic era, God left them with a substitute, the *bath qol*, which means literally "daughter of the voice" or "echo". It is usually said that in the voice from heaven at the baptism of Jesus we have an example of the *bath qol*. But this is quite mistaken. The *bath qol* was an inferior substitute for the Word of God formerly given by the Spirit to a prophet. But this voice was no feeble substitute; it was a direct address from the God who had been silent. It is inconceivable that at his juncture when Mark is heralding the return of the Spirit in Jesus he should introduce it with anything so banal and second-hand as an echo. And the content of this voice is even more amazing than its occurrence. "Thou art my beloved Son; in thee I am well pleased," seems to be a deliberate combination of two famous Old Testament texts. "Thou art my Son" comes from Psalm 2: 7, where the king of Israel is addressed as "Son" of God. The kings had been pretty poor specimens as "sons": they showed little enough of Yahweh's family likeness, and there was a long-standing hope in Israel that one day God would bring into the world a messianic Son, a worthy ruler to sit on David's throne. We

2

know people were treasuring this hope at the time of Jesus, because in the caves of Qumran there has turned up a messianic anthology which includes the prophecy given to David in 2 Samuel 7: 14. There God undertakes to give an everlasting kingdom to the boy "and I will be his Father and he shall be my Son". The voice from heaven, recorded by Mark, announced that the ultimate messianic ruler had arrived in Jesus.

But that was only half the message. The other half "with thee I am well pleased" comes from that picture of the Servant of Yahweh in Isaiah 42: 1 which we looked at in the last chapter. At his baptism, then, Jesus publicly assumed a double rôle: the rôle of the Messianic Son, and the rôle of the Suffering Servant. Such was the destiny he willingly undertook.

But the baptism of Jesus did not merely see the end of the long silence, and God's declaration that in Jesus the rôle of the Servant and the Son had converged: the age-long drought of the Holy Spirit was ended too. As we saw in the last chapter the anointed king of Israel was equipped with the Spirit to enable him to carry out his work; hence the expectation of Isaiah 11: 1ff that the Messiah would also be equipped, in fuller measure, with that Spirit. It was just the same with the Servant. "I have put my Spirit upon him; he will bring forth justice to the nations", says God through the prophet. And now the Spirit had come, and Mark's account of the baptism makes it abundantly clear that he sees Jesus as the Messianic Son and the Suffering Servant, equipped for his stupendous task with the Spirit of God promised for the end-time. The last days are no longer entirely in the future; in the person of Jesus the end has dawned. No wonder Jesus's first recorded words in Mark's Gospel are "The time is fulfilled: and God's kingly rule has drawn near" (Mark 1: 15).

St. Mark on the Battle with Satan

Mark has two ways of emphasising the fact that Jesus is fully and uniquely endowed with the Holy Spirit in his rôle as Son and Servant of Yahweh, who brings in the kingly rule of God in the end-time. First, he makes a great deal of the struggle with Satan in which Jesus is involved both in the temptation in the wilderness into which the Spirit thrusts him (Mark 1: 12) immediately after his baptism; and also in the healings and exorcisms which follow during the ministry. He does so in a very subtle manner.

In the Old Testament there was a use of *ruach* which I did not mention. It concerns evil spirits which are seen as rebellious creatures of Yahweh, bent on wrecking his purposes but ultimately subject to his control. In the earlier books of the Old Testament we read of these evil spirits (1 Samuel 16: 14, Judges 9: 23, 1 Kings 22: 21); later they are personalised in Satan, whose name does not appear before the rather late books of 1 Chronicles (21: 1ff), Job (1: 6ff) and Zechariah (3: 1ff). In the intertestamental period there is a great deal about these evil spirits and their prince. It is important to bear in mind that there is no absolute dualism in the Hebrew religion. Even the devil is God's devil: he is on a chain held by God, even though the chain is a long one. The devil and his spirits are seen as a distortion of the original good creation of God, and though they are allowed to tempt and hurt men because of men's wickedness (see, e.g. *Jubilees* 10: 7–11) in the last time they will be bound and punished. Now against that background of thought we must set Mark's emphasis on the binding of Satan by Jesus. Jesus, filled with the Spirit, goes off into the wilderness, the place where Israel had been tested for forty years after the Exodus, and tries conclusions with the tempter for forty days. He wins, where Israel's forebears failed. In him the days of fulfilment, the days of Satan's defeat, have dawned.

And so it continues throughout his ministry. Time and again we find him casting out unclean spirits from afflicted people: it is one of the well-known characteristics of Mark's Gospel, which on the whole contains little teaching, but a great deal of action by Jesus. That action includes many miracles of healing, the most important being the curing of people who were possessed. The meaning is clear. Jesus is the conqueror of demonic forces through the power of the Spirit. He is the victor over Satan, and he tells a gem of a story to drive the point home. "No one can enter a strong man's house and plunder his goods unless he first binds the strong man; then indeed he may plunder his house." The context in Mark 3: 20–30 makes it abundantly clear that by his cures and exorcisms Jesus is driving out the demons. The man endued with the Holy Spirit is more than a match for the unclean spirits which are such a feature in Mark's account. Jesus is the conqueror. And men are amazed. They see in the presence and power of Jesus a cameo of the final victor over the forces of evil. "With authority he commands even the unclean spirits and they obey him" (1: 27).

But it is not only through his healings and exorcisms that Jesus shows himself as the bearer of the Spirit: he claims it explicitly in the controversy with the scribes about Beelzebul (apparently another name for Satan, conceived of as "Lord of the House"). In response to their charge (Mark 3: 22) that it is through demonic power that he casts out demons, he replies that no divided house can stand: if Satan casts out Satan, his empire is doomed. And then he makes that terrifying statement about the sin against the Holy Spirit, over which many people have needlessly tortured themselves.

"All sins will be forgiven the sons of men, and whatever blasphemies they utter; but whoever blasphemes against the Holy Spirit never has forgiveness . . . for they said 'He has an unclean spirit'." More light is shed on this verse by the form in which it occurs in the "Q" material (sayings of Jesus preserved in Matthew and Luke independently of Mark). "Whoever says a word against the Son of Man, it shall be forgiven him. But the man who blasphemes against the Holy Spirit will not be forgiven" (Luke 12: 10). It is one thing to mistake and misrepresent Jesus, clothed in all his humility as Son of Man; it is one thing to misread his parabolic teaching, coming as it does in riddles. But it is quite another thing to see the truth clearly and wilfully to reject it; quite another thing to ascribe the power of the Holy Spirit to the devil — which is what the scribes were doing. If men firmly reject the saving work of God in Jesus, they forfeit the very possibility of rescue, not because God will not have them, but because they say, like Satan in Paradise Lost, "Darkness, be thou my light".

Jesus, then, is the bearer of the Spirit: he, and he alone during the period of the ministry. It is a mark of the extraordinary faithfulness of St. Mark to the historical situation of the life of Jesus that he does not read back into those days the experience of the Spirit to which he and his friends were used in the post-resurrection era. There is one place only where he lifts the curtain. In the "apocalyptic discourse" of Mark 13, Jesus promises the disciples that in the coming days when they are out preaching the Gospel, they will be put on the spot time and again when arrested and unjustly accused. And then the Holy Spirit will give them words to say. He will equip them for witness-bearing. The promise refers to the post-resurrection days; it does not provide an exception to Mark's sharp portrait of Jesus alone as the man uniquely possessed by the Holy Spirit.

The teaching of Matthew

Matthew is equally convinced that Jesus is the focus of the Spirit's activity. He brings it out in a number of ways, in addition to those we have noticed in Mark. For one thing he carries the story of Jesus back far beyond the baptism to his very conception. This too was specially brought about by the Holy Spirit (Matthew 1: 18, 20). Just as the Spirit was active in breathing life into the first man (Genesis 2: 7), so here he is associated with the birth of the last Adam. But Matthew is claiming more than this. He knows that the Messiah is uniquely endued with the Spirit, and he stresses that from the outset of Jesus' life this was the case.

Matthew makes quite explicit the way in which Jesus fulfils the rôle of the Servant. He quotes Isaiah 42: 1–4 in full, and says that Jesus' works of healing are the fulfilment of that prophecy. In other words, the power of the Spirit is specifically set out as the energising principle in Jesus' healing ministry.

Finally, this evangelist is as well aware as Mark that the Spirit was during the ministry concentrated, as it were, in Jesus, and will only be available to the disciples when they, too, are engaged in the mission. Then they will baptise those they evangelise in the name of the Father, the Son, and the Holy Spirit (28: 19), but in the meantime they are given one trial run, if we may so call it, when they are sent out on a missionary journey (Matthew 10: 20). Mark's promise that the Holy Spirit will look after their words when arraigned before councils for the sake of the gospel is brought into the Mission Charge by Matthew: it seems clear that he is looking forward from an isolated incident in the ministry of Jesus to the continuing mission of the post-resurrection church of which he was a member.

The teaching of Luke

Luke has a lot to say about the Holy Spirit, both in the Gospel and the Acts. At present it is sufficient to notice his agreement with the other evangelists that Jesus is the unique messianic bearer of the Spirit. He makes a very special point of emphasising the presence and activity of the Spirit in the birth stories of John and Jesus, and in underlining the new outbreak of prophecy, which had been silent so long, but as we have seen, was confidently expected afresh in the Age to Come. Right at the start of the gospel story we find the Spirit active in full vigour. The new age had dawned, and the signs of its presence were experienced. It is a weakness in Dunn's useful book *Baptism in the Holy Spirit* that he sweeps aside these dozen or so references to the Spirit in the first three chapters of Luke and insists that the Kingdom did not come until the baptism of Jesus. In fact, Luke could hardly go to greater lengths in stressing that the Age to Come dawned with Jesus' birth. The Spirit active in an upsurge of prophecy, active in the birth of John and Jesus, rests upon Jesus and in its power he carries out his mighty works and after the resurrection imparts that same Spirit to his disciples. From Bethlehem at the beginning of his Gospel to Rome at the end of Acts it is the one Spirit active throughout: first showing us the nature of that messianic salvation brought by Jesus, and then showing us how it was spread.

Luke lays even more stress on the Spirit activating the whole life and ministry of Jesus than any other evangelist. By the Spirit he went into the wilderness, by the Spirit he was led there, and in the power of the Spirit he returned to Galilee to begin his ministry (Luke 4: 1, 14).

Luke persistently links the coming of the messianic age with the gift of the Spirit in various subtle ways. There is an ancient variant in the Lucan version of the Lord's prayer, which is attested as early as Marcion in the second century and reads, "May thy Holy Spirit come upon us and cleanse us", instead of, "Thy kingdom come". This, if it is original, would suggest that Luke saw the Holy Spirit as the supremely desirable object of prayer (as in his version of the saying of Jesus, recorded in 11: 13, "If you, being evil, know how to give good gifts to your children, how much more shall the Heavenly Father give the Holy Spirit to those who ask him" — compared with Matthew who reads "good gifts" for "the Holy Spirit"). It also suggests that he saw the gift of the Spirit as the supreme characteristic of the kingdom. But the experience of this Spirit must wait for the disciples until after the death and resurrection of the man filled with the Spirit. As in Matthew, the isolated promise of the Spirit in the Mission Charge points beyond the resurrection to the days when they really are engaged in the mission. Meanwhile, it is Jesus alone on whom the Spirit rests in his fulness. And the prophecy of Isaiah 61: 1, "The Spirit of the Lord is upon me, for he has anointed me to preach the good news to the poor . . ." stands in Luke's Gospel (4: 18), as a beacon shedding light over the whole of his ministry. It is the passage he reads in the synagogue of his home town at the outset of his work. It contains all the great themes of the Gospel. It identifies the Spirit with the anointed one. And he calmly tells them that "Today this scripture has been fulfilled in your hearing". Could anything stress more strongly the concentration of the Spirit in the person of the Messiah for his mission? It is exactly the same point as John makes by his assertion that "the Spirit was not given by measure" to Jesus, but rested upon him and remained—in fulfilment of the promises of the Old Testament (3: 34, 1: 32, 33).

There is a striking passage in the early second-century *Gospel according to the Hebrews* which may serve as a summary of this point. The *Gospel* itself has perished, though it was very popular in the early Jewish Christian community. This fragment of it survives, however, because it is quoted by Jerome— significantly in his Commentary on the messianic prophecy of Isaiah 11: 1. It runs as follows:

> It came to pass that when the Lord had ascended from the water, the whole fountain of the Holy Spirit descended and rested upon him, and said to him "My Son, in all the prophets I looked for thee, that thou mightest come and I might rest in thee; for thou art my rest, thou art my Son, my first-born, who art king for evermore".

2. *Jesus is the unique Dispenser of the Spirit*

If, then, all the evangelists agree that Jesus is the unique *bearer* of the Spirit, in whose power he ushers in the Messianic Age, they are no less agreed on a second vital point. And here the *Gospel according to the Hebrews* is silent. The whole fountain of the Spirit is indeed his, but not for himself alone; rather that he should shower it upon his followers. And this the canonical evangelists stress, each in his own way. The point is that Jesus is the unique *dispenser* of the Holy Spirit. You cannot get him except through Jesus, or get to Jesus except through him.

All four evangelists record the promise of John the Baptist that whereas he baptises in water, the One who comes after him will baptise with the Holy Spirit (and, according to Matthew and Luke, "with fire"). Precisely what John expected, it is difficult to know. But it is evident that John's work was preparatory: to get men ready for the forgiveness of sins which his baptism foreshadowed but did not profess to provide, and to warn men of judgment, the wrath to come. His baptism

exemplified these two themes of his teaching. The prophet
Ezekiel had given this oracle from God, looking ahead to the
age of fulfilment:

> I will sprinkle clean water upon you, and you shall be clean
> from all your uncleannesses, and from all your idols I will
> cleanse you. I will give you a new heart, and a new spirit
> will I put within you.
>
> (Ezekiel 36: 25f)

John saw his baptism as the preparation for this new era.
He was under no illusions that water could convey forgiveness.
In common with the men of Qumran, with whom he seems to
have had some links, John saw washing with water as merely a
preparatory rite, while the great cleansing and the gift of the
Spirit lay in the future (1QS: 9–10f and 4: 21).

But judgment as well as mercy was presaged in John's baptism. The Old Testament had a lot to say about God administer-
ing fire. And it always means either destruction or cleansing.
Daniel 7: 10 had spoken of the stream of fire issuing from the
throne of God, and this too is picked up in one of the Qumran
hymns which describe the molten river of judgment that will
befall the world in the last day (1QH 3: 28ff). Probably this
idea was in John's mind. In the very book of Malachi from
which he derived the understanding of his own mission to
prepare the way of the Lord, he would have read of fire both
burning up evil-doers and also refining and purifying the
faithful like a refiner's fire (Malachi 4: 1f, 3: 1–4). Perhaps
those who came in repentance and were prepared for the
running waters of Jordan to flow over their heads in judgment
were thought of as undergoing the judgment of God in symbol
so that they would not have to undergo it in its awful reality
on the Day of Judgment.

At all events, John knows that his baptism is merely preparatory. The coming Messiah will baptise with the Holy Spirit
and fire. T. E. Yates has tried to maintain in *The Spirit and
the Kingdom* that this prophecy was fulfilled in the ministry of
Jesus, for he was not only filled with the Holy Spirit but
constituted the fire of judgment to his hearers by means of his
teaching and miracles. It is of course true that the coming
of Jesus did bring a fire upon the earth, a fire of judgment;
men judged themselves by their response to him. But he did
not baptise with the Holy Spirit until after his death and
resurrection. We do not have to rely on the verse which

embarrasses Yates ("the Spirit had not yet been given, because Jesus was not yet glorified", John 7: 39) for this, though that is unambiguous enough. It is the concerted teaching of the whole New Testament that the Christian experience of the Holy Spirit is possible only after the death and resurrection of Jesus. We have seen the evidence for this clearly enough in the preceding pages. Mark emphasises it by only allowing one reference in his Gospel to Christians having the Holy Spirit, and that in a prophecy about what would be their lot in the days after the passion (13: 11). Matthew and Luke in their Gospels speak of the Holy Spirit for Christians only in the Mission Charge which anticipates their future rôle as ambassadors of Christ. Furthermore, Matthew stresses that the task of telling men the good news and baptising them into the possession of the Holy Spirit will only be theirs after the cross and resurrection have given them a gospel to proclaim and a Spirit to receive (28: 19). Luke, as we have seen, makes the prayer for the Holy Spirit the supreme blessing of the Messianic Age, and shows how wonderfully it is shed upon the thirsty disciples of Jesus from the day of Pentecost onwards— but not before. And John, whose Gospel scheme does not include, except by implication, the story of what the Church, equipped with the Holy Spirit, achieved, and therefore could not make room for Pentecost (as Luke does at the outset of his second volume), nevertheless makes the same point with considerable clarity. In the first chapter of his Gospel he stresses that the Spirit rests exclusively upon Jesus, the fulfilment of the messianic hopes of the Old Testament for the bearer of the Spirit. In the twentieth chapter, significantly after the cross and resurrection, he shows how Jesus fulfils the second part of Old Testament expectation for the Messianic Age by breathing upon his disciples, charging them with his mission, bidding them continue his rôle of proclaiming remission of sins to the penitent and judgment to those who refused to hear, and saying to them "Receive the Holy Spirit" (20: 22f). The Spirit which rested upon him is now made over to them, along with the mission on which he was engaged; this too is theirs. As we shall see, the mission and the Spirit belong together. The important point is not to try to harmonise this account with that of Luke in the Acts—after all, John in all probability never read Luke's work, and presents the material in a very different manner and with different aims. I do not think we get much further by supposing that Jesus gave two insufflations of his Holy Spirit, one in John's upper room, and one at Luke's

Pentecost. No, the point they both make is that Jesus was equipped for his messianic mission by the Spirit promised for the last days; that this Spirit was not available to others in the days of his flesh; and that after his death and resurrection the last days were extended, so to speak, by the followers of Jesus inheriting his mission, his authority and his Spirit. On this point the evangelists are agreed.

3. *Jesus stamps a new character on the Spirit*

This leads us on to a third important point about the relation of the Holy Spirit to Jesus. We have seen that the Spirit of God which appeared fitfully, in a variety of forms, and prophetically in the Old Testament days shone steadily, personally, and fully in the Man of Nazareth. No longer is the Holy Spirit encountered as naked power; he is clothed with the personality and character of Jesus. If you like, Jesus is the funnel through whom the Spirit becomes available to men. Jesus transposes the Spirit into a fully personal key. Jesus is the prism through whom the diffused and fitful light of the Spirit is concentrated. Jesus is *the* prophet (Luke 7: 16, Acts 3:22, 7:37) the long-awaited prophet of the end-time, through whom the prophetic Spirit, so active in the Old Testament, gave full and final revelation. We have seen that Jesus gave this Spirit to his disciples in virtue of, and subsequent to his death and resurrection. What follows is that the Spirit is for ever afterwards marked with the character of Jesus. Indeed, he can be called "the Spirit of Jesus" (Acts 16: 7).

This is the common teaching of the New Testament, but no writer brings it into sharper focus than St. John. In the fourth Gospel Jesus tells his followers, heart-broken because he is going to leave them, that it is better for them that he should do so:

> I tell you the truth: it is to your advantage that I go away; for if I do not go away, the Paraclete will not come to you; but if I go, I will send him to you.
>
> (John 16: 7)

In a word, it is the task of the Paraclete to universalise the presence of Jesus. In the days of his flesh Jesus was limited by space and time. His physical departure made possible the coming of the Spirit as Paraclete and there would be no barriers of space and time to prevent disciples being in intimate

THE SPIRIT OF JESUS

contact with him. Indeed, they would find the relationship even closer than companionship with Jesus in the days of his flesh. They have known Jesus as their Paraclete (we will examine the meaning of the word in a moment) during his ministry. He has dwelt *with* them, but the one whom he promises as another Paraclete will dwell *in* them (John 14: 17). There it is in a nutshell. The Spirit universalises the presence of Jesus in the hearts of disciples.

The Spirit as Paraclete

It is well worth taking a careful look at the teaching of St. John's Gospel about the Spirit as Paraclete. There are five references to him in the farewell discourses. They are 14: 15–18; 14: 25–7; 15: 26, 7; 16: 7–11; 16: 13–15. Once only in the rest of the New Testament do we meet this title, in 1 John 2: 1. And this, I think, is very significant. In the Epistle of St. John we find that Jesus is the Paraclete. He is the one who represents us before his heavenly Father. The righteous Lord Jesus having dealt with the defilement of our sins, represents us—stands in for us if you like, before his Father. As such he is the guarantor of our acceptance. In the Gospel, too, Jesus alludes to himself as Paraclete: for when promising "another paraclete" or "another as paraclete" in 14: 16 (it makes no difference which way you take the Greek) Jesus is clearly insisting that he is their Paraclete already, just as the Epistle says he is. The identity between Jesus and the Spirit could scarcely be more strongly stressed, particularly as he goes on to say "I will not leave you orphans: *I* will come to you" (14: 18). Nothing of the personality of the Spirit as embodied in Jesus will be lost when the disciples come to experience him as Paraclete. Indeed, John breaks all the rules of Greek by referring to the Spirit (a neuter word in Greek) by the masculine pronoun. The Spirit is as personal as the Jesus at whose behest he comes.

A great deal of discussion has centred around the meaning of this word Paraclete. It has been understood as "Comforter", "Intercessor", "Interpreter", "Preacher" and either "Prosecutor" or "Defence Counsel". The basic meaning of the word is "One called alongside to help". Jesus is the one called to the Father's side to help us, according to the Epistle. The Spirit is the one called from the Father's side to help us, according to the Gospel. The way in which he helps will be best discovered by looking at the text, not by speculating about the meaning of the term. But before we do so, it is worth mentioning the shrewd suggestion of Professor Raymond Brown that foremost in the complex imagery behind this word is the idea of what he calls a "tandem relationship". Sometimes in Old Testament days God granted a man signally endued with his Spirit to pass it on to his successor. Thus Moses passes on the Spirit of the Lord to Joshua (Deuteronomy 34: 9) and Elijah does the same to Elisha (2 Kings 2: 9, 10, 15). So Jesus passes on to his disciples the Spirit which has "rested" upon him throughout his ministry.

What do we find when we look at the detailed promises about the Paraclete? Precisely what this tandem relationship and the reiterated link with the historical Jesus would lead us to expect. Namely, that the Spirit acts for, and in, and against men in precisely the same way as Jesus had done when on earth. Just as Jesus had come forth from the Father into the world as the Father's gift to mankind, so it is with the Paraclete (5: 43, 16: 28, 3: 16f). Just as the Father sent the Son into the world as his representative, so the Paraclete will be sent in Jesus' name (5: 43, 14: 26). Just as Jesus remained with and guided the disciples, so will the Paraclete (14: 16–18). Just as Jesus taught them the truth because he was Truth, so the Spirit of Truth would lead them into all the truth about Jesus (14: 6, 17, 15: 26, 16: 13). Just as Jesus did not draw attention to himself but set out to glorify his Father by passing on the Father's message to men (8: 28, 12: 28, 17: 4), so the Paraclete "will not speak on his own authority . . . but will take what is mine and declare it to you" (16: 14). Jesus bore witness to the Father (8: 14) and the Spirit would bear witness to Jesus (15: 26, 27). For Jesus had still much to teach the disciples which they could not understand before his passion; so he assured them that the Spirit would continue his teaching function among them when he had left them (16: 13).

Not only was the Spirit to universalise the person of Jesus to future believers, he was to do the same to the unbelieving world. One of the prime purposes of his coming was to nerve the disciples themselves to witness to Jesus in the face of a hostile or apathetic society. Look at 15: 26, 27: "He will bear witness to me . . . and you also will bear witness." Through the witness of the disciples which he will apply to the hearts of the hearers, the Spirit will convict men of being in the wrong. Three of the great themes of the apostolic preaching are then mentioned; sin, righteousness and judgment. Through the witness of the apostles and the witness of the Spirit (now seen as Accuser), men are shown that they are wrong with their moralistic ideas of sin: sin is essentially the refusal to commit themselves to Jesus, God's saviour. They are wrong in their views of righteousness, supposing Jesus to be a sinner like themselves—and worse, because he ended up in the place of cursing on a cross (cf. Deuteronomy 21:23): his sinlessness had been vindicated by the resurrection ("I go to the Father"). And they are wrong in thinking that the judgment lay entirely in the future: the decisive battle which dethroned Satan had been won on the cross, and from now on he was a defeated foe, and believers were ransacking his empire. But is this triple message taken home by the Paraclete in the apostolic mission not precisely what the Johannine Christ proclaims throughout the Gospel, and particularly in a passage like 9:35–41? In a word, the Paraclete takes over the rôle of Jesus. Just as the world refused to accept Jesus, so it will refuse to accept the Paraclete (1:10, 11 and 14:17). Just as Jesus had to bear his witness against a background of hate because he told men the unwelcome truth (7:7) so will the Spirit (16:8). Whether we look at the Paraclete's rôle in the world or among the disciples the answer is the same. The Holy Spirit is "another Jesus". He is sent to replace Jesus among the disciples and to do for them what Jesus had done on earth. More, he is to equip them for their mission just as he had equipped Jesus for his. Yet there is no complete autonomy for the Spirit, just as there had been none for Jesus. He had lived his life in dependence on his heavenly Father: if he was to give a true representation in human terms of the nature of Yahweh, then he needed to live, as man, in constant obedience to Yahweh both as his anointed Ruler and as his obedient Servant. And if the Spirit was truly to represent Jesus, he had to remain bound to the person and character of Jesus. Jesus was God's Last Word to man; and the function of the Spirit was not to give some new revelation of his own, but to bear witness to Jesus, to draw out the implications of God's Last Word. We shall look at some of them in the next chapter, but before closing this one it might be pertinent to speculate why it was in St. John's Gospel, of all places, that we get such stress laid on the Spirit as Paraclete. The reason is probably twofold.

The Spirit Replaces the Apostles

There is good reason to suppose that St. John's is the latest of the Gospels to be written. Chapter twenty-one, which seems to have been composed as an afterthought to the main body of the Gospel with its climax in 20: 31, indicates that there was a tradition doing the rounds in Christian circles to the effect that John would not die: he would be there until the Second Coming of Christ. Imagine the feelings of the Christians when the old man died!

On the one hand the last of the apostles had passed on; the last of those authorised interpreters of the person and work of Jesus had left them bereft: on the other hand the promised Advent had not materialised. What would help them most in such a situation? Well, the record must first be set straight. Jesus did not actually say that John would survive until the Second Coming, but "If it is my will that he remain until I come, what is that to you?" (21: 23). After doing that, the problem must be faced head on, in both its aspects. And the Holy Spirit, the Paraclete, provides the answer to both problems. Christians were distressed because the age of revelation was over (and they were acutely conscious of this with the passing of the apostolic generation, as is made clear not only by the speedy recognition in the second century that their writings were determinative for the Christian faith, but also by the deep sense of nostalgia to be found in the earliest of the sub-apostolic writers like Polycarp and Ignatius): and to them comes the promise that they are not worse off, but if anything better. They may have lost their apostles, but they have the Spirit of the Lord himself remaining with them to teach and to inspire. The risen Christ carries on his teaching work through the Spirit whom he has given to the Church. Sometimes people today bewail the fact that they were not contemporaries of the historical Jesus, and imply that it would be much easier to believe and much more advantageous generally if they had been. To them the words of Jesus still apply. "It is to your advantage that I go away, for if I do not go away the Paraclete will not come to you. But if I go, I will send him to you." And that is what he has done. The Spirit is his parting gift to the Church to make his presence as real to them as if they were listening to him teaching beside the Sea of Galilee: and the Spirit can do more for us than ever Jesus could have done had we been his contemporaries. He can come within us, and take up residence within our very beings. He can not only bring to our remembrance what Jesus taught, but can reveal to us the deeper significance of his person, his death and resurrection which we could never have grasped by historical contemporaneity. We are indeed not worse off but better.

The Spirit anticipates the End-time

The second problem that would have troubled the faithful at the death of the last apostle was this. Why had the promised Advent not happened? It was a problem as early as 1 Thessalonians which was partly written in order to meet it. It was a more acute problem by the time of 2 Peter: chapter three of that Letter is specifically directed towards those who have given up hope in the Return of Christ. But when the last apostle died, and Jesus, who had uttered the mysterious words "There are some of those standing here who will not taste death before they see the kingdom of God come with power" (Mark 9: 1), had not returned—what were they to think? Had they been misled? No, they had not. In a very real sense, though not the sense they were expecting, the Kingdom *had* come in power. It came in the power of the Holy Spirit on the Day of Pentecost, and that power had never been withdrawn, and never would be. The previous chapter in St. John had drawn attention to it. Jesus had breathed his Spirit upon his disciples. This was the gift through which the Messiah had accomplished his work. This was the endowment of the end-time which he had lived and died with—and yet the last page of the last chapter of human history had not been written. Were the disciples to be any different from their Lord? No. To be sure, the last page of the last chapter had not been written at the death of the last apostle any more than it had at the death of the Messiah; but, like him, the disciples enjoyed the characteristic gift of the end, the Holy Spirit whom the prophets knew would be poured out in the last days. Let them not therefore bewail the delay of the Parousia. Jesus had not left them orphans: he had come to them in the person of the Spirit, who was not only the special gift of the Messiah to the messianic people in order to enable them to know his continued presence with them, but was the first instalment of the Age to Come, the pledge that the last days which had dawned with Jesus of Nazareth would, one day, come to God's perfect conclusion.

CHAPTER 4

The Spirit and Jesus

YOU MAY WELL be wondering why I have taken such pains
to show that the Spirit of God, his active intervention on the
human scene which took such varied forms in the Old
Testament, became concentrated in the person of Jesus the
Messiah, and then was poured out by him upon the messianic
community. Why does it matter?

It matters a great deal, and I want in this chapter to sketch
out some of the implications of this inviolable link which the
New Testament writers make between Jesus and the Spirit.

The Spirit in the Gospels?

For one thing, it gives an answer to an otherwise very
puzzling problem. Why is it that there is so little about the
Holy Spirit in the Gospels? We know that the early Church
was intoxicated with the experience of the Spirit, and the
comparative silence of the Gospels about him is a great credit
to their historical trustworthiness in not reading back the
conditions of their post-resurrection situation into the days of
Jesus' life. This in itself is highly significant, particularly since
many New Testament scholars seem to believe that the early
Christians had no sense of historical propriety and would be
perfectly happy to dream up some saying and attribute it to
Jesus, or to listen to a message from one of the Christian
prophets in the congregation, and then put that into the
mouth of the historical Jesus. It is a staggering compliment to
their historical reliability that we find almost nothing of the
major concerns which engaged the primitive Church written
back into the Gospels. How easily they could have tried to
solve their problems about law keeping, Spirit possession,
circumcision, law and grace by inventing "words of Jesus" to
settle the matters in question.

But granted the credit for historical reliability which accrues to the evangelists through their reserve about the Spirit, that still does not help us with the problem of why there is practically nothing in the Gospels about men and women being filled with the Holy Spirit now that he was clearly in business again. If he was active in Jesus, why not in the disciples? The answer is clear. Because the Spirit was tied up with the person of Jesus. He was the funnel through whom all subsequent experience of the Spirit of God would be mediated. That is why other men do not receive the Spirit between his baptism and Pentecost. The gift of the messianic Spirit, promised to the people of God in the end-time, depends upon the Messiah accomplishing his mission. Until he had died for man's forgiveness, until God had raised him from the dead by way of vindication, the Spirit which rested upon him was not available to be passed on to others.

The Spirit in other faiths?

A second problem is this. Why is there nothing said in the New Testament about the Holy Spirit disclosing himself in other faiths, in the struggles of men to find God, and in the ethical endeavours of decent people? In our day, as mentioned in chapter one, we are constantly being told that the efforts of our statesmen, the voting procedures of our councils, the ethical advances of our humanitarians, are being governed by the Holy Spirit. We go further, and it is often said that God has revealed his Spirit as much in Buddhism and Hinduism as in Christianity; indeed, as much in atheism as in theism. In these days when inter-faith dialogue can easily slip into syncretism, and when man's search for God can easily supplant all idea of God's self-disclosure to man, it is most important to remember the emphatic union which the New Testament asserts between the Holy Spirit and Jesus. If God really has disclosed himself in a Son; and if that Son was characterised by his possession of the Holy Spirit which he has passed on to his followers, then we cannot without denying Christ maintain that God has revealed himself as much in Buddhism as in Christianity; we cannot make an amalgam of religions as if we were all honest seekers after a God who hides himself. I think it is of the utmost significance that the New Testament writers do not assign to the inspiration of the Holy Spirit the noble elements in pagan ethics or in other religions. For the task of the Spirit is to bear witness to Jesus. He is the Spirit of Christ.

This does not mean that there is little truth in the tenets of other faiths. Of course there is much that is true, alongside much that is not. It does not mean that God has failed to give any indication of his person through "the moral law within and the starry heaven above". It does not mean that the Holy Spirit cannot work on men of other faiths and draw their inner longings to Christ. John Taylor, in *The Go-Between God* says rightly, "The eternal Spirit has been at work in all ages and all cultures making men aware and evoking their response, and always the one to whom he was pointing and bearing witness was the Logos, the Lamb slain before the foundation of the world. Every religion has been a tradition of response to him, however darkly it groped towards him, however anxiously it shied away from him." He goes on to give a splendid example of the thing he has in mind, when an old Muslim tribesman went on urging a drug-addicted English hippy to "pray to Jesus the Messiah", until he was converted and delivered. The old man explained his views on the matter afterwards to a Christian friend, "For an ordinary man in normal circumstances it is enough that he believe faithfully in God. But when anyone is beset by such evil power as this, nothing can save him but Jesus Christ: this I firmly believe."

Dr. Taylor gives another example of the Spirit of God drawing a man to Jesus in circumstances that were very unpropitious and through a medium that was to say the least opaque. The first missionaries to preach in the Muslim north of Nigeria were greeted by a handful of people who were already believers in Jesus and claimed to follow him. They were the disciples of one Malam Ibrahim, a teacher of the Koran whose studies had slowly convinced him that the Jesus of whom he read in its pages was the mediator through whom the prayers of the faithful are offered up to the All-Merciful. So he gathered around him a group who began to pray regularly in the name of Isa Masih, Jesus the Messiah. When the Islamic authorities discovered, he was charged with heresy, refused to recant, and was crucified in Kano market place thirty years before a Christian preacher arrived in the country.

Under such circumstances it is thoroughly in line with the teaching of the New Testament to ascribe such leanings among non-Christians to the agency of the Holy Spirit. Is it not his task to convince the world of sin, righteousness and judgment? Is it not through his agency that anyone makes the Christian confession "Jesus is Lord" (1 Corinthians 12: 3) and is born again (John 3: 5)? After all, it is the rôle of the Paraclete to bear witness to Jesus, and he does it with and without our testimony, to men of any faith or none. But that is a very different matter from the exegetically unjustified expedient adopted by some modern students of mission, of divorcing the Spirit from Jesus, evading the scandal of his particularity, and attributing to the Spirit's agency whatever seems to them to be admirable in the beliefs and practice of other faiths. If we wish to claim the leading of the Spirit of God with any assurance, we shall find that the leading is always towards Jesus. As Professor Moule has written in an unpublished paper, "to generalise the Holy Spirit and use the term to denote God's activity anywhere and everywhere, is to miss the biblical theme of election for service, and to ignore God's strange way of particularising in order to universalise".

Bishop Stephen Neill, in an article in *The Church Quarterly* for April 1971, makes the same point. The Spirit in the New Testament is "not found anywhere outside the realm of direct and personal encounter with the risen Christ . . . It would be an advantage if Christian writers would take as their example the actual usage of the Christian Scriptures".

The Spirit in person?

There is a third problem to which this link between Jesus and the Spirit provides the key. In the Old Testament, as we have seen, the Spirit of God was manifested in a variety of ways—strength, wisdom, ecstasy, even frenzy being attributed to the wind or Spirit of Yahweh. By the time of the New Testament Epistles, on the other hand, the Spirit is the fully personal embodiment of the Godhead. How comes this change?

It is simply due to the fact that the diffused, little-defined, fitfully-manifested and sometimes sub-personal presence of God as Spirit which we found in the Old Testament, becomes clearly focused for the first time in Jesus of Nazareth. No longer is this presence diffused; it is sharply localised in Jesus. No longer is it ill-defined: it is marked with the lineaments of his character. No longer fitfully-manifested, the Spirit rests upon him with unwithdrawn steadiness. No longer sub-personal, the Spirit is stamped with the personality of Jesus. From now on the Spirit is seen as a person within the Trinity, though the New Testament is not interested in doctrinal formulations of this type. The sheer facts of experience, however, drive the Christians to acknowledge the deity of Yahweh, Jesus, and the Spirit, whilst distinguishing between

them. Thus, Jesus is divine, but he is not all of God that there
is: he lived his earthly life in dependence on Yahweh. The
Spirit is divine, marked with the very stamp of Jesus, and yet
distinct: for Jesus was anointed by the Spirit, lived in the Spirit
and passed his Spirit on to the Church. A growing and almost
unreflective recognition of the diversity and unity within the
Godhead led the New Testament writers to make the assertions
which became the raw material for later Trinitarian orthodoxy.
Thus in 1 Corinthians 12: 4–6 Paul correlates the work of the
Spirit, the Lord (i.e. the Lord Jesus) and God. He does it
again in Ephesians 4: 4–6, 2 Thessalonians 2: 13, 14, Galatians
4: 4–7, Romans 8: 9–11 and in the well-known "grace" of
2 Corinthians 13: 14. We have already mentioned the baptism
into the name of "the Father, the Son and the Holy Spirit"
which is enjoined upon the disciples by the risen Christ in
Matthew 28: 19. In various other places and strands of the
New Testament we find similar unselfconscious allusions to
the three persons in the deity. One of the most interesting is
attributed to the sermon of Peter on the day of Pentecost, where
he maintains that "This Jesus God raised up, and of that we are
all witnesses. Being therefore exalted at the right hand of God,
and having received from the Father the promise of the Holy
Spirit, he has poured out what you now see and hear" (Acts
2: 32ff). You find the same thing brought out in 1 Peter 1: 2
and Revelation 1: 4, 5.

If, then, the Spirit is fully personal, and the personality he
wears is the personality of Jesus, two very important consequences follow. We cannot rightly attribute to the Spirit any
teaching which does not shed light on Jesus, or any religious
experience which is not congruous with the life of Jesus. There
is a danger of falling into both these traps in the present spate
of Christian enthusiasm for the Spirit. Let me enlarge on this
a little.

A criterion for doctrine

In contrast to a few years ago when one would rarely hear
any teaching on the Holy Spirit, it seems that some people can
speak of nothing else these days. There is a cult of the Holy
Spirit, and often it has precious little to say about Jesus.
Now in view of the past neglect, this is understandable enough.
But it is none the less dangerous. The Holy Spirit does not
draw attention to himself. He is there to glorify Jesus, to show
Jesus' attractiveness, and not to take the centre of the stage.

One of the wisest criteria we can apply to any of the claims made for the Holy Spirit and any of the teaching about the Spirit which is being advanced from all sides today is this: does it glorify Christ? It is the characteristic of the Paraclete to bear witness to Jesus, to glorify Jesus, to take the things of Jesus and declare them to us (John 15: 26, 16: 13f). In contrast to this emphasis of the New Testament writers, much of the stress on the Spirit today dishonours Jesus, tends to squeeze him out of the picture, and infers that allegiance to Jesus is only the lower reaches of the Christian life, the heights of which belong to the Holy Spirit. Imbalance of this sort is only to be expected; for we are very human and our understanding is limited and our perspectives often determined by what has particularly struck us. But it is a salutary reminder that nothing less than a fully Trinitarian Christianity can stand. Some strands in Christendom, particularly the Catholic, have laid stress on God the Father almost to the exclusion of the Son and the Spirit. They need to remember that the Father said, "This is my Son, my beloved, in whom I am well pleased. Listen to him", and to reflect on St. John's assertion, "No man has ever seen God. The only begotten one, himself, God, has made him known" (John 1: 18).

Other strands, particularly the Evangelical, have so concentrated on "the Lord Jesus" in their teaching and worship that they have virtually made an idol of the flesh of Christ instead of coming to the Father through him. They need to remember that even Jesus did not primarily draw attention to himself, but taught men that they could find the Father through the way he showed, the truth he revealed, and the life he lived.

Other strands, particularly the Pentecostal, make the mistake of concentrating on the Spirit to the prejudice of the Father and Jesus. At the end of the second century, Montanism was a Spirit-centred movement which had great strengths but fell into terrible error because it lost sight of Jesus as the controlling factor in spirituality. If I may quote Professor Moule's wise words again, "Authentic Christianity finds itself uttering, in the power of the Spirit of God, the address of Jesus Christ the Son of God to God the Father, and thus bearing witness about Jesus to the world. It is this balance that keeps it authentic".

A criterion for experience

If remembering that the Spirit is the Spirit of Jesus keeps

doctrinal formulation authentic, the same may be said for experience. There is real danger in prizing, let us say, speaking in tongues (which I believe can be a real gift of the Holy Spirit) so highly that those who lack it are regarded as second class Christians if Christians at all. So far as we know, Jesus never spoke in tongues. And the Spirit is the Spirit of Jesus. It cannot, therefore, be a *Christian* insight to urge that speaking in tongues is an indispensable mark of life in the Spirit of Christ; whereas it is an undeniably Christian insight to insist that love and holiness, so manifest in the life of the incarnate One, should mark those who claim to have his Spirit. In a word, the Spirit of Jesus points us back to Jesus. If we want to understand and possess the Spirit in his fulness, we need to keep our eyes firmly on Christ himself, for it is to him that all the Spirit's authentic witness is directed. If we do this we shall not claim as the teaching of the Spirit what does not relate to Jesus. And we shall not claim as experience of the Spirit what cannot be shown to flow from Jesus.

There is a further sense in which the very strong link between the Spirit and Jesus will determine our experience of the Spirit. The Spirit of Jesus is the Spirit which marked him out as Son of God, as Servant of Yahweh, and sent him on his mission to Israel and the world. If the Spirit of Jesus is the gift bestowed on his followers, we shall expect to find the same characteristics marking authentic Christian life in the Spirit. And that is very much what we do find in the pages of the New Testament.

The Spirit of Sonship

Take first the question of Sonship. Now there is a very obvious difference between us and Jesus. He was born by the express agency of the Holy Spirit; we are not. He was Son of God by right: we are sons only by adoption. Nevertheless it was the possession of the Spirit that set Jesus apart as the messianic Son of God, and brought the voice from heaven at his baptism "Thou art my Son". As Son, Jesus coined a new word for God. He called him "Abba" (Mark 14: 36). Jeremias has shown in *The Central Message of the New Testament* that nowhere in pre-Christian literature does anyone dare to call God by this intimate, family word which could better be translated as "Daddy" or "Dear Father". It was a word for the intimacies of the family, not for the worship of God. Jesus, the one set apart by the Spirit as *the* Son of God, dares to call God by this name. He alone has the right to, for he alone enjoys the intimate relation of sonship with God the Father. And it is into this sonship that he installs us. He enables us to pray the Lord's Prayer, which, in the form known to Luke, begins simply "Abba", "Father". It is the Spirit who adopts us alongside Christ into this sonship with God, and who enables us to cry the "Abba" of little children in the family of God. "You have received the Spirit which makes you sons," exults the apostle Paul. "When we cry 'Abba! Father', it is the Spirit himself bearing witness with our Spirit that we are children of God, and if children then heirs, heirs of God and fellow-heirs with Christ, provided we suffer with him in order that we may also be glorified with him" (Romans 8: 15ff). That is the incredible privilege and status of the Christian. He possesses the Spirit of God's Son, which makes him a son of God, and enables him to utter the family cry to God as "Abba". Well may Jeremias conclude that the whole of the good news is concentrated in that single word, Abba.

The Spirit of Servanthood

But even in that word of highest privilege and relationship there lie hints of another aspect of the Spirit-filled life of Christ that devolves upon his followers. "Provided that we suffer with him", says Paul, reminding us, perhaps, that the agonising context in which Jesus is actually recorded as calling God "Abba" is in the Garden of Gethsemane. Unlike the kings of Israel who had aspired to the title of "Son" of Yahweh, Jesus displayed utter trust in his heavenly Father though the outlook was black as night; utter obedience to his Father, even though it would take him to a cross; and utter readiness to suffer—in bloody sweat there and then, and the blood, sweat and hell of crucifixion thereafter. Sonship could not be divorced from servanthood. The Messianic Son was appointed by the Spirit at his baptism to be also the Suffering Servant.

In this respect, too, authentic Christian experience is stamped with the mark of the Servant. In the enthusiasm of the renewed emphasis on the Spirit these days he is sometimes presented as the pathway to power in the Christian life, the secret of success in personal living and in service. There is truth in this, but it is only a half truth. The other side of the coin is the agonising trust in the dark, the utter obedience when all our inclinations go the other way, and the willingness to suffer which marked our Lord. It is when they first suffer for Christ

that the earliest apostles return to their friends, pray (not for
safety but for boldness), and find the place shaken by the Holy
Spirit (Acts 4: 29–31). It is the Spirit who not only convinces
Paul that "imprisonment and afflictions" await him if he goes
to Jerusalem, but constrains him to accept that destiny
(Acts 20: 22, 23). Peter, too, stresses that the Spirit calls us
into the experience of suffering which Christ underwent. He
calls on his persecuted readers to rejoice when they suffer as
Christians and so share Christ's sufferings, for "the Spirit of
glory and of God rests upon you" (1 Peter 4: 13–16). But perhaps
the most striking example of the sombre side of suffering in
obedience to God which the Spirit of Jesus calls us to is
provided by Paul in the Corinthian correspondence. Käsemann
has perceptively observed, in *Jesus Means Freedom*, that this
church at Corinth was infatuated with a theology of the Spirit
whilst allergic to a theology of the Cross. They revelled in
charismatic experiences of the Spirit, so richly was their
community endowed with tongues, miraculous healings and
prophecy. They reckoned that they had already entered into
their reign with Christ: they were already rich, already filled
with the powers of the Age to Come (1 Corinthians 4: 8).
Paul comes down immediately like a ton of bricks on this
attitude which regards the Spirit as a medium of religious
experience or an embodiment of supernatural power, rather
than as the vocation to and equipment for the rôle of the
Servant. He contrasts their position of self-satisfaction with
his own. "God has exhibited us apostles as last of all (like
gladiators in the arena), as men sentenced to death. For we
have become a spectacle to the world, to angels, and to men
(like the dying gladiators)." He goes on to speak of the hardships he endured, the thirst, the hard work, the opposition, the
homelessness, the abuse, and concludes, "we have become and
still are, the refuse of the world, the offscourings of everything"
(1 Corinthians 4: 8–13). He could scarcely put more vividly
the truth that the Spirit who has come upon Christians is the
Spirit of Jesus, and that our destiny will involve the suffering
and the hardship of the Servant of the Lord. That is why he
is determined to know nothing among these Corinthian
enthusiasts but "Jesus Christ, and him crucified" (1 Corinthians
2: 2). For the power of Christ's resurrection, as he puts it
elsewhere, is available only to those who are willing "to share
his sufferings and become like him in his death" (Philippians
3: 10). The era of the Spirit in which Christians may exult
(2 Corinthians 3 throughout) leads inescapably to the

rejection, the hardship, perplexity and physical sufferings of which the Apostle speaks in chapter four, for he carries about in his body the death of Jesus, so that the life of Jesus may shine through his personality (2 Corinthians 4: 10). In short, no crown without thorns. No exultant, joyous experience of the Spirit of Christ without a corresponding taste of Christ's suffering.

The Spirit of Witness

Son, Servant, and Witness. This was the third notable characteristic of the Spirit in Christ, and this too is everywhere to be noted in the early Church's experience of the Spirit. It was in the power of the Spirit that Jesus carried out his work of proclaiming the good news of God's kingly rule (Luke 4: 18): and it was in the power of the same Spirit that the disciples got to work after the resurrection. They were told by Jesus not to speculate about the time when God would bring in the Kingdom in all its fulness, but, once they had received the Holy Spirit, they were to witness to Jesus in Jerusalem, Judaea, Samaria, and throughout the world (Acts 1: 8). That is precisely what they did, and we shall be examining it more closely later. It is sufficient here to notice the pronounced link between the Spirit and power to witness which can be seen both in the life of Jesus and that of the post-ascension Church.

In drawing these three threads together, it is fair to say that if, as we have shown, the Spirit is the Spirit of Jesus, we shall expect similar marks in the Church of our age and every age as the Spirit displayed in the life of our Lord. We shall expect the Spirit to bring us assurance that we are indeed the sons of God, and conversely we shall be careful not to deny that any Christian people, any sons of the Heavenly Father, possess the Spirit of adoption. Secondly, we shall be very suspicious of any claim to spiritual blessings which does not render the man who claims it willing to tread the path of the Servant, and endure suffering joyfully. And thirdly, we shall be unimpressed with any claims to the Holy Spirit's presence where men are unwilling, in the power and joy of that same Spirit, to go and bear witness to Jesus. To crown it all, we shall realise that this strong link between the Spirit and Jesus leads us to think of him in personal terms, as the one who makes Jesus real to us and works out in the common clay of our lives the priceless treasure of Christ's character.

CHAPTER 5

The Spirit in Mission

WHY DID GOD send us his Holy Spirit? It is a fair question, and allows of more than one answer. The Spirit of God came upon Christian individuals in order to create in them a quality of life that would otherwise be beyond their powers. The Spirit of God came upon the Christian community in order to unite them in a fellowship which could not be paralleled in any other group. We shall be looking at both these important functions of the Holy Spirit in the next two chapters. But there can be no doubt from a candid examination of the New Testament accounts that the prime purpose of the coming of the Spirit of God upon the disciples was to equip them for mission. The Comforter comes not in order to allow men to be comfortable, but to make them missionaries.

This is so contrary to our general assumptions (namely that the Holy Spirit, however vaguely we conceive of him, is an internal gift for the faithful, appropriate only to be mentioned in church) that it is important for us to see the crucial link between the Spirit and mission which is presented to us in the pages of the New Testament. The evangelists make the point in their own characteristic ways.

The Age of the Spirit and the Mission

Mark's only mention of the Holy Spirit for Christians is, as we have seen, placed in the Apocalyptic Discourse in Chapter 13, where Jesus is looking ahead to the tribulations which will face his followers in the years running up to the fall of Jerusalem, and, interwoven with that theme, up to the end of the world. They will be hard times, with opposition, persecution, famines, wars and distress. Yet against this sombre background (so matching the experience of the hard pressed Christians in Rome of the 60s A.D., for whom Mark wrote his

Gospel) two clear and closely linked rays of light shine out. The coming age will be the age of the gospel being preached among the nations: equally, it will be marked by the presence of the Holy Spirit enabling the Christians to bear faithful witness to Jesus, despite the costly consequences (Mark 13: 9–13). Only the one reference, it is true: Mark is recording the story of Jesus, not of the Church. But that one reference speaks volumes. The age of the Church to which Jesus looked forward is to be marked by evangelism and the Spirit. He is the power for mission.

Matthew's way of expressing the same point is this. He makes a great deal, as we have seen, of the gift of the Holy Spirit to Jesus: but only once in the Ministry does he speak of the disciples having the Spirit. In 10: 1ff. he solemnly names the twelve disciples, and tells how Jesus sent them out on a mission. He then makes two very significant points. First, for the only time in his Gospel, he calls them apostles. Second, he says that Jesus gave them power over unclean spirits, and that when they were under pressure the Spirit of their Father would speak within them (11: 20). Whatever the meaning for those twelve disciples on that short mission (and the Spirit may well have come upon them temporarily as he did upon the Old Testament of God to equip them for a special purpose), it is hard to mistake the shadow this event casts towards the time of the Church, when men sent out by Jesus ("sent one" is the root meaning of the word "apostle") would be equipped by the Spirit given them by Jesus, for carrying out Jesus' own mission in the world. The Holy Spirit is for mission. As if to emphasise the point, Matthew ends the Gospel by Jesus' mission charge to the disciples, "Go therefore, and make disciples of all nations." How is this to be done? Why, it is in the power of Jesus to whom all authority in heaven and earth is entrusted; this Jesus is with them always in their mission, to the end of the age; and naturally, therefore, they baptise men not only into the possession, the "name", of God the Father and the Lord Jesus, but into the sphere of that Holy Spirit who makes real to them the presence of the risen Christ, and empowers them for their work of making him known (Matthew 28: 18–20). If we turn to St. John, it is precisely the same picture that meets us, although painted in very different colours. The Paraclete will come upon the disciples when Jesus is taken from them. He will bear witness against the world, as Jesus did, and he will bring conviction (John 16: 8). But he will not do it on his own. "The Spirit will bear witness to me . . . and you will bear witness" (15: 27). So when Jesus breathes his Spirit upon them after the resurrection, it is to enable them to enter into his own mission received from the Father and proclaim forgiveness of sins to believers, and doom to the impenitent (20: 20–23). John is saying, loud and clear, that the coming of the Spirit upon the Church is to equip it for evangelism.

If we turn to Paul, we find him characterising his missionary work at Christ's behest among the Gentiles as a sort of priestly offering, sanctified by the Holy Spirit (Romans 15: 16). Unusual and striking imagery, but the same linking of the Holy Spirit with evangelism at Christ's command. If we turn to 1 Peter 1: 11, 12, we find that the Spirit, once active in the prophets, led towards the suffering Christ, at whose instigation and in whose Spirit evangelists have brought the readers of the Epistle to faith.

But the man who gives us the clearest picture of the link between the Spirit and evangelism is St. Luke in his two-volume work. In volume one he showed how Jesus was the bearer of the Spirit: he was conceived and born in an atmos-phere where the Spirit had been poured out afresh, in the days of messianic salvation. He was baptised and, as Peter put it later, "God anointed Jesus of Nazareth with the Holy Spirit and with power" (Acts 10: 38). The word "anointed" (*echrisen*) is the one from which Messiah (Greek *christos*) is derived. Jesus was designated as Messiah or "Christed" by the coming of the Spirit to rest upon him, and he could claim that the prophecy of Isaiah 61: 1 had been fulfilled—"He has anointed me (*echrisen*) to preach the good news" (Luke 4: 18). In Jesus the Spirit destined for the messianic days, the days of salvation, *had come to stay.* That is why there is so much stress in Luke's account of the life of Jesus that his deeds and words were at the inspiration of the Spirit (Luke 4: 1, 14, 10: 21, 23: 46, etc.). Accordingly, as he leads up to the day of Pentecost Luke is at greatest pains to maintain that the Spirit who equipped Jesus for his mission, equips the disciples to carry it on.

Beginning at Jerusalem

Notice, first, how Luke links the ascension of Jesus with the Spirit and evangelism. In the Gospel we have been told that Jesus will bring about a new *exodus* (9: 31) by his death and resurrection at Jerusalem: a release from a worse bondage and a more terrible death than that which befell the Israelites in Egypt. Three times Luke tells us that Jerusalem was Jesus' goal (9: 51, 13: 22, 17: 11). It is to Jerusalem that the Spirit of the Suffering Servant leads Jesus. At the end of the Gospel, therefore, we find the resurrection appearances that Luke records are confined to the city where these climactic events have taken place. No mention of the Holy Spirit, you notice: merely a foreshadowing of the rôle of the disciples in being witnesses to the Messiah who had to suffer and rise from the dead so that repentance and forgiveness could be preached to the nations, *beginning from Jerusalem* (Luke 24: 46f). And with that the curtain comes down on the Gospel. The volume telling us of the coming of salvation to Israel is complete with the death and resurrection of Jesus. His ascension to the place of power at God's right hand is the fitting conclusion.

But at the beginning of Acts, volume two in the drama, we find the story of the ascension related agin, and from a very different point of view. This time the ascension does not bring down the curtain on the life of Jesus; instead, the curtain goes up on the life of the Church. The exaltation of Jesus to the Father's right hand is not only God's vindication of his person and his achievement; it is the precondition of the coming of his Spirit upon the witnesses who are to carry on his mission (Acts 2: 32f). Volume one tells of what Jesus began to do and to teach until his ascension to the right hand of God; volume two tells of what Jesus continued to do and to teach through the apostolic Church after his ascension, through the gift of the Holy Spirit which he shed upon it. That, surely, is the implication of Acts 1: 1ff, with its studied throw-back to the beginning of the Gospel. Just as there was a great outpouring of the Spirit at the coming of the Messiah—prophecy, divine begetting, voice from heaven, baptism and so forth; so at the beginning of the age of the Church's witness-bearing to Jesus we find a similar intensive manifestation of the Spirit. As the Spirit equipped Jesus for his ministry, so it is with the people of Jesus.

Luke makes part of his point through the misunderstanding of the disciples. They were still thinking of the Kingdom in materialistic terms. When was Jesus going to fulfil his promise and bring it in? They had to learn that the final day of God's victory might be long delayed, and they could not tell its date (a point to which successive generations of enthusiastic date-guessers have remained remarkably blind). However, the first instalment of the Kingdom would soon be sent them by the

ascended King himself. Until God's final day when he will
bring in the Kingdom, two characteristics would mark the
age of the Church: the Holy Spirit, and witness to Jesus.
The Spirit, who had inspired Jesus to teach and heal and
proclaim the good news of God's kingly rule among men, would
come upon them, marked with all Jesus' character. The
mission on which Jesus had been engaged would devolve on
to their shoulders. "You shall receive power when the Holy
Spirit comes upon you, and you shall be my witnesses"
(Acts 1: 8). Precisely as in Mark, we find the Spirit and mission
being the two notable marks of the Church in the age stretching
between the advents. The Spirit, mediated in evangelism, is
the mode of the Kingdom's presence among men until the
return of the King.

Spreading from Jerusalem

And just as the Gospel had concentrated on Jerusalem, the
location of God's great exodus for man, so the Acts shows the
mission spreading out from that centre in ever widening circles.
As Jesus insisted in Luke 24: 47, it was all to *begin* in Jerusalem:
hence the emphasis on Jerusalem as the place where the
Pentecostal gift arrived. It was *never to lose touch with Jerusalem*:
hence the repeated journeys of Paul back to the metropolis
(e.g. Acts 18: 22, 19: 21) and the supervisory visits of Jerusalem
leaders to various parts of the expanding Christian arena
(e.g. Acts 8: 14, 11: 22). But *it was to move out from Jerusalem.*
The Acts is the story of that moving out. First within Jerusalem,
where three thousand are converted on the day of Pentecost
itself; it would be hard to stress more emphatically the link
between the Spirit and mission than by showing such effective
evangelism as the result of the reception of the Holy Spirit on
that notable day! Then the good news spreads out in the
pattern outlined in Acts 1: 8. At every point in the advance, it
is the Holy Spirit of God who takes the initiative. It is the
Spirit who inspires Peter to withstand the rulers of Israel
(4: 8ff) and proclaim to them the Messiahship of Jesus. The
Spirit marks out Stephen as a special vehicle of God when he
refuses to remain restricted to the static categories of the
temple and moves into broader pastures (6: 3, 5, 10, 7: 55).
It is the Holy Spirit who so signally lays his mark of blessing
upon the preaching of the good news to those untouchables
(from the traditional Jewish viewpoint) the Samaritans in
the first half of Acts chapter 8, and the eunuch in the second

part of that chapter. For it was the Spirit who called Philip from his successful mission in Samaria to reach the Ethiopian eunuch with the gospel (8: 29 and probably 26), and led him on his further preaching tour as far as the very Hellenised city of Caesarea. It was here in Caesarea that Peter had his memorable lesson not to call any man "unclean"—which, as a Jew, he would instinctively have done to all Gentiles. In order to drive home the point that the messianic Spirit, the Spirit of the days of salvation, was really available to all believers, the Spirit had first of all to inspire Peter with his vision of the unclean animals in the sheet which were intended for him to eat, and then to apply that vision to a Gentile officer whose men were at that very moment waiting in the courtyard for Peter to accompany them to Cornelius so that he might receive the good news of Jesus. Even then, such is Peter's Jewish prejudice, the Holy Spirit has to take the initiative in falling upon Cornelius and his company before ever Peter had got round to making any appeal to repentance, faith and baptism (10: 44f).

The Spirit has shown that he validates the Christian mission among Jews, proselytes, "Godfearers" (as Gentile adherents on the fringe of the synagogue were called), and even outsiders like eunuchs and Samaritans. But more was to come. The second part of Acts is dominated by the mission to the Gentiles, under the leadership of Paul. It is the Spirit who leads the Antioch church to send out Saul and Barnabas on the first missionary journey (13: 2, 4) which enabled them to return and report that, "The Lord has opened the door of faith to the Gentiles" (14: 27). This is a keystone in the expanding arch of mission in Acts. The Holy Spirit has broken through all the man-made obstacles, and has incorporated all types and backgrounds of people in the messianic community. "The greatness of Luke's view", wrote Eduard Schweizer in *Church Order in the New Testament* (p. 75), "lies in his showing more impressively than anyone else that the Church can live only by evangelising, and by following whatever new paths the Spirit indicates". Those paths lead ever wider and wider afield in the cause of Christ. The evangelist who tells us three times that Jesus contracted his perspective to concentrate on Jerusalem and that at Jerusalem the disciples had to await the coming of the Spirit that would equip them for mission, ends his second volume with a triple reminder that this good news, beginning from Jerusalem (Luke 24:47) reaches Rome (19:21, 23: 11, 27: 24). The butterfly of the gospel has broken out of its chrysalis at Jerusalem and has flown to the centre of the civilised world. The Spirit that dwelt in the Messiah of Israel is available to the citizens of Rome. The faith of Israel is good news for the world.

It is one of the remarkable indications of the balance of St. Luke that he manages to stress the initiative of the Spirit in ever-expanding circles of evangelism with the reminder that the mission is one. The Paul who receives his mission to the Gentiles does so in a trance in the temple at Jerusalem (Acts 22: 17ff). The apostle who brings the Acts to an end by preaching unhindered in the capital of the pagan world is also shown as arguing all day with the leaders of the Jews "declaring to them the kingdom of God" and "persuading them about Jesus" by appeal to the law and the prophets (28: 16–31). To the Jew first and also to the Greek, the Spirit of the Messiah is available through the preaching of the good news of what the Messiah has done. There is neither Jewish nor Gentile bias in this chronicler of the Holy Spirit's initiative in mission throughout the world, though his application of the famous "blinding" passage of Isaiah 6 to Jewish leaders who refused to receive their Messiah, and his assertion "Be it known to you that this salvation of God has been sent to the Gentiles: *they* will listen" (28: 25–28) is suggestive of the direction in which the Christian mission would, for the most part, go.

The Spirit initiates Mission

Now all this emphasis on the Spirit as the author, the controller and the energiser of the Church's mission is highly significant. It reminds us that mission did not originate, in the earliest days, in the leadership of the Church. It was not a matter of Peter and subsequently Paul saying "What about a bit of evangelism?". Luke does not teach us that the apostles initiated mission. They sat quietly in Jerusalem until the Spirit came upon them at Pentecost; then they could not keep quiet about the mighty deeds of God. It was not the twelve who fulfilled their Lord's command to go and teach all nations the good news. It was rather an ex-Pharisee opponent of the gospel, converted through the direct agency of God and thrust out on the mission at the direct leading of the Lord the Spirit. It was not the apostles at Jerusalem who ever dreamed of reaching eunuchs or Samaritans with the good news: the Holy Spirit led the way. It was not the Jerusalem leaders who agreed to the first widespread dissemination of the Word. That came through their being cooped up at Jerusalem in the persecution which followed on the death of Stephen: as a result of the ordinary followers of Jesus being scattered by that persecution, they were able to preach the good news along the Phoenician seaboard until they came to Antioch, later to become the home of the Gentile mission. And so one could go on. The initiatives in evangelism were always those of the Holy Spirit. So much so that the crucial coming of the Holy Spirit on Cornelius is recorded three times in Acts, so that no one might miss the message. The Holy Spirit was not to be confined to the narrow straits of Jewish respectability, nor was he the perquisite of the Church leadership. He was sovereign, and he was the leader of the whole Christian outreach as well as its energising power. The Church was only effective when it broke through its old taboos and shibboleths and followed the Spirit who could come upon Samaritans and Gentiles as well as Jews. So far from the Church being the possessor and dispenser of the Spirit, as Käsemann would have it with his astonishing reading of primitive Catholicism into Acts (see *Essays on New Testament Themes* p. 89ff), it is the Spirit who energises the evangelism of the Church and drives its often unwilling members into the task for which God laid his hand on them: mission.

This sovereignty of the Spirit is worth dwelling on. It humbles us, as God intended it to do, to find that there is no tidy doctrine of the Spirit to be found in Acts or, for that matter, in the whole of the New Testament. He always retains that unpredictable, mysterious otherness of the *ruach adonai*. Utterly unmediated in his coming on the day of Pentecost, and on what has been called "the Gentile Pentecost" to Cornelius and his entourage, the Spirit works in many varied ways. He leads through a committee at the Council of Jerusalem (15: 28), through a prophet in 11: 28, through a trance in 10: 19. In 13: 2 he reveals his will to the community gathered at worship. Sometimes it is through a mysterious inner constraint that he makes his presence felt, as when he guided Paul's evangelistic direction away from the province of Asia in 16: 6, 7 and towards the hardships and opposition he realised he would have to face if he went up for that last journey to Jerusalem (Acts 20: 22, 23). It is impossible to get the Holy Spirit taped, and to fit his movements in the Acts into any tidy ecclesiastical or doctrinal pattern. He remains the sovereign Spirit, but always the Spirit who is bent on leading the people of Jesus out into mission.

3

The Spirit universalises Mission

We have already seen some of the emphasis on this in the
account Luke gives of Pentecost. But there are more subtle
nuances in that story. Luke clearly interprets Pentecost as the
fulfilment of the prophecy of John the Baptist, which he
quotes in Acts 1: 5. It is the fiery baptism of Holy Spirit which
John looked forward to. Hence the emphasis Luke gives on the
physical manifestation to the disciples of tongues of fire and
rushing wind, which equipped them for their mission, just as
the physical coming of the Spirit upon Jesus "in bodily form,
as of a dove" (Luke 3: 22) equipped him for his ministry.
Once baptised in the fiery power of the Spirit which had been
in Jesus, the disciples at once interpret it as the fulfilment of
Joel's prophecy about the availability of the Spirit in the
last days, and proclaim the good news to the representative
crowd from "every nation under heaven" which had gathered
in Jerusalem for the feast of Pentecost (2: 16ff). Now Pentecost
did not only mean the offering of the firstfruits to God (and
what remarkable firstfruits of the Spirit were offered to the
Lord that day as 3,000 people believed, were baptised, and
joined the company of the disciples praising God in the
temple): first-century Jews would also have recalled the giving
of the law on Mount Sinai (see *Jubilees* 1 : 1, 6 : 17). According
to one rabbinic tradition (preserved in Midrash *Tanchuma* 26)
when the law was given on Sinai, "the ten commandments
were promulgated with a single sound", yet it says 'All the
people perceived the voices' (Exodus 20: 18). This means
that when the voice went forth it . . . went into seventy
tongues, and every people received the law in their own
language". The nations of the world were reckoned to number
seventy, after the indication in Genesis 10. It may be that Luke
is referring to this tradition, and if so, he will mean us to
understand that on the day of Pentecost, the gathered
representatives "from every nation under heaven" heard the
mighty deeds of God being proclaimed, "every man . . . in his
own language". The Christian Pentecost would thus not only
reverse the Curse of Babel (Genesis 11 : 9) but be the antitype
of the covenant inaugurated on Sinai through the giving of the
law. What was there external to men has now, in the new
covenant, become interiorised through the Spirit.

Such an interpretation is attractive but speculative. It would
fit the teaching of Paul, who makes just this contrast between
the law and the Spirit in 2 Corinthians 3; it would fit Hebrews

chapters 8 and 10. But Luke nowhere speaks of the new
covenant unless Luke 22: 19b and 20 are original (against the
main weight of manuscript attestation). He prefers to see
believers as the heirs to the one Abrahamic covenant which
inaugurated the Old Testament people of God (Acts 3: 25).
At all events we shall not go wrong in assuming that it is not
without good reason that he tells us of so impressive a roll call of
nationalities on the day of Pentecost (2: 5–11). At the very
least he is showing us that the Christian good news is for the
whole world.

The Spirit uses testimony

The agents in this mission inaugurated by the Spirit are, of
course, the disciples of Jesus. But this rôle is by no means
confined to the twelve. "The great mission of Christianity was
in reality accomplished by means of informal missionaries",
wrote Harnack long ago (*The Mission and Expansion of
Christianity* p. 368). He was right. As early as Acts 6 we find the
apostles seeking deputies to manage the administration of the
church, while they give themselves to prayer and the ministry
of the word. The seven, sometimes improperly called deacons,
are accordingly appointed. But the next thing we find is one of
these administrators, Stephen, preaching his heart out! As
soon as he has been liquidated, another of the seven, Philip, takes
over. And he has four daughters with the gift of prophecy:
doubtless they engaged in the mission too. That same eighth
chapter of Acts records the spread of the gospel by informal
missionaries, men and women evicted from Jerusalem by the
persecution which followed Stephen's death. The message is
clear. All disciples are expected to bear their testimony to
Jesus. That is what the Holy Spirit is given them for.

The word "witness" is significant. Its root figures over thirty
times in the Acts, in one form or another. The apostles, the
folk who had known Jesus in the old days in Galilee, Stephen,
Paul; all are "witnesses of these things; and so is the Holy
Spirit whom God has given to those who obey him" (Acts 5: 32).
The witness attests his own experience: he does not necessarily
preach. The Acts gives us many examples of Christian people
bearing witness to Jesus, in particular his death and resurrection, to soldiers and governors, princelings and mediums,
crowds and individuals. Witness in the New Testament is
neither the silent churchgoing that passes for witness among
many Christians, nor the sickening self-advertisement that

often results when a believer "gives his testimony"; but simple, factual reference to the historical Jesus, his death and resurrection, his gift of the Spirit, and his present availability and power.

This emphasis on testimony is one of the great strengths of the present Pentecostal revival in South America. You are scarcely accounted a Christian in Chile until you have got up in the street and given testimony to Jesus. This is not necessarily the best way of passing on the good news, but it does stir the passers-by to find not the paid priests but the cobbler, the miner, the man who sells meat fritters telling them about Jesus. In his book, *Haven of the Masses* (p. 47), Dr. d'Epinay describes the impact of such witness. It offends the élite, of course. "These men", said a teacher, "do not even speak in Castilian, but in slang; sometimes they don't even know how to write, and can hardly read. And they quote epistles of St. Paul so difficult that the theologians, who have been working on them for two thousand years, have not got to the bottom of them. By what authority do they teach?" That is just the reaction provoked by Jesus and by the informal missionaries in the Acts (Mark 1: 27, Acts 4: 13). The élite were offended, but the common people loved it. If the language is slang what does it matter so long as the preachers are radiant with the experience they speak of, and live in the midst of the same social situation, with all its problems and difficulties, as the listeners? When ordinary men and women are fired by the Spirit to bear witness to "a Lord who pardons and loves, a Lord who is just as powerful as the landowners, the mine-managers or the trade union secretaries, because he is God, a God who desires to be called Father, and who treats the most wretched of men as his son" (d'Epinay) then people will sit up and take notice. They did in the first century, and they do still when the Christians come out of their ghettos and chatter the good news in the streets to passers by, as the Jesus People in the States are accustomed to doing.

The Spirit enlivens the Word

It is not only this informal witness to Jesus which is promised the aid of the Holy Spirit. So is the more formal proclaiming of the Word. "The Word" is as common in the Acts as "The Spirit", and they belong very closely together. One of the great merits of C. K. Barrett's book, *Luke the Historian in Recent Study* is the weight he gives to the Word as the prime agency through which the Spirit extends the good news of Christ. It is expressed in a number of ways: "the Word of God", "the Word of salvation", "the Word of the gospel" or quite simply "the Word". It means the message about Jesus. Wherever the early Christians went, it was the Word they carried (Acts 8: 4). When Paul was encouraged at Corinth by the fellowship of Priscilla and Aquila we read that he became gripped by the Word (18: 5). During the two years and more of his mission in Ephesus "all the residents of Asia heard the Word of the Lord" (19: 10). When Luke wants to indicate the success of evangelistic work, he can say that "the Word of the Lord grew and prevailed". So it was in Judea (6: 7), Samaria (8: 4-7, 14), on the first missionary journey (13: 49) and in Asia (19: 10). The Word makes its own impact on Theophilus (Luke 1: 1, Acts 1: 1), Cornelius (10: 44), the proconsul of Cyprus (13: 7), and on the citizens of Antioch (13: 44). No wonder the twelve made it their priority, and the nameless missionaries of 8: 4 took it as their great weapon. For if a man believes, it is because the Word brings faith (4: 4). If a man receives the Spirit, it is because he has responded to the Word (10: 44). It is no exaggeration to say that the Word is the prime tool used by the Spirit of God in advancing the Christian mission.

It would take us too far afield to examine the content of this apostolic "Word". Essentially it was concerned with Jesus. Many people have tried to summarise it, and perhaps the most celebrated attempt is that of C. H. Dodd in *The Apostolic Preaching and its Development*. He maintained that the good news about Jesus had a clearly defined form. This form is discernible in Mark's Gospel, the Acts sermons, the Pauline Letters and in certain other parts of the New Testament. The kerygma of the early Church, contained in that outline, amounted to something like this:

The age of fulfilment has dawned. This has taken place through the ministry, death and resurrection of Jesus of Nazareth. By virtue of the resurrection Jesus has been raised to the right hand of God, as messianic head of the Israel of God. The Holy Spirit in the Church is the sign of Christ's present power and glory. The Messianic Age will shortly reach its culmination in the return of Christ. Hence the importance of repentance, faith, baptism into the messianic community, and the reception of God's offer of forgiveness and the Holy Spirit.

Footnotes in plenty have been added to Dodd, but his pattern remains a fair summary of the early preaching so far as we can reconstruct it. But such summaries will inevitably remain speculative since we have only one source in the New Testament for determining the content of the early preaching to people who were not Christians, and that is the sermons in Acts. And it remains a matter of debate to what extent Luke is exercising editorial privilege in his accounts of the apostolic preaching. Furthermore, as I have tried to show in my book *Evangelism in the Early Church*, there was considerable flexibility in the way the gospel was preached to different audiences in different circumstances, coupled with great unity in presenting men with the person of Jesus, the offer of forgiveness through his death on the cross, the promise of the Holy Spirit, and the challenge to repent and believe and be baptised. Such, in essence, was the Word that the Holy Spirit could confidently be expected to take home to the hearts of the hearers. He still does.

Preaching is a very humbling thing. You feel such a fool. Paul catches the feeling precisely in 2 Corinthians 4: 1–6. The preacher is involved in a titanic confrontation, in which he is a tiny Lilliputian. He becomes aware that "the god of this age (i.e. the devil) has blinded the minds of those who do not believe, lest the light of the glorious gospel of Christ, who is the image of God, should shine on them". Every effective preacher knows that proclamation involves not mere communication, but confrontation. "For we are not contending against flesh and blood, but against principalities and powers, against the world rulers of this present darkness" (Ephesians 6: 12). We don't get anywhere by what Paul calls "preaching ourselves": gimmicks do not help. It is by being prepared to be people's servants for Jesus' sake so that the light may shine through to them. For light is not lacking: "the God who commanded light to shine out of (primeval) darkness has shone in our hearts to give the light of the knowledge of the glory of God in the face of Jesus Christ" (2 Corinthians 4: 6). But how is this glory to shine through to others? Only as the Holy Spirit takes the "foolish" message of the gospel home to people's hearts, and convinces them of its truth; that it is indeed "the wisdom of God to every one who believes" (1 Corinthians 1: 18ff). We come back to this theme of the double witness, by the Holy Spirit and ourselves, which the New Testament continually brings before us. A preacher can talk till he's blue in the face, but he can never bring anyone to faith in Christ. Yet the Holy Spirit can take his words home to the conscience of the hearer and bring that person low in repentance and faith before the crucified and risen Christ. Anyone who has been instrumental in this transformation of another person's life through the impact of the Word of God and the Spirit of God will know that it is not his own doing. I have on occasion preached the same sermon in two different churches. In one, between twenty and thirty people professed conversion. In the other, nobody did. The Spirit and the message and the messenger all combine to carry out this strange alchemy of new birth. But only the Spirit is indispensable. I heard a remarkable story recently from a leading Indian Christian, the Revd. Samuel Kamelesan. A friend of his, who was engaged in Christian colportage work, decided to go to the heart of Brahmin country in Kumbbakoman in Southern India. He wanted to bear witness to Jesus in this tough spot, and invited some of the nearby Christians to accompany him. They declined. "We have to live here", they replied! So he went alone.

This brave man entered the courtyards of the main temple, and began to preach Jesus. He expected to be killed. Instead, he had hardly begun before he was embraced by a Brahmin woman and was asked, "Why did you not come sooner?" Her story was a fascinating one. This rich, high-caste woman had had terminal cancer. She was given a very short expectation of life by the doctors. So she went to Madras, in whose pleasant climate she would live out the few remaining weeks of her life. Then, apparently, she died. She was laid out in the mortuary. But she was not dead, only deeply unconscious. In this state she had a vision of Jesus, about whom she knew nothing. In the vision the Lord looked on her with love. "If you will let me live again, Lord, I will give my life for you" she promised.

While the woman was lying there in the mortuary unconscious, a crossing sweeper happened to notice a faint movement in this supposed corpse. She went immediately to the doctor who had signed the death certificate. The doctor examined her, found a faint pulse, and immediately swung into action to resuscitate the patient. A blood transfusion was necessary. It so happened that the crossing sweeper had blood of the same group as this rich Brahmin lady. And she happened to be a Christian. She gladly gave her blood for a substantial blood transfusion, and the patient was told afterwards by the doctor, "You owe the fact that you are alive today to the crossing sweeper who first detected a movement in you when you were in the mortuary and then gave her blood for you".

The Brahmin lady was as good as her word. From that day onward she worshipped Jesus only, and renounced her Hinduism. This provoked intense opposition, not least from her own family, in a militantly Hindu city like Kumbbakoman. The woman began to bear witness to the Jesus of whom she knew almost nothing, and was physically beaten up for her pains. Indeed, her own brothers knocked two of her teeth out. Yet her simple witness led three of her five brothers to Christ. And when the colporteur started to preach Jesus in that temple courtyard the lady ran out and embraced him, delighted to find a fellow believer in that unexpected place. He taught her much more about the Lord in whom she believed, rather as Paul, Aquila and Priscilla did to Apollos.

Now in that story only one of the normal evangelising agencies was present, the Holy Spirit. There was no proclamation of the word to bring the Brahmin woman to belief. And there was no human messenger to tell her about Jesus, though the part played by the Christian outcaste crossing sweeper was of the utmost importance. The Spirit of life not only revived the woman, and caused a spontaneous remission of the cancer, but brought her to trust in Christ—which from that background was quite as great a miracle. In more senses than one we can say with the Creed, "I believe in the Holy Spirit, the Lord, the Lifegiver".

The Spirit convicts and attracts

At every point the Holy Spirit is involved in the process of a man becoming a Christian. As we saw in discussing John 16: 8, it is the Holy Spirit who acts as prosecuting counsel, and convicts a man of sin. No man can do that to another. If this conviction arises through my preaching, it is frequently through some phrase or thrust that I had not intended. I well recall one tough Yorkshire girl who was on drugs at the time, coming to a service where I was preaching, and being pierced to the heart by a throwaway line I had never intended saying, about God hardening Pharaoh's heart. I knew nothing about this convicting work of the Spirit in her, until a week later when she rang me from Halifax and asked, "Does God really harden people's hearts?". It was through this most improbable passage of Scripture, taken home to her by the Spirit, that she in due course became a Christian. I think of another man, to whom I had said something about Jesus Christ while marching down alongside him to an army parade! He had seemed very uninterested, and I had not pursued the conversation. In any case, the conditions were scarcely suitable. To this day I cannot recall what it was I said to him. Nevertheless, the Spirit took it home with unerring aim. A day later he came to see me, unable to sleep and distraught. He had begun to see what he looked like to God, and now he was not in the least uninterested to hear what Jesus Christ had done about it. Before that night was out he had surrendered himself to Christ.

Not only is the Spirit the one who convicts a man of sin: it is he, and only he, who can make Jesus attractive. As we have already seen, it is the Spirit who bears witness to Jesus and glorifies him (John 15: 26, 16: 14). Sometimes this happens over a long period, as a person finds himself constrained to attend a Christian place of worship, or drawn to read the Christian scriptures. Time and again I have met folk who have been warmed by the Spirit to perceive the beauty of Christ in the life of a group of believers or in the story of the New Testament, and have come to faith that way. Sometimes this attraction to Jesus happens instantaneously. The penny suddenly drops, and he is revealed as the one who makes sense of life. I remember an English don once coming to me at the end of a meeting, and saying that she had suddenly seen that evening in Jesus Christ the answer to the rather negative existentialist framework into which her life had been cast. That was the work of the Spirit, revealing Christ to her.

The Spirit brings repentance and faith

The Spirit is probably meant by passages of the New Testament which speak of repentance as a gift of God. Acts 11: 15–18 is a case in point. Peter is recounting the Cornelius episode. He tells how the Holy Spirit fell on Cornelius, and points out that God had given Cornelius the same gift as the Jewish believers. Their response is "Then God has given the Gentiles also the gift of repentance leading to life". The plain inference is that it is through the operation of the Spirit that these Gentiles have come to repentance. The same is probably intended by Acts 5: 31 and 2 Timothy 2: 25.

When it comes to faith, we are left in no doubt that this is a gift of God brought about by the Holy Spirit. No man can make the Christian confession "Jesus is Lord" without the Holy Spirit enabling him to do so (1 Corinthians 12: 3). Seen in its context, that is a most significant verse. For the Corinthians were fascinated with the charismatic and ecstatic aspects of the work of the Spirit. St. Paul tells them at the outset of his three-chapter discussion on spiritual gifts, that ecstasy is no sure mark of inspiration by the Spirit. So-called spiritual men could, and did, call Jesus accursed in ecstatic cries in the Corinthian assembly (12:3). The true mark of the Spirit's operation is when a man can say from his heart that Jesus is his Lord. Once again we see the Spirit is related securely to the person of Jesus, and it is when the Spirit enables a man to see who Jesus is and respond to him in allegiance that faith is born. It is the Spirit who takes the things of God and reveals them to us (1 Corinthians 2:12), and Paul can rightly say that the very capacity to respond in faith is a gift of God and no man-made attribute of which we can boast (Ephesians 2:8). The Spirit can therefore be called "the Spirit of faith" (2 Corinthians 4:13). And to possess the pledge of the Spirit is interpreted as living the life of faith (2 Corinthians 5:5, 7).

In other words, it is due to the work of the Holy Spirit that we become Christians at all. He is the Spirit who adopts us into the family of God alongside Jesus (Romans 8:15, Galatians 4:6). Though by nature we Gentiles are "without Christ, aliens from the commonwealth of Israel, strangers from the covenant of promise, having no hope and without God in the world", the Holy Spirit has given us access, through Christ's self-sacrifice for us (Ephesians 2:12–18). "Now you are no longer strangers and foreigners", Paul exultantly reminds his readers, "but fellow citizens with the Old Testament believers, and in the very household of God". The New Testament writers use a variety of terms to speak of the Holy Spirit's work in making us Christians. "You received the Spirit", says Paul to the Galatians. "You began in the Spirit." You accepted "the gracious provision of the Spirit", or "the promise of the Spirit" (Galatians 3:2, 3, 5, 14). Sometimes this initial encounter with the Spirit is seen as a great washing (1 Corinthians 6:11). Sometimes it is a new birth (Titus 3:5, John 3:3, 5) brought about by the entry of the Spirit into our lives. Whatever the imagery, one thing remains constant. It is only through the agency of the Holy Spirit, enabling us to repent and believe, convicting us of sin and making Jesus attractive to us, that we ever become Christians. It is the Spirit of Christ that unites us with Christ: so much so that Paul can say "If any man does not have the Spirit of Christ, he does not belong to Christ" (Romans 8:9).

We shall be looking further at this vexed question of Christian initiation and the relation of the Holy Spirit to baptism in a later chapter. But we have seen enough to be able to frame a clear answer to the question formulated at the outset of this chapter. God sent the Spirit of Jesus to his followers in order to equip them to carry on the mission of his Son in the world. Empowered by that Spirit, and bearing witness to the crucified and risen Jesus, the early Christians and succeeding generations alike have found hard hearts softened, strong men brought to repentance, sceptics coming to faith, and people of all ages, backgrounds and classes coming to taste the salvation of the messianic community, and being born into the very family of God.

CHAPTER 6

The Spirit in the Individual

IF GOD'S OVERALL strategy in sending us his Spirit is to equip the Church for mission, and bring people into the messianic kingdom, the sphere of salvation — we may well ask what he does when he has got them there? Why does he give his Holy Spirit to the individual?

1. The Spirit in Christian Initiation

The Spirit initiates us

As we have seen, it is the Spirit who brings men to repentance, faith and incorporation into Christ. To believe the gospel, respond to Jesus or receive the Spirit are three ways of looking at the same thing (2 Corinthians 11: 4). The whole Godhead is involved in the rescue and restoration of mankind, and so we read of Paul giving thanks over Christians for "God chose you from the beginning to be saved". How was that achieved? When "the Spirit set you apart" — that was God's side; and "when you believed the truth" — that was your side. "To this he called you through our gospel, so that you may obtain the glory of our Lord Jesus Christ" (2 Thessalonians 2: 13). Christians are people who have tested the "grace of our Lord Jesus Christ, and the love of God, and the fellowship of (better 'joint participation in') the Holy Spirit" (2 Corinthians 13: 14). The three experiences cannot be divorced. As Peter puts it, "you are chosen by God the Father, and set apart as his own by the Spirit for obedience to Jesus Christ and sprinkling with his blood" (1 Peter 1: 2). In other words, any experience of Christ is also an experience of the Holy Spirit who mediates Christ to us. In that fascinating passage in Romans 8: 9–11 Paul recognises "the Spirit of God" from Old Testament days to be none other than "the Spirit of Christ", the Spirit who indwelt Christ and who is given us from Christ. Thus to have the Spirit is to have Christ, and vice versa. The Spirit is the one who makes Christ real to us. So "if any man have not the Spirit of Christ he is no Christian". It is right to say, "If Christ is in you" and in the next verse to say, "If the Spirit of him who raised Jesus from the dead dwells in you", for it is by means of the Spirit, the Spirit of God, the Spirit of Christ, that Jesus makes his home in the believer. The Spirit is the mode of the divine indwelling. That is why Jesus in St. John's Gospel can promise that through the arrival of the Paraclete not only he himself will come back and indwell the disciples, but so will the Father (John 14: 17, 18, 21, 23). We are back to the three act drama with which we began. Act Three reveals the deity actually resident within believers; and it is through the Spirit that this takes place.

The New Testament writers sometimes speak of Christ living within Christians, sometimes of the Spirit doing so (Galatians 2: 20, Colossians 1: 27, Romans 8: 10, 8: 11, 1 Corinthians 3: 16). They sometimes speak of Christians being in Christ, and sometimes of being in the Spirit (Philippians 1: 1, 1 Corinthians 3: 1, Romans 8: 1, 8: 9, Colossians 1: 8, Ephesians 2: 22). It does not seem to matter very much which way we look at it. If you intertwine your fingers together, it is equally true to say that your right hand is in your left, or that your left hand is in your right. The point is that they are firmly connected. And that is what the New Testament wants to say about our relationship to Christ and his Spirit. On the whole, as M. Bouttier has shown in his book *En Christ: étude d'exégèse et de théologie pauliennes*, there is a tendency to speak of us being in Christ, and of the Spirit being in us. That is the predominant emphasis, and it is a helpful one. Christ is the new man, the last Adam (1 Corinthians 15: 45), and Christians are members of his body (1 Corinthians 12: 12ff). The Spirit comes and takes up residence in our bodies, which he wants to use as his temple (1 Corinthians 6: 19).

Very well then. The Spirit comes and takes up residence in a man once he is invited in. What is his task then?

The Spirit assures us—through sacraments

The first requirement, when a man passes "out of darkness into light, from the power of Satan to God" (Acts 26: 18) would seem to be that he needs assurance. He needs to know he belongs to the new family, that he is "accepted in the beloved one" (Ephesians 1: 6). And that is just what the Spirit does. St. John tells us that this is one of his main functions. "This is how we know that he remains in us, by means of the Spirit whom he has given us" (1 John 3: 24). He repeats it in 4: 13, "This is how we know that we remain in him, and he in us, because he has given us a portion of his Spirit". And in chapter 5 he expands his meaning. There are three grounds for Christian assurance, he tells us: "the Spirit, the water and the blood". This passage should be seen against its background. The Gnostic teacher, Cerinthus, was active in Asia Minor at the time when John wrote, and he taught that the heavenly Christ came upon the human Jesus only at his baptism, and left him before his passion: the union between them only *seemed* to be real—actually it was merely temporary. Had this been the case, there would have been no Christian gospel to preach: no incarnation of the Son of God, no real solidarity between him and us, no expiatory death upon the cross. John therefore opposes it strongly. Jesus, the Christ, is the one who has come through the water of his baptism, through the blood of his cross, and is mediated to us through the Holy Spirit. The coming through water, the cross, and the gift of the Spirit are all thoroughly historical events: and yet they are more than that. They are continuing factors in the life of the Church through the experience Christians have of the Spirit, and through the sacraments of water (baptism) and blood (the eucharist) which seem to be alluded to here. Baptism is a mark of belonging, a ground of assurance, which the Spirit can take home to our hearts. It was so to Martin Luther when he was tempted to despair of his spiritual state: "*Baptizatus sum*" he recalled with joy. Joy, because it did not rest upon his own faith, strongly though he valued that: but when in the morass of doubt, one has no confidence in subjective attitudes such as faith. But his baptism, administered to him by another, sealing physically upon him the objectiveness of what Christ did for him on the cross, that was indeed a ground of assurance. It was the sacrament of justification by grace; the physical, palpable reminder that God acted for him without his aid and prior to his response.

The eucharist, too, is one of the ways in which the Spirit gives us assurance. This is strongly implied in John chapter 6 where the Spirit is brought closely into relation with "eating his body and drinking his blood" and so being confident of dwelling in Christ, being fed by him, and being raised up by him at the last day (6: 54, 56, 63); just as he is in chapter 3: 3–8 in connection with the new birth. Of course the sacraments can be completely empty, like the marriage ceremony. But just as it is proper for me to look back to my wedding day as assurance that I am really married, so it is proper to look back to my baptism as a mark given me by the Holy Spirit that I am really born again in Christ, and to the eucharist as a pledge that I do partake of his life, feed on him, and shall in the last day share his resurrection.

The Spirit assures us—through signs

But it is not only through the sacraments that the Spirit assures us we belong to Christ. 1 John gives several other ways which enable us to be confident of our new status. The Spirit means us to know where we stand (1 John 3: 24, 5: 13) and the Epistle is at pains to point out various signs which give confidence to true believers, while breaking down false assurance.

The Christians should expect the indwelling Spirit to make a difference. If there is no difference, there is good reason to suppose that the Spirit has not been received into the man's life. Thus a believer begins to "keep God's word" or "walk as Christ walked" (2: 5, 6): "he does not go on sinning, because God's seed remains in him, and he cannot go on sinning, because he is born of God" (3: 9). Of course John does not mean that the Christian becomes sinless overnight. He knows full well that Christians can and do sin, and if we pretend otherwise we are lying (1: 8, 10). But he is insisting, in black and white terms, that the divine sonship, mediated by the Spirit, must show itself in changed behaviour. We cannot go on untouched in the old self-centred ways if the Holy Spirit has made his residence within us.

Another of the marks of belonging is a willingness to face the opposition of "the world" (a technical term in the Johannine literature to indicate society which has left God out), and to get involved in the loving fellowship of the family of Christ. "Do not be surprised, my brothers, if the world hates you. We know that we have passed from death to life because we love brother Christians" (3: 13f).

What is more, the Spirit who has become resident in the followers of Jesus mediates to them the victory over the world which Jesus had (4: 4) as they trust him for the power to overcome temptation (5: 3, 4). Joyous fellowship, too, is a mark of the new life which the Spirit initiates in us (1: 3, 4), and so is the experience of answered prayer (5: 14). Most of all, perhaps, the love for God and for our fellows which the Holy Spirit produces in our hearts, a quality which we do not possess independently of him (4: 18ff). Over and above all this, John tells us of the internal testimony of the Holy Spirit with the Spirit of the believer, assuring him that God's testimony to his Son is reliable, assuring him that the Christian experience is real. Christians are meant not only to *believe* in Jesus, but to *know* that we have eternal life (5: 13) and it is the task of the Spirit to bring this quiet confidence home to us.

After all, we need to know we belong. No man can erect a building of any serious dimensions on a rickety foundation. It would not be possible to live a Christian life on the shifting sand of doubt as to our relationship with our Lord. Accordingly, it is not modesty to say "I hope I am a Christian, but I cannot say more". That might indeed be the proper thing to say if being a Christian were the result of my own efforts, goodness or achievements. But the New Testament writers insist with one voice that it is nothing of the kind. I am saved by God's gracious intervention on my behalf, not by "works" of whatever type. So I have nothing to boast of. "It is all of God that you are in Christ Jesus", says Paul to the Corinthians (1 Corinthians 1: 30), "and God makes Christ to be our wisdom, righteousness, sanctification and redemption, so that, as the Scripture says, 'He that boasts must boast in the Lord' ". It is not, therefore, presumptuous to say with quiet confidence, "I know that I belong to Christ. I have not done anything to earn it, but God has given me the Spirit and accepted me into his family; and he means me to know that I belong".

Five aspects of belonging to the Spirit

There are five words in particular which the New Testament writers use to describe different aspects of this work of assurance which the Holy Spirit does for the believer.

The first is the metaphor of "adoption". Paul alludes to a pagan custom, rare indeed in the Jewish world, whereby a man might adopt the children of another family into his own. It was quite common for the Emperor to adopt his putative successor in this way. And this, says the apostle, is what God has done for us. Jesus died to redeem us, and adopt us into the Father's family; and because we are sons God has sent the Spirit of his Son into our hearts, enabling us to call "Abba,

Father" (Galatians 4:5, 6, Ephesians 1:5, Romans 8:15). The Spirit of Jesus, entering our lives, comes to us as God's adoption present, so to speak, and enables us to call God by the intimate family name which Jesus used and which we have already considered. The Holy Spirit accomplishes and applies to us our sonship, and all the privileges that flow from it: "for if children, then we are heirs, heirs of God and joint heirs with Christ" (Romans 8: 17).

The second word is "seal". Paul tells the Ephesians that having heard the word of truth and having believed the good news of salvation, they are "in Christ" and have been sealed with the Holy Spirit who was promised long ago (1. 13, cf 2 Corinthians 2: 21). "Seal" is a property word. It speaks of belonging. The Holy Spirit is given us to identify us as belonging to Jesus, just as the seal on a letter or the brand on a sheep identifies it as mine. There may even be a double nuance in the assurance of ownership that is mentioned here. The seal of the Spirit is meant to assure us that we belong to Christ, and to let others also know the fact. It is perhaps an anachronism to read back into New Testament times the usage of second-century Christians whereby this word "seal" was explicitly used of baptism, or sometimes confirmation. Paul uses it of the Spirit, without any indication of any outward sign. But in view of passages in Revelation like 7: 3 which speak of "sealing the servants of God in their foreheads", and Romans 4: 11 which speaks of circumcision as "the sign and seal of being in the right with God through faith", it is not impossible that baptism may have been in the apostle's mind when he spoke of this sealing with the Spirit. What circumcision was to men of faith under the old covenant, assuring them that they belonged to Yahweh, so baptism is to the Christian; and Colossians 2: 11, 12 brings the two ordinances together round the cross of Christ which alone gives them meaning.

Another word which Paul uses of the Spirit who assures Christians of their position is "earnest". Two of its three occurrences go with the "sealing" work of the Spirit (2 Corinthians 1: 22, Ephesians 1: 14. The other one is 2 Corinthians 5: 5). If "seal" is the property word, "earnest" is the prophetic word. It looks forward to a greater gift in the future while stressing a real gift in the present. Often used in commerce for a "down-payment", or "first instalment", it is a highly appropriate word for the Holy Spirit. He is God's first instalment of the future salvation that awaits us; the part of the future we have now in the present; the pledge of the fuller life that is to come. Indeed, the modern Greeks use that word for an engagement ring, and that gives not a bad idea of the Holy Spirit's work as "earnest" in Paul's thought. He is the Heavenly Lover's engagement ring given to us. We shall carry that engagement ring with us into God's future, when we have the full wedding ring of final union with Christ. At present, the Spirit is the pledge of blessing to come. He is a real part of the age to come that is available to us here and now: he will never be supplanted. But there is more to come, in the fulness of God's time. Such is the nuance of the Spirit's as "earnest of our inheritance".

. The fourth word is "firstfruits". This is a word from farming. If the firstfruits are good, so will the main crop be. The metaphor is used in the New Testament in a variety of ways. Epaenetus was the firstfruit of the harvest of converts in the province of Asia (Romans 16: 5). Christ's resurrection is seen as a firstfruit from the grave, and pledge of the great harvest to come when those who are in Christ will share his risen life in heaven (1 Corinthians 15: 20, 23). Paul takes comfort from the firstfruits of Jewish believers that the whole nation will, in God's time, turn back to the Lord (Romans 11: 16). And the Holy Spirit is given us as a firstfruit of the harvest God has in store for us (Romans 8: 23).

A final word to describe this witness of the Spirit with our spirit that we are indeed sons of God (Romans 8: 16) is "assurance". In 1 Thessalonians 1: 5 Paul reminds his readers how the gospel was first preached to them: "it came not in word only, but in power and in the Holy Spirit and in full assurance". The literal meaning seems to be that a man is so full of the Holy Spirit that he carries conviction when he speaks about Christ. Christian assurance is no merely intellectual persuasion, but an overwhelmingly convincing experience of the indwelling Spirit welling up within us and flowing out to others. Such is the confidence that the Spirit means to give believers.

But a final word is needed before we leave this side of the Spirit's work. There is an "already" and a "not yet" about the Spirit's witness of assurance. This reminder of the "not yet" is clear in the word "earnest". God has not yet come back to buy up his possessions (the Christians), for whom he has paid the down-payment of the Spirit (Ephesians 1: 14); and it is in the context of our future inheritance beyond death that Paul speaks of the Spirit as our "earnest" in 2 Corinthians 5: 5. Similarly "seal" has a future look to it. Ephesians 4: 30

tells us that the Spirit seals us in preparation for the day of redemption: the "already" and the "not yet" are united in that phrase. To speak of a "firstfruits" inevitably takes one's eyes to the "not yet" (and this is made explicit in Romans 8: 23). Even our sonship, mediated to us by the Spirit, has this ambiguity about it. On the one hand we can be sure that the Spirit makes us sons (Romans 8: 15). On the other, we have still to wait for our final adoption at the Second Coming (Romans 8: 23). And to match our assurance, our being so full of the Spirit that he bubbles over from us, there is the other side of the picture: we also groan in the Spirit, and he groans with us (Romans 8: 26). For the Spirit's work in assurance is to give us a firm foundation to build on, not to make us arrogant; the "already" and the "not yet" of the Spirit's internal witness enable us to be sure without being cocksure.

2. *The Spirit in Christian Character*

After assuring us of our sonship the Spirit sets out to reproduce in us the character and graces of the Family into which we have been adopted. First and foremost he brings us into an entirely new dimension of freedom.

The Spirit of Freedom

Paul in particular found that when he preached the forgiveness and gift of the Spirit which Christ made possible he ran up against a deeply entrenched problem. The Jews of his day had come to see the Old Testament law not as a pointer to the life of trusting obedience in God which it was meant to be, but rather a code to be scrupulously followed in every detail. If you managed to do this, you would earn, indeed almost compel from God, a favourable verdict at the Last Day. It all depended on human effort. Justification would come from law-keeping. This belief, though not taught in the Old Testament, was widely held in the Jewish constituency among whom Paul worked: it is widely believed today that if only you try hard and do your best, God will accept you at the last. The apostle attacks this belief with a battery of arguments. Galatians 3: 10–14 is a good example.

First, he shows scathingly that it cannot be done, this perfect law-keeping. If you do not keep *all* the things written in the book of the law, you remain under its curse as a lawbreaker. As James put it in his Epistle, "whoever shall keep the whole law, and yet offend in one point, is guilty of all" (2: 10). If legal contract is what you are after, one slip in the contract is sufficient to invalidate it. And which of us has not broken the law of God not just once but thousands of times? So getting in the right with God is impossible for human beings to achieve by their own efforts. As guilty failures we all come beneath that "curse" imposed on lawbreakers. "All the world is guilty before God", Jew and Gentile, virtuous and wicked alike (Romans 3: 19). All have come short of the divine standard for human life; none can lay claim to earning the verdict of acquittal by keeping the law in its entirety: "for there is no distinction, since all have sinned and come short of the glory of God" (Romans 3: 23). It is not only overt actions which are reprehensible, but rather the thoughts of the heart and that attitude of rebellion against God which characterise us all (Romans 3: 9–20).

Secondly, even if man could achieve the impossible and live a perfect life, fulfilling the divine requirements in all particulars, a doctrine of merit would remain unacceptable to the God of the Bible. For, according to the prophets, "he who by faith is righteous shall live"; and the law does not rest on faith, for "he who does them shall live by them" (Galatians 3: 12). The whole principle of merit militates against the personal God whom Scripture depicts as wanting to have personal relations with his creatures. The father in a family can never be satisfied if his children clean his shoes and lay the table, but never talk to him, and never hug him. How could the heavenly Father be satisfied with mechanical obedience devoid of love and trust?

And thirdly, Paul argues that the way of self-commendation to God by merit is not the way of God's heroes in the Old Testament. The Jews of Paul's day could draw no credit for being sons of Abraham unless their attitude was like that of Abraham. God gave his inheritance to Abraham by promise, not as a reward for law-keeping (3: 18). He graciously appeared to Abraham, who had no claim on him, and offered to give him a posterity like the stars of heaven: Abraham responded to this grace by an act of faith which issued in a life of obedience. The whole thrust of Paul's argument at this point, and again in Romans, is that the true Jew follows the example of Abraham, and responds in faith and obedience to the God who meets him in grace: and that is precisely the terms of the gospel which Paul preaches. The only difference is this. Abraham was accepted by God in virtue of what Christ *would do* upon the cross by bearing the curse of the broken law upon his representative shoulders: men living after the cross could be accepted by God as they put their trust in what God *had done* for them through Jesus. That is the only difference. "Christ redeemed us from the curse of the law, having become a curse for us—for it is written 'Cursed be every one who hangs upon a tree'—so that in Christ Jesus the blessing accorded to Abraham might come upon the Gentiles, that we might receive the promised Spirit through faith" (Galatians 3: 14). The mysterious irony of salvation lay in this paradox: Jesus, the only one who kept the law in its entirety, paid the penalty of lawbreakers, by being exposed upon that accursed cross and subject to the judgment of God. He acted as the substitute and the representative for the whole human race. As a result believers under the old covenant and under the new are accepted before God as if they were sinless, for they are incorporated in the sinless Messiah who stood in their place of sin and judgment (2 Corinthians 5: 21). They are "justified" by the grace of God that gives them what they do not deserve, and by the "faith" which grasps that proffered gift and responds in obedient dedication to that proffered love. God's way of salvation is shown to be the same throughout the ages: men respond in faith to his initiative in grace. Through the crucial action of "Abraham's seed, which is Christ" (Galatians 3: 16) even the despised Gentiles can become children of that archetypal believer, Abraham, and receive the promised Spirit.

Away, then, with all attempts at self-justification before God. They are impossible, immoral, and out of step with the whole history of salvation. The Messiah has done for us what we could never do in putting us in the right with God; and the gift of his Spirit releases us from the need to try to justify ourselves. "Did you receive the Spirit by works of the law, or by hearing with faith?" asks Paul of the Galatians who were being tempted to go back to legalism (Galatians 3: 2). The Spirit brings new life, new freedom from those old legalistic attitudes. "We serve not under the old written code, but in the new life of the Spirit" (Romans 7: 6). "The written code kills, but the Spirit gives life" (2 Corinthians 3: 6); new life, and liberation from this whole depressing attempt to justify ourselves. "Where the Spirit of the Lord is, there is liberty" (2 Corinthians 3: 17).

The Spirit of Power

But liberty does not mean licence. If Jesus died in order to

make the unjust justified, he also endowed them with his
Spirit in order to make them just. God has done for us what
law-keeping, weakened by the frailties of our own fallen
nature, could never do. He sent his own Son in human flesh,
identical with us except for sin, and he condemned man's
sinfulness in Christ's person, hanging upon the cross, as a
sin-offering for us. He did so in order that the just requirement
set out in God's law might be fulfilled in us who live our lives
not after the principle of self-effort but in the power of the
Spirit. That is a rough paraphrase of Romans 8: 3, 4. It shows
that Christ's work of sinbearing did not abrogate the moral
claims of the law, but was the precondition to men being able
to face up to them. In other words, we are not forgiven because
we keep the law: but once we are forgiven we are called to
keep it. The claim of a holy God that those who have fellowship
with him should not only be acquitted and accounted righteous,
but actually and progressively be made righteous in an ethical
sense is strongly brought out in the Pauline letters. He will not
for a moment allow that the doctrine of justification through
free grace, received by faith, can lead to antinomianism
(Romans 6: 1ff). Far from it. For justification, and the very baptism which is its outward symbol, means dying with Christ and
rising again; dying to the old sinful ways, and being prepared
to see them as characteristics of the unregenerate nature that
was dealt with on the cross by Jesus and must be kept there.
And it means rising with Christ too; rising to share in the new
life which he makes possible, and which in the fullest detail
Paul in Romans chapter eight ascribes to the Spirit of Jesus,
resident within us.

The law of God had demanded holiness, but could not
enable it. The law remained an external authority expressing
God's requirements, but providing no power to keep them.
The demand and the requirements still stand. But through
the Spirit, God has given us the ability to fulfil those requirements. Not only is there "no condemnation for those who are in
Christ Jesus", but "the law of the Spirit of life in Christ Jesus
has set me free from the law of sin and death (Romans 8: 1, 2).
Paul finds himself not only with a new pardon now he is
united with Christ: but also with a new power. The Spirit of
Jesus has come within him, and provides a higher law than the
law of sin and death. By this he means that the principle he
had known as dominant in his life was the principle of sin and
the death to which it inevitably led. Now in Christ, he has
a new principle active within him, a higher law, the life-giving

power of the Spirit. Just as the higher law of life stops an apple held in my hand from obeying the law of gravity to which it would otherwise be subject, so the law (as he daringly calls it) of the Spirit overcomes the sin-death principle to which the Christian would otherwise be subject.

There is nothing automatic about this. Paul knows, not only from pre-conversion experience but, as a careful reading of Romans 7 will show, from painful experience of struggle and failure *as a Christian*, that when he relies on himself and his own resources (such seems to be the nuance of "I of myself" in Romans 7: 25), he remains subject to the law of sin. But, thanks to what God has made available through Jesus Christ our Lord, Paul knows that we need not remain defeated. Though the sinful propensities remain in us till our dying day, they need not be dominant. Through the Spirit we can put to death the deeds of the "flesh" (by which he means unredeemed human nature, alienated from God, Romans 8: 13). And at the end of our human course, the Spirit who can overcome sin, will also prove his ability to transcend death. "If the Spirit of him who raised Jesus from the dead dwells in you, he who raised up Christ Jesus from the dead will also give life to your mortal bodies through his Spirit which dwells in you" (8: 11). In other words, it is the Spirit of Jesus who reproduces in us the crucifixion and the resurrection of our Lord. The old unregenerate "I" is nailed to the cross with Christ (Galatians 2: 20): we "live in the Spirit" or "walk in the Spirit" precisely in so far as we allow the Spirit to "crucify the flesh with its affections and lusts" (Galatians 5: 24). And equally it is the Spirit who liberates Christ's risen power in us and enables us to share in his triumph. So "walk in the Spirit, and you shall not fulfil the lusts of the flesh" (Galatians 6: 16). In Romans 8 and Galatians 5 Paul makes it very clear that a battle royal rages in the lives of believers; a far greater battle than before their union with Christ. This is because the Spirit is opposed to the fallen human nature I am born with (and do not lose after my incorporation into Christ). The two principles are opposed to one another. And the ensuing battle, of which all Christians are aware in their experience, means either that they cannot achieve the good intentions they have or, if the Greek is taken in another sense, that the presence of the mighty Spirit prevents them doing what, if they followed the dictates of mere self-will, they otherwise would (Galatians 5: 17). In any case, we are reminded of the spiritual battle. Power over the inclinations of the fallen "flesh" is possible only when the

Spirit is given control by our act of deliberate choice. He has the power to overcome my fallen appetites, but he will not use it in me unless I ask him. Mercifully, the Spirit works deeply within my subconscious self. When I am so self-centred that I would not dream of asking the Spirit for his strength, preferring to go my own way, I am encouraged to recall that "God is at work in you both to will and to work for his good pleasure" (Philippians 2: 13). We shall not be mistaken in seeing that as a reference to God the Holy Spirit. He it is who not only empowers us to do right, but works in us the desire to want to do right, without which we would never dream of turning to ask him for his strength.

But that strength is available to all who are in Christ. It is none other than the superhuman power which raised Christ from the dead which is let loose within our human bodies (Ephesians 1: 18f). Paul is evidently referring to the Spirit when talking of this power, since he not only prays that the Spirit will reveal it to his readers, but he, in common with other New Testament writers, associates the Spirit with the resurrection of Christ from the dead (1 Timothy 3: 16 cf, 1 Peter 3: 18). In Ephesians 3: 16 Paul makes it quite explicit. He prays that "according to the riches of his glory, the Father may grant you to be strengthened with might through his Spirit in the inner man".

The Spirit of Christlikeness

This power given to individuals by the Spirit is not the naked *ruach* that we sometimes met with in the Old Testament days in men like Saul and Samson. It is the powerful application to believers of the character of Christ. Thus when Paul is talking about the spiritual battle in Galatians 5, the content of the Christian freedom he advocates is defined by the character of Jesus. This powerful, victorious Spirit which indwells believers, and can keep their sinful natures nailed upon the cross, is like a seed planted in the soil of the believer's life. If cultivated and nourished, this seed will grow into a lovely fruitful tree; and this is what the fruit is like:

> love, joy, peace, patience, kindness, goodness, faithfulness, gentleness, self-control (Galatians 5: 22).

And what is that, but a description of the character of Jesus? A holy God requires his people to be holy. But the God who "has called us for holiness . . . gives us his Holy Spirit"

(1 Thessalonians 4: 7, 8) to enable us to fulfil his requirement. This holiness is not merely a devotion to the deity (there was plenty of such attachment in the ancient world that was far from holy—for instance the cult prostitution that was so common in the temples), nor a mere adherence to ethical rules (there were plenty of those current in antiquity, too, and they possessed all the disadvantages, while lacking the advantages, of the Jewish law). Christian holiness involves both devotion and ethics; it springs from allegiance to Jesus, who embodies in himself the ideal of human conduct. Consequently we find the characteristics of Jesus being stressed time and again throughout the New Testament as the qualities which the Holy Spirit seeks to produce in Christ's people. The kingly rule of God which Jesus proclaimed and so signally embodied is not a matter of mere externals, what you eat or drink; but righteousness, peace and joy in the Holy Spirit (Romans 14: 17), and all three were pre-eminently to be found in Jesus. Power marked the apostolic preaching in the Holy Spirit at Thessalonica, and joy marked its reception by the new believers (1 Thessalonians 1: 5f). The Spirit that rested upon the suffering Messiah rests upon suffering Christians (1 Peter 4: 14). Just as Jesus' life was the embodiment of God's love, so we find that the Holy Spirit is particularly given to believers to live out God's own love in their loveless lives. "God's own love has been poured out into our hearts by the Holy Spirit who has been given us", says Paul in Romans 5: 5, and he rejoices to hear of that "love in the Spirit", which is to be found in the church at Colossae (1: 8). So cardinal a quality is this, so clear a mark of a man being filled with the Spirit of Christ, that in the middle of his three chapters on spiritual gifts (1 Corinthians 12–14), Paul sets the crowning gift of love. One has only to substitute the name of Jesus for "love" in that chapter to see that the whole thing is a pen picture of Christ's way of life. The first and foremost fruit of the Spirit is that outgoing love for others, irrespective of their deserts, which marked the Giver of the Spirit in his earthly life. True holiness, into which the Spirit calls us, is nothing other than Christlikeness. And in one marvellous passage, in which he contrasts the old dispensation with the new, Paul reaches this point as the climax of his theme. The Lord who had revealed himself fitfully and alternately under the old covenant, when Moses commuted between the Lord on Sinai and the people on the plain (with the glory reflected from his communing with God waxing and waning correspondingly), has now revealed himself steadily

and with unwithdrawn accessibility. Under the new covenant Yahweh makes himself present to his people as Spirit (which seems to be the meaning of "Now the Lord is the Spirit" 3: 17); and as such his presence is constant, unwithdrawn and steady. The divine presence, concentrated in Christ, and universalised through his death and resurrection, becomes available to transform his people. As we fix our gaze upon the Lord Jesus, worship him, and reflect on his character brought before us in the Gospels, our faces will shine, as Moses' did when he went in to seek the presence of the Lord. But the glory will not fade from the Christian as it did from Moses. It will increase. God's purpose is to change us by his Spirit within us (the word "change" is used in the Gospels to denote Jesus' trans-figuration!); and to change us from one degree of glory to another. "Glory" indicates the person and character of God, under the imagery of light. If we want to see the glory of God (which no man can do in all its unmediated radiance, and live, Exodus 32: 20) then we must seek it in the person of Jesus. In him the glory of God shines out in human form (John 1: 14, 2 Corinthians 4: 4). Well, the work of the Spirit in the believer is supremely to transform us from one degree of glory to another: that is to say, to make us more and more like Christ. In Titus 3: 5 the Holy Spirit is said to be the one who not only regenerates us, but who renews us; and this work of renewal of our natures from within is stressed in Romans 12: 2 (as we present our bodies a living sacrifice to God) and in Colossians 3: 10. There Paul explains that the new kind of life they live through union with the crucified and risen Christ involves having done with "anger, wrath, malice, blasphemy, filthy talk" which characterised "the old man" (i.e. their fallen human nature). Instead they are to put on, as if it were a suit of new clothes, the new humanity that is brought to them in Christ and is constantly renewed by a deepening knowledge of Christ, into the Creator's original image in man, a likeness to God himself: hence the "compassion, kindness, lowliness, meekness, patience, forbearance", love, peace and gratitude of which he goes on to speak (Colossians 3: 1, 5–16). It is the work of the Spirit, then, to make us progressively reflect the character of Christ, himself the Last Man who demonstrates the image of God which God intended for us when he made us. The process of Christlikeness is a progressive one: let nobody think he has attained it. Paul himself after decades of knowing Christ could still say that he had not attained the purpose for which Christ laid hold of him; he was still following on (Philippians 3: 8–15). But as he grew older, and felt the signs of decay in his mortal body, he rejoiced to think that his inner man was being renewed every day, until he should attain that "being at home with the Lord" to which his whole Christian life was directed and of which he had been given the Holy Spirit as a guarantee (2 Corinthians 4: 16f, 5: 1ff, 5, 8).

So in our sanctification as in our assurance, there is always an "already" and a "not yet" about the work of the Spirit. He is indeed given us to actualise in us the character of Christ: but that process will not be complete until we see him as he is, either at death or the Parousia. Let St. John have the last word on the subject. "Beloved, we are now the sons of God, and it does not yet appear what we shall be, but we know that when he appears we shall be like him, for we shall see him as he is. And everyone who has this hope in him purifies himself" (1 John 3: 2f).

3. The Spirit in Christian Growth

The Holy Spirit, who is both one with God and resident in us, has a further rôle in the life of the believer. He is indeed, as John Taylor has aptly called him, "the go-between God", for he both takes the things of God and makes them real to us on the one hand, and takes our faint longings and prayers and brings them to the Father on the other.

The Spirit illuminates God

Paul develops an interesting and original line of argument in 1 Corinthians 2. He is explaining that the Christian message is no earthly wisdom, such as the travelling philosophers of the day peddled, and with which some of the Corinthians were confusing it. No, it is nothing less than God's truth mediated to them by God's Spirit (2: 9). And just as human wisdom is only perceived and passed on by the human spirit inside us, so it is with the truth of God. No man can comprehend the things of God: if there is to be any comprehension on our part, then the onus is on God to reveal himself. That he has done. The Spirit has been given us to enable us to understand not the future, but the gracious gifts God has already made over to us (2: 12). But did we not read in St. John that it is Jesus who makes the Father known and discloses to us his nature (John 1: 18, 3: 13 etc.)? Certainly. But the same Gospel makes it plain that the Spirit will interpret Jesus as the focal point of all God's revelation. That is why "the Spirit of truth, who proceeds from the Father" is shown in his rôle of bearing witness to Jesus who is the truth of God incarnate (John 15: 16, 16: 14, 15 and 14: 6). Paul sees it in precisely the same way as John. In 1 Corinthians 2 he can say almost in the same breath that it is the Spirit who shows believers the deep things of God, and that we have the mind of Christ. Once again we come up against the indissoluble link between the Spirit and Jesus. He does indeed reveal to us God's gracious provision for us. But the name of that provision is Jesus. In many other places in the New Testament the Spirit who was active in the prophets is promised to the Christians to guide them, but always that guidance centres upon Jesus in whom the truth of God took personal form. Thus in Romans 8: 14 we are promised the guidance of the Spirit, but it is along the pathway of sonship wherein we follow Jesus in addressing God as "Abba", and share his mortification and risen life. In Ephesians 1: 17f Paul prays that the readers may have the spiritual illumination afforded by the Spirit. But this illumination is granted by the God of our Lord Jesus Christ and is possible only "in knowing him". The Spirit enables us to know the Master, to sense his will, to grasp his mind and to see things his way. In particular it is Paul's prayer that the Spirit would reveal to them three things. First, "the hope of his calling". In that phrase the Spirit characteristically mediates between the "already" and the "not yet". The calling is past. The hope of the calling is future. The first instalment of heaven, the Spirit himself, enables us to see the reality of our calling and its future consummation. Second, "the wealth of the glory of his inheritance in the saints", a deliberately ambiguous phrase which could mean that the saints have God as their inheritance—and what inexhaustible riches lie there! But it could also mean the even more staggering truth that the saints are God's inheritance, and pose the question to what extent he is allowed the freehold of that inheritance which is our lives. Third, Paul prays that they may perceive "the extreme greatness of his power to aid believers, the very power that raised Christ from the dead to God's right hand". And so we are brought by the Spirit's revelations back to Christ again. No further light has broken nor will break from God than Christ: the Spirit's task is to illuminate him to us. And to make this centrality of Christ even more emphatic the apostle ends his paragraph by reminding the readers that this mighty, risen, ascended Christ is the head of the body constituted by the Church, and his fulness fills their lives (or, perhaps, their lives are the complement of his fulness, Ephesians 1 : 23).

When in Colossians 1 : 9ff Paul prays for Christians he has never met, his first request is that the Spirit would give them understanding of the Lord's will for their lives; then, that they should live their lives in accordance with that will by pleasing the Lord in everything; then, that they should increase in their knowledge of God; and finally, that they should be strengthened with all might according to the measure of his glorious power which should result for them as it did for Christ, not in arrogance but in patience and longsuffering. Such was the Christian path of *imitatio Christi* on which the Spirit could be relied to shed the light of his illumination. The Christocentric nature of his revelation is once more to the fore; so is the characteristic Hebrew emphasis on knowledge leading to obedience.

In the Gnostic situation to which 1 John was addressed, "knowledge" was the "in" word, and false teachers were laying exclusive claims to it. John's response is to say that they did not need false teachers, or any other teachers for that matter: "you have been anointed (lit. 'Christed') by the Holy One, and you all know" (2 : 20). There is no doubt about the content of this divinely imparted illumination: "who is a liar but he who denies that Jesus is the Christ?" (2 : 22). They are warned not to believe every spiritual manifestation, because the authentic disclosures of the Spirit always bear witness to the incarnate Jesus. "By this you know the Spirit of God: every spirit that confesses that Jesus has come in the flesh is of God, and every spirit that does not confess Jesus is not of God" (4 : 2). Confident that the anointing they have all received is the person of the Spirit of the Anointed One, who remains with them (2 : 27), John knows he can safely leave their instruction to that same Spirit who is true and who shows them how to abide in Christ, the Christ who will one day return (2 : 28f). It is thoroughly in line with this that the author of Revelation can say, "Witness to Jesus is the Spirit of prophecy" (19 : 10). For Jesus is God's final word to men; and the Spirit illuminates and interprets but does not add to that word.

This means that if a man is truly brought to faith in Christ, he is not dependent on human teachers to lead him on, helpful though these may be. He has the heavenly Spirit to be his teacher. And he can safely set down to the Spirit's guidance anything which brings Jesus into sharper focus. I learnt this

lesson some years ago when the soldier to whom I referred
earlier came to Christ. I was at the time very concerned,
because he was posted almost immediately to North Africa,
and there was no chance of helping him forward in the early
days of his Christian life. I heard some months later that he
was organising a Bible study in his quarters in North Africa
to which not only fellow subalterns were coming but even
such exalted members of the Army hierarchy as majors! He
had no human teacher, but he had the Spirit of Christ and the
Scriptures, and through them he grew in knowledge and in
spiritual stature.

The Spirit guides believers

The problem of how the Spirit of God guides us is one which
confronts every humble Christian. There is no easy answer, for
the Spirit blows where he wills, and man can neither prescribe
to him nor control him. In practice, two tendencies are
discernible in the Church. The first is to suppose that God
always guides by the majority vote, by the reasonable thing,
by sanctified common sense. This can easily deteriorate into
prudential judgment, worldly planning and manipulation of
voting procedures. The second is to suppose that the guidance
of God is always extraordinary, individualistic, and sudden.

David Watson has some wise words to say on the matter in
his *One in the Spirit* (p. 54ff). He draws together from the Bible
four strands in divine guidance which, taken together, provide
a confident basis for action, and avoid excessive recourse to
that overworked claim, "The Lord told me to do such and
such".

First, God guides through circumstances (Acts 16: 10).
God closes some doors and opens others; our responsibility is
to be sensitive to his leading, and to follow through the doors
when they open.

Second, God guides through other Christians, as he did in
Acts 6 when the whole multitude chose the Seven, or in
Acts 13 when the Spirit spoke to the Church at Antioch about
the need for Paul and Barnabas to go abroad. Personal
convictions should be open to testing by the guidance of other
Christians. If our conviction really comes from God, others,
who are in touch with God, will confirm it. "The Christian
who will not listen to reason is a fool", says Watson forthrightly.
To be sure, this is not the only criterion: the voices of other
Christians may be very confused. But at least we must be

willing in principle to receive guidance through other members of the Body of Christ.

Third, God guides us through the Scriptures. The Spirit who inspired their writing is perfectly well capable of taking some part of them and writing it on our hearts so that it becomes an inescapable pointer to a particular course of action. This method, also, taken by itself is liable to abuse. To pick verses at random from the Bible proves nothing at all, except that we are gullible and are not using the Scriptures as we are intended to. Paul's advice is very different: "Let the word of Christ dwell in you richly, as you teach and admonish one another in all wisdom" (Colossians 3: 16). An increasingly broad appreciation of the Scriptures will give us a developing ability to scent the will of God in any given situation.

Fourthly, God guides us in prayer. Watson points to Colossians 3: 15, "Let the peace of Christ rule (i.e. be the arbiter) in your hearts". There is such a thing as praying a situation through until one is virtually sure of the will of God on the matter. One has a deep inner peace about it; not absolute intellectual certainty, but practical confidence, which allows one to proceed to action with joyful assurance. These are some of the ways in which we may expect the Spirit of God to illuminate not only the person of God but his will for us. He is the supreme Teacher for Christians who are growing in grace and in knowledge of their Lord.

The Spirit empowers prayer

As go-between, the Spirit not only teaches us the truth of God, he opens our eyes to the one in whom that truth became incarnate, and guides us in our lives. He also enables us to approach God in prayer. We have already seen that it is through the uniting Spirit that Jew and Gentile alike have access to the Father (Ephesians 3: 18). We have noticed that it is the Spirit who enables the adopted sons to call God "Father", "Abba", that intimate form of address first found on the lips of Jesus. Bearing in mind that "Abba" is the opening word of the Lord's Prayer in Aramaic, we could rightly say that only through the Spirit can we pray and live out that prayer. Indeed, in the immediate context of the Lucan Lord's Prayer, Jesus promises that the Father will give the Holy Spirit to those who ask him. The Spirit is thus the supreme object of prayer. And it is interesting to see how Luke works this theme out in his two-volume work. He tells us that as Jesus was praying before his baptism the Spirit came upon him. As the disciples were at prayer in Jerusalem awaiting Pentecost, the Spirit came upon them. Saul of Tarsus after his Damascus road experience spent three days in fasting and prayer; that showed he was in the receptive mood which invited the Spirit to come. It was the same with Cornelius, another great landmark in the spread of the gospel in Acts. It was as Cornelius waited humbly and receptively in prayer, that God's supreme gift, the Holy Spirit, was poured out upon him before ever Peter who was preaching the good news to him, reached the climax of his sermon! Luke could scarcely underline more strongly that the supreme object of prayer is the Holy Spirit of God.

But that is not all. The Spirit who is the supreme object of prayer is also the prime inspirer of prayer. Not only does he enable us to cry "Abba" with the joyous obedience and trust of newly adopted members of the family; not only does he enable us to pray the articulate words of the prayer that Jesus taught us. He initiates prayer within us on at least three other levels.

In the first place, we read of Christians "praying in the Holy Spirit" (Jude 20, Ephesians 6: 18). This seems to indicate a deep, free, and intensive time of prayer, when the Spirit takes over and controls and leads the prayers, and one can go on praying for several hours without being aware of the passage of time. Those who have taken part in nights of prayer can, no doubt, all recall such times when the Holy Spirit has led people to pray in harmony, with intensity, with breadth, with perseverance and assurance. "Pray at all times in the Spirit", writes Paul, "with all prayer and supplication. To that end keep alert with all perseverance, making supplication for all saints, and also for me . . . that I may declare the gospel boldly, as I ought to" (Ephesians 6: 18f). It is fascinating in this context concerning the spiritual warfare in which we are engaged to notice how he ascribes the work of the Spirit to two juxtaposed concepts: prayer, and the Word of God which he calls the sword of the Spirit. The go-between God addresses us primarily through the Word or message enshrined in the Scriptures; and he enables us to address God with freedom and confidence in prayer.

A second way in which the Spirit inspires prayer is by giving to the man in question the gift of tongues. We shall be examining this in another chapter. It is sufficient to notice here that speaking in tongues is one of the gifts of the Spirit to his people (1 Corinthians 12: 10), and that the primary purpose is to enable the recipient to pray to God from the depths of his being and not merely from the conscious levels of his mind. Indeed, the conscious mind is not employed when the Christian prays in tongues to the Lord (1 Corinthians 14: 14). But perhaps we have grown over-concerned about the conscious levels of rationality and suppressed for too long the reservoirs of subconscious feeling which the Spirit seems to touch and use when a man prays in tongues, with the result that he is built up, even though he cannot understand what he is saying (1 Corinthians 14: 4). There is no doubt among those who have been given the gift of tongues that their prayer life and their ability to praise God in all circumstances has grown dramatically. It is one of the ways in which the Spirit evokes prayer in the people of the Messiah.

The third level at which the Spirit undertakes for us in our weakness is brought movingly before us in Romans 8: 26f. "The Spirit helps us in our weakness. For we do not know what to pray for as we ought, but the Spirit itself intercedes for us with sighs too deep for words. And he who searches the hearts of men knows what is the mind of the Spirit, because he intercedes for the saints according to the will of God. And we know that in all respects he co-operates with those who love God." There are some profound depths here for the Christian to ponder. For many of us, prayer in the Holy Spirit is something about which we know very little. Our prayers tend to be mechanical or at best self-centred, and prayer in the Holy Spirit means allowing the Spirit of Christ to pray in us, to pour into our souls his overflowing life of intercession. I came across a striking example of this recently in the story of John Hyde—nicknamed "Praying Hyde", a missionary to India early in this century. A man once asked him to pray for him. "He came to my room, turned the key in the door, dropped on his knees, waited five minutes without a single syllable coming from his lips. I could hear my own heart thumping and beating. I felt the hot tears running down my face. I knew I was with God. Then with upturned face, down which the tears were streaming, he said 'O God'. Then, for five minutes at least, he was still again, and then, when he knew he was talking with God, his arm went around my shoulder and there came up from the depth of his heart such petitions for men as I had never heard before. I rose from my knees to know what real prayer was." Prayer in the Spirit need not, I think, always have that emotional intensity. It does need to have that direct meeting with God. And this is where the

4

Spirit's aid is so crucial in our prayers. For the Holy Spirit understands not only the mind of the Lord, as we saw in I Corinthians 2, but the mind of struggling Christians. He knows we find it hard to pray. He knows there are times when we feel so deeply and yet so confusedly that we cannot frame petitions, but simply come in silent pleading to the Lord. He knows that we are often very unsure what is the will of God, and therefore cannot pray with clarity and confidence about it. He knows the varied and perplexing circumstances in which we are placed. And he helps — the very word in Greek is highly suggestive. It means he grasps the situation *for* us and *with* us. He frames the petitions in our lips; and he prays within us to the Father, with sighs too deep for words. As for the variety of circumstances to which we are exposed, the Spirit works with us in them all, and his aim is to promote our good.

What a tremendously encouraging thing this is. We have in the Spirit a divine intercessor, resident within us, to teach us to pray and to pray alongside us. Perhaps this is the reason why we rarely if ever find a prayer in the New Testament addressed to the Spirit. The Holy Spirit is that part of the deity given us to enable us to pray. Christian prayer is normally offered *to* the Father *through* the Son, or "in his name", and "*in*" or at the instigation of the Spirit.

There is a fascinating passage in Hebrews 7: 25, where the Lord Jesus is said to be able to "save to the uttermost those who come to God by him, because he is always alive to make intercession for them". The word for "make intercession" is the same in Hebrews 7: 25 as in Romans 8: 26; except that in Romans it has a prefix which indicates intensity, or, perhaps, stresses that it is done *for* us. But the basic thought is the same in both cases. It does not say that the Spirit or the Son begs the Father to give us what he otherwise might not. The usual word for "ask" is not used; instead, we have this strange, rare word which literally means "to be around". Is that, perhaps, significant? What higher confidence could a Christian have than to reflect that in heaven the risen Christ in his ascended manhood "is around" on our behalf? His presence at the Father's side is the silent guarantee that we are accepted. There is in the Godhead in heaven one who fully understands us and is there as our representative and our head. Equally, what an encouragement it is to know that there is, in struggling Christians on earth, one of the Godhead who "is around" on our behalf; and that when we are agonising in prayer, we do not approach the Almighty on our own, in all our poverty.

We have the Spirit as the divine representative in our hearts who enables us to pray acceptably.

This has been a long chapter on the work of the Spirit in the individual Christian. But it is no use making out an extensive list of the treasures in our inheritance if we do not make use of them. The Holy Spirit is God's gift to us, and he means us not just to read about him but to make use of him. God means us to know that we are in Christ, and has given us the Spirit to assure us. God means us to grow in Christlikeness, and has given us the Spirit to change us. God means to free us from the bondage to the self-centredness and self-vindication which marked us in the old days, and has equipped us with the Spirit of the Messiah to set us free to serve him unselfconsciously, effectively and joyfully. God has set the seed of his Spirit in our hearts and intends to produce in us a crop of lovely qualities of character if we do not grieve the Spirit (Ephesians 4: 30) by wilful disobedience or neglect. God undertakes to teach us through the Spirit if we will allow him to lead us into a closer understanding of and obedience to Jesus Christ. And God will not only listen to our insignificant prayers, but has given us his Spirit to enable us to pray and to share with us in that most demanding task. Nor is that the full extent of God's generosity. The Spirit groans (Romans 8: 26): we, who have the firstfruit of the Spirit, groan as we await the redemption of our body (8: 23); indeed, the whole created order groans (8: 22), as on tip-toe it awaits the day when it will be redeemed from all its anguish and frustration and share in the glorious liberty of the sons of God. The Spirit, then, is fully involved in the anguish of our world-in-the-making, and of us Christians-in-the-making; and he points towards the day when the pains of travail will give way to the joys of birth. His very presence in our world and in our lives is guarantee of that future day: he is the one part of God's future present here and now. That is why time and again in the New Testament he is linked with hope. We can only "abound in hope through the power of the Holy Spirit" (Romans 15: 13). For the Holy Spirit and hope are two sides of the same coin; respectively the objective and the subjective modes in which the future is made real to us in the present. No wonder that in that same verse Paul bids us be filled with all joy and peace in believing. With so powerful and so complete an equipment as the Holy Spirit, the Christian has every reason for peace and joy in believing.

CHAPTER 7

The Spirit in the Church

WHAT IS THE function of the Holy Spirit within the Christian Church? Historically speaking there have been two main tendencies. Sometimes the Church has tried to exercise proprietary rights over the Holy Spirit, confining him to its basis of faith, its ministerial orders, its sacraments. Sometimes the "spiritual people" have reacted against the institutional church of their day, and broken off to form a "pure church" consisting of themselves and likeminded friends—and before long this new church has usually become as encrusted with barnacles as the one from which they broke away.

In the New Testament era the Christians had to face similar problems, and yet they managed to live with them and surmount them. This chapter will, therefore, examine the ways in which the early Christians were conscious of the Spirit's presence in their community; the next four chapters will glance at some of our contemporary problems concerning the Spirit in the Church, when set against this background.

The Spirit creates unity

One of the notable ways in which the Spirit expressed himself in the Christian community was through creating unity. When in Ephesians 4: 3, 4 Paul is sketching some of the things all Christians have in common, he has this to say: "Endeavour to keep the unity of the Spirit in the bond of peace. There is one body, and one Spirit, as you are called in one hope of your calling; one Lord, one faith, one baptism, one God and Father of us all, who is above all, and through all, and in all. But grace was given to each of us according to the measure of Christ's gift." He then goes on to outline some of the gifts of the ascended Christ. "His gifts were that some should be apostles, some prophets, some evangelists, some pastors and

teachers." Whilst therefore making full allowance for the
diversity of gifts God has given to his Church in the varying
capacities he has accorded to different members, Paul insists
that the Spirit creates unity, and that it is the job of the
Christians to keep that unity and not spoil it. Paradoxically,
like so much in the Christian life, unity is a gift of God, and
yet we have to work at it.

This given unity is not surprising. As we have seen, the first
Christians were aware that the Spirit of the Messiah had come
to indwell them. Hardly surprising, then, that with this Spirit
of their Master making them into sons of God, they should be
conscious of the closest ties with other members of the family.
In this family, seen as one body indwelt by one Spirit, there was
no place for distinctions of wealth or station, sex or nationality;
no room for pride in education or religious privilege (Colossians
3: 11, James 2: 1ff). After all, not one of them had anything
to boast about. All had been rescued by their Lord when they
could never have earned their salvation. As for their differing
gifts, well, they were God's gifts to them, and no reason for
pride. "Who makes you different from anybody else? And
what have you that you did not receive? If, then, you received
it, why do you boast, as if it were not a gift?" (1 Corinthians
4: 7). This concern to preserve the unity the Spirit had created,
accounts for so much in the life and teaching of the early
Church. It accounts for the determination of the Jerusalem
leaders that there must be no independent Samaritan church
growing up without the age-old split from Judaism being
healed (Acts 8). It accounts for the decision of the Council of
Jerusalem that the issue of circumcision must not be allowed to
split the Church (Acts 15). It accounts for the constant visits
of the Apostle to the Gentiles back to the Jerusalem church
(Acts 18: 21, 20: 16, 25: 1 etc.), and his organisation of a great
collection for their benefit, little though he could have approved
of their theology (Romans 15: 26, 1 Corinthians 16: 1,
2 Corinthians 8: 1ff). It accounts for Paul's repeated call to
the Christians at Philippi to pull together and stand together
(Philippians 1: 27, 2: 1ff, 4: 1-3). It explains why Paul will
not allow that there are specially illuminated, "gnostic"
Christians at Colossae: the divine mystery of the gospel is an
open secret, and Paul warns "*every* man, and teaches *every* man
in *all* wisdom so as to present *every* man mature in Christ"
(Colossians 1: 26, 28). John does the same, with his emphasis
that "You all have knowledge . . . you do not need anyone to
teach you" (1 John 2: 20, 27). This unity in the Spirit bridges

the gap between Jews and Gentiles once they become
Christians (Ephesians 2: 15) and breaks down the hostility
between men of different colours and backgrounds. There is a
splendid example of this in the church at Antioch (13: 1ff).
Its leadership was corporate, unlike that of most modern
churches; it comprised an equally unusual feature, prophets
and teachers in the leadership together—and they are not
always the easiest of bedfellows. But more amazing still is the
composition of this group. There is Barnabas, who used to be
a rich, landowning Cypriot Levite: Symeon, called "Swarthy",
who seems to have been a negro; Lucius of Cyrene, no doubt
a Jew from the dispersion in North Africa; Manaen, who was
educated in court circles alongside Herod the tetrarch; and
Saul of Tarsus, the Jew from the Levant who had studied under
Gamaliel. What a varied leadership! Their very names speak
volumes for the unity which the Spirit creates. Christ's will
for his Church, that they should be one (John 17: 21), was
being carried out in the Christian community at Antioch.
That is why Paul was so angry and distressed when he heard
of the divisions in the Christian church at Corinth.

The first three chapters of 1 Corinthians are dominated by
this problem. Thinking of the faith as though it were a
philosophical position, and of those who had come to preach
to them as if they were travelling intellectuals, led the
Corinthians to imagine themselves as judges between the
various emphases they heard. The catch cries of "I belong to
Paul", "I belong to Peter", "I belong to Apollos" and perhaps
"I belong to Christ" (1: 12) were merely subtle forms of self-
advertisement. Paul hammers this savagely. The gospel is not
analogous to philosophical wisdom; it is folly to the worldly.
Its teachers are not like travelling philosophers: they are
co-operating labourers in God's vineyard, and one plants while
another waters, but God is the only one who can make
anything grow (3: 6). The Corinthians are not in the privileged
position of judges between theological niceties. To think they
are, shows that they are governed not by the Spirit but by the
attitudes and outlook of their unregenerate days (3: 1, 3).
Disunity is utterly repulsive to Christ. The Church can no
more acquiesce in being divided than Christ or baptism can
(1: 13). God has built his Church into a temple for the Spirit
of God to indwell (3: 16). The thought is that the Spirit of God
whose glory filled the temple of Solomon, then shone out
through the temple of Jesus' life (see John 2: 18–22), now
resides in the Christian community. Though he does not

develop the metaphor, Paul would, I think, agree with the fuller details to be found in 1 Peter: individual Christians are spiritual stones which go to make up the spiritual temple which is built on Christ (1 Peter 2: 5). At all events he is very strong in this passage in 1 Corinthians 3. The man who spoils the temple of God by encouraging disunity will be destroyed by God (3: 17). That is how highly Paul rates the unity of the Christian Church.

The Spirit brings reconciliation

Reconciliation is closely allied to this concept of unity. It is well brought out in Ephesians 2: 14, 18. A great wall separated Jew from Gentile in the ancient world: the law. This was graphically symbolised by the notice in the outer court of the temple threatening death to any Gentiles who went beyond that point. The "unclean" might not enter the sanctuary of the Lord. That barrier bred emnity. Jews despised and hated Gentiles: despised them because they did not belong to the elect; and hated them because they lorded it over God's chosen people. Gentiles returned the compliment with interest, as can be seen by the references of Martial, Horace and Juvenal to the Jews. Yet in Christ that barrier has been broken down, along with the far bigger wall separating both Jew and Gentile from God. Both have been reconciled in one body by Christ on the cross. Indeed, by incorporation into him the two have become one new humanity. The peace of the Messianic Age belongs both to those who once were outsiders and to those who prided themselves on being the elect. "For through him we *both* have access by one Spirit to the Father" (2: 18). That is no mere theological idealism. We see it happening in a crucial passage in the Acts, the conversion of Cornelius. There his reception of the "one Spirit" convinces Peter, the orthodox Jew, that Cornelius, the Gentile soldier, has been accepted by God into his family on just the same basis as the original disciples. The Spirit brings intractable barriers down. The Spirit reconciles men who were at variance. This is a standing characteristic of his work in the Church.

The Spirit makes fellowship

A third and closely allied way in which the Holy Spirit manifested himself in the early Church was through fellowship. Indeed, the Spirit is constitutive of Christian fellowship. On

two occasions we actually read of "the fellowship of the Holy
Spirit", once in the grace of 2 Corinthians 13: 13 and once as
the ground for Paul's plea that the Philippians should stand
united (Philippians 2: 1). The phrase may mean "the fellowship
which the Holy Spirit gives" or "joint participation in the
Holy Spirit" which all Christians enjoy. Actually, these two
are not far apart, for the Holy Spirit gives a share of *himself* to
all believers, so all alike are partakers of the Spirit. The quality
of this fellowship is best gauged by the early chapters of Acts.
The new converts, having responded to the offer made by
Peter of forgiveness and the Spirit, were baptised, and "devoted
themselves to the apostles' teaching and fellowship, the
breaking of bread and prayers" (2: 42). Their fellowship was
no mere glow of warm feeling. It involved communalism of
living, financial sacrifice and sharing, the care of those in need,
and making time just to be together (2: 44f). You would find
them revelling in each other's company, sharing their
possessions, praising God in the temple, regular at the meetings
for prayer, vigilant to see that widows and other defenceless
folk in the Christian community did not get overlooked in the
share-out of money and food. In 4: 32 we find the same picture.
"Now the company of those who believed were of one heart
and soul, and no one said that any of the things which he
possessed was his own, but they had everything in common . . .
There was not a needy person among them, for as many as
were possessors of lands or houses sold them and brought the
proceeds of what was sold and laid it at the apostles' feet; and
distribution was made to each as any had need."

It is one of the ironies of history that a movement which
professes to follow a penniless carpenter-rabbi and his needy
bunch of disciples; a movement which cherishes among its
foundation documents an image of communal living like this,
should have become so opposed to communism and so closely
associated with capitalism's deification of personal possessions!
Of course, Christianity can have no truck with communism's
atheism and indifference to truth and the value of persons;
but their communalism of possessions is very much more
Christian than our glorification of wealth and our obsession with
individualism. No doubt the primitive attempt at communal
living at Jerusalem was a failure, but what a glorious failure!
Until there is a real sharing of money and possessions, an
equitable distribution of resources and living conditions in so
far as the Christian Church can achieve it, unbelievers are
unlikely to remark on the quality of our fellowship. Real

koinōnia in the Holy Spirit means that we cannot stand apart from those with whom we have this fellowship, no matter what it costs. I am told that three or four years ago President Nyrere of Tanzania sent out a copy of these verses in Acts on communal living to all the clergy, with the brief appended comment: "That is the policy of the President." There is a man who from Christian principle is attempting to apply communalism of possessions to an emerging African state. He is an example to Western, capitalist Christendom.

The Jerusalem experiment was a failure. The church went broke, and richly merited the name in which they gloried, the *ebionim*, God's poor. A few years passed. The Gentile mission sprang into being and produced a flourishing church at Antioch, hundreds of miles away. This church received a prophetic warning from a Jerusalem prophet Agabus, that there would be a widespread famine. So what did they do, these Gentile Christians of Antioch? They did not even wait till the famine happened; on the word of the Jerusalem prophet (whom they might well have thought was prejudiced!) they had a collection; each of the disciples contributed according to his means; and they sent it to Jerusalem by the hands of Saul and Barnabas (11:28ff).

This seems to me a most remarkable thing. They could well have said, "Those Jerusalem folk are a long way away; what do we owe them, anyway? Let us make sure that our own churchmen are all right when the famine comes, and not bother our heads about them". They might have said, "Those fools at Jerusalem will be taught a lesson by this famine. They will learn the hard way that when you realise your assets and share out your capital it does not last very long. They will learn some business sense for a change. And a good thing too." They might have said "We don't see why we should do anything to help those most unsatisfactory Christians (if the name is not too good for them) at Jerusalem. Their theology is narrow; their ritualism is offensive; and they even attempt to mount a counter mission and force circumcision and food laws on our mixed church at Antioch." They could have made these strictures, and with no small justification. But they did not allow theological differences, differences of churchmanship, differences in church organisation, and sheer distance to prevent them from making a most moving and eloquent expression of fellowship in the Spirit. It is hardly surprising that such a quality of life could find no parallel in antiquity, and drew many into the Christian fellowship.

The Spirit enables worship

A fourth way in which the Spirit showed his presence in the Church was in their worship. The earliest disciples were led by the Spirit not only to a sharing of possessions but to a tremendous depth of worship. They "broke bread from house to house" or "at home": this seems to indicate house communion services. They ate their meals with generosity of disposition and exultation (a word which Luke uses to characterise the joy of the messianic community as it delights in what Christ has done for them, what they are now experiencing of his goodness, and what will await them at his return). They were notable for their praise of God even when threatened or in prison (4: 24ff, 16: 25). Indeed, praise is one of the special results of the Spirit coming on them (Acts 2: 47, 3: 8, 9). They were to be found in the formal worship of the temple as well as the warm informality of the home meetings. They were regular in synagogue worship; sometimes in a great Jewish centre like Antioch in Pisidia (13: 14ff): sometimes in a place like Philippi, which had too few Jews to form a synagogue. The tiny congregation went down to a prayer place by the river, and Paul and his company joined them to such good effect that they led Lydia to faith (16: 14). When we find the Christians organising their own worship, the Spirit of the Lord is often mentioned. In Acts 13, before the first missionary journey, we find the church united in worship (and probably liturgical worship at that—*leitourgountōn*, 13: 2) and showing their earnestness by fasting. It is in such a context that the Spirit could make known his leading. Perhaps he inspired a prophet to call for Barnabas and Saul to be set aside for special service; perhaps it was a conviction that he impressed upon the hearts of those present. At all events the mission from Antioch was born in that time of worship where the Spirit of God was so signally present. Paul expects visitors to a church where the people are gathered together for worship, and are open to the Spirit speaking directly through prophets in the assembly, to be conscious that God is in that place, and to be constrained to worship too (1 Corinthians 14: 25). The Book of Revelation springs from John's being in the Spirit on the Lord's day— doubtless in the context of worship (1: 4). And in chapter 4, and repeatedly throughout the book, we find the author joining in worship in the Spirit before the throne of God (4: 2. 5ff). True worship is in the Spirit, as Jesus made clear to the Samaritan woman (4: 24). This passage is often misunderstood;

as if it means that locality does not matter in worship, and that our human spirits have an affinity with God's Spirit. But this, as G. S. Hendry has pointed out in *The Holy Spirit in Christian Theology* (p. 32), is the precise opposite of the truth. "Spirit" for John, as for Paul, is the opposite of "flesh", and "flesh" stands for all our fallen human-ness. To say that God is Spirit, and that the only way to worship him is in Spirit and in truth, is first and foremost to slam the door in the face of our approach to God in our own strength or goodness. How can "flesh" approach God who is "Spirit", how can sinners approach the Holy One? They cannot. But the good news is that God has opened a way. God has made himself accessible in the Word become flesh, and he is now to be worshipped in the place where he has revealed himself, i.e. Jesus Christ, who proclaimed to the woman, "I who speak to you am he". Hendry concludes, "God actively seeks men to worship him in spirit and in truth, by making himself accessible to them in his Son, who is truth incarnate, and by the mission of the Spirit, who is the Spirit of truth. The worship of God in spirit and truth is, therefore, Trinitarian worship; it is to worship God through Jesus Christ, in the Holy Spirit."

Before we leave this aspect of the Spirit in the Church, we ought not to neglect the classic case of Acts 4: 23ff. Peter and John have been released from prison, after being grilled by the Sanhedrin, and told not to say any more about the resurrection of Jesus. They returned to the Christian fellowship, and their immediate action was significantly different from what would happen in most Christian circles today. We might organise a petition for civil liberties, or approach our Member of Parliament, or at least appoint a committee to look into the matter of these unwarranted threats by officialdom. They did nothing of the kind. They gave themselves to prayer. This seems to have been a mixture of liturgical and free prayer. The prayer as recorded is dependent to a very large extent on Psalm 2, and to it they appended their brief request. But they did not prescribe to the Almighty what he should do. They did not ask for protection. They spread the matter before the Lord and asked him to "behold" it. They claimed his sovereignty over every threat of man. And they asked for boldness in proclaiming the gospel of Jesus. "And when they had prayed, the place was shaken in which they were gathered, and they were all filled with the Holy Spirit and spoke the word of God with confident assurance" (4: 31). Such was the reality of the Spirit's presence in their worship.

The Spirit inspires Scripture

Closely associated with the Spirit's presence in worship is his inspiration of the Scriptures. As we have seen, the prophets of old claimed to have been sent and inspired by the Spirit of the Lord. Jesus himself set his seal on the Spirit's inspiration of Psalm 110, for instance, "For David himself said by the Holy Spirit" (Mark 12: 36). We find the same attribution of the Old Testament to the inspiration of the Holy Spirit in Acts 1: 16, 4: 25 etc., and it is entirely in keeping not only with Christian but with Jewish orthodoxy when we find the blanket claim in 2 Timothy 3: 16 that "All Scripture is inspired by God". We never get any nearer to an explanation of the divine inspiration of the human writers than in 2 Peter 1 : 20f where the author tells us that prophecy came from God, not from the prophet's own ideas. It came as the human writers were moved or carried along by the Holy Spirit. This is a fascinating maritime metaphor in the original Greek, suggesting the way a ship is carried along by the wind. The prophets raised their sails, so to speak (they were obedient and receptive) and the Holy Spirit filled them and carried their craft along in the direction he wished. The writers were not robots but men; men of their time, men of varied backgrounds and intellects, prejudices and outlooks. But those men were yielded to the leading of the Holy Spirit in such a way that he could speak through them. Co-operation between the human author and the divine Spirit is perhaps the key word; there is no suggestion that the personality or individuality of the writer was suppressed in any way. The Holy Spirit did not use instruments; he used men, holy men, through whom he could speak to men in ages yet unborn. "Whatever was written in former days was written for our instruction", wrote Paul. "The prophets who prophesied of the grace that was to be yours . . . inquired what person or time was indicated by the Spirit of Christ within them when they predicted the sufferings of Christ and the subsequent glory" wrote Peter (1 Peter 1: 10ff). It was therefore to the inspired Scriptures of the Old Testament that the early Christians went as they wrestled with the meaning of Christ and his work. The passages they found particularly illuminating, and their handling of them have been superbly set out in books such as C. H. Dodd's *According to the Scriptures* and F. F. Bruce's *This is That*. That inspiration by the Spirit, is, of course, why the Old Testament became the Bible of the early Christians. It was not only that they

took it over with their original Jewish heritage; they were per-
suaded that the Old Testament pointed forward to the days of
salvation brought in by Jesus, and that it is impossible to
understand Jesus or his salvation except against the background of this Old Testament. The Spirit that had been active
in the prophets was the Spirit which had become embodied in
Jesus.

It was, however, impossible to leave the matter there. Had
not Jesus promised the Spirit to his followers? The Spirit who
would teach them and lead them into all the truth about him?
And had that Spirit not become their inalienable gift from the
day of Pentecost onwards? Then did it not follow that the same
Holy Spirit who inspired the prophets to point forward to
Jesus, no less inspired them as they bore apostolic witness to
Jesus? This was undoubtedly the belief of the apostles. Peter,
in the passage 1 Peter 1: 10–12 already referred to, not only
declared that the Spirit of Christ inspired the prophets to look
forward to the Messiah, but claims that the good news, fulfilling
what the prophets had said, was brought to his readers by the
apostolic witness and "the Holy Ghost sent down from heaven".
The same Holy Spirit who was active in the prophets was
active in the apostles. There was, therefore, no anachronism
when 2 Peter 3: 16 sets Paul's letters alongside the other
Scriptures. They had to wait another three hundred years for
the formal promulgation of the books of the New Testament
in precisely the form we have them today, but from the days
of the apostles themselves it was quite clear to the Christians
that the Holy Spirit who inspired the prophetic writings was
also standing behind the words of Jesus and his apostles. Paul
could claim to have the very mind of Christ, to proclaim not
the word of men but of God, and to teach not merely in broad
outline but in detailed words imparted by the Spirit of the
Lord (1 Corinthians 2: 16, 1 Thessalonians 2: 13, 1 Corinthians
2: 13). Hence his abrupt challenge to any who thought
themselves "inspired" to recognise and abide by what he said
(1 Corinthians 14: 38). Hence his expectation that his letters
would be read in the Christian assembly at worship, alongside
the inspired writings of the Old Testament (Colossians 4: 16).
It is, therefore, in the Scriptures of the Old and New Testaments, with Jesus as the centrepiece, that the Spirit is most
readily to be encountered. That is why Bible reading both in
church and for the individual, occupies so prominent a place
in Christianity. There is no sniff of bibliolatry about it. It is
simply the fact that the Spirit who inspired the Scriptures is

to be met there. We read them in order to gain illumination from him and be transformed by him into greater likeness to our Lord. 2 Corinthians 3 is the classic chapter for the rôle of the Spirit as illuminator of the Scriptures. It is when men turn to the Lord the Spirit that the veil is taken away from the eyes of their understanding. One sees once again the aptness of John Taylor's name for the Spirit as the go-between God. He is the one who inspired the Scriptures in the first place. He is the one who interprets them to the humble, seeking reader.

The Spirit speaks through preaching

There is one point that ought to be added to the way the Spirit manifests himself through the Scriptures. He does so through another enterprise undertaken in the context of the worshipping congregation by one or more of its members, namely preaching. Acts 4: 8 is typical: "Then Peter, filled with the Holy Spirit, said . . ." and he launched into his address. As we have seen in chapter 6, it is part of the work of the Spirit to convict a person of his need, and to make Christ attractive to him; this very often takes place in the course of preaching, particularly biblical preaching. One of the great weaknesses in contemporary Christianity is the poverty of preaching. Many clergy consider it a chore, and many congregations complain if it lasts more than ten minutes. There seems to be little expectation that the Spirit of God might be present and active, to take home the words that one would hope have been prepared and prayed over in his presence, so that the message (or some part of it) becomes luminous, indeed life-changing, for one here and another there in the congregation. But that is in fact what happens when there is prayerful, believing, biblical preaching, delivered in the power of the Spirit and in dependence on God to use it. Time and again after preaching people have said to me, "I felt you were speaking precisely to me" or asked, "How did you know about me when you said such and such?" That is the work of the Holy Spirit. I may know little or nothing about their needs: but he who searches the hearts does, and he takes the preached word and applies it to the needs of those present.

I remember a student recently discovering this while he was actually preaching. He did not previously have great confidence in the value of preaching, and he certainly did not think he was much good at it. But he had prepared this sermon on prayer with great care and much prayer, and he got up in fear and trembling to preach it. To his amazement he found that the people in this down-town city congregation were gripped by the Word of God, and one non-churchgoer who had been dragged into the service by another student had to go out because he was so convicted by what was said. That student will never again doubt that the Spirit of God can use the preached word. When he is ordained he is not likely to scrap the sermon in favour of more music or discussion. There is room for music, room for discussion, but the Holy Spirit uses preaching in a quite special way. And it is by no means a one-man effort. The congregation can "meet" the preacher by the way they respond, the way they support him in prayer, the way they assess what is said, and the way they worship. They create the atmosphere in which the Spirit of God has ease of communication, if I may put it that way. I well recall an evangelistic service in the North of England at which I preached. I *knew* that God was going to lead many people to Christ in that service by the time we had got half-way through, long before we reached the sermon: the sense of worship was so real, the love and dedication to Christ so obvious. It was moving to stand in the aisle for half-an-hour afterwards and meet a steady flow of individuals who had been brought to the service by friends, and those same friends had stayed with them to help them on in the early days of their Christian life after many of them that night committed their lives to Christ and asked his Spirit into their hearts. No wonder many of the Barthian theologians maintain that the Bible is not so much the Word of God, *tout simple;* but that it *becomes* the Word of God when the Spirit uses the Word preached or read to create an encounter with the hearts of men.

The Spirit enlivens the Sacraments

If the Spirit of God is active in the Word in the Church, he is no less concerned to bring life to the sacraments. It seems probable that there is an allusion in John 3: 3, "born of water and the Holy Spirit", to Christian baptism, and in John 6: 53, "unless you eat the flesh of the Son of Man and drink his blood, you have no life in you" to the eucharist. If so, it can scarcely be accidental that the Spirit is mentioned emphatically in both contexts. In John 3, the "born of water and the Spirit" in verse 3 becomes merely "born of the Spirit" in verse 5, and it is the Spirit in regeneration that is the subject of the subsequent discussion. Similarly in chapter 6, alongside the extremely harsh sayings about literally "munching" his body and his blood goes the assertion in verse 63, "It is the Spirit that gives life, the flesh is of no avail; the words that I have spoken to you are Spirit and life". Clearly, the Spirit is vital to effective baptism and meaningful communion. And there is a lovely passage in 1 John 5: 7, 8 which seems to indicate that the Spirit uses the sacraments to assure his people that they belong and to act as a physical vehicle of spiritual blessing. "The Spirit is the witness, because the Spirit is the truth. There are three witnesses, the Spirit, the water and the blood; and these three agree." This letter of John is written, among other reasons, to combat Docetism, an early heresy which maintained that the heavenly Christ was too holy and spiritual to be soiled by permanent contact with human flesh. The heresy had a number of variations, but they would all have repudiated the idea that the Christ of faith could have been identified with the Jesus of Palestine. But John's point in these verses is that that identification is essential to the gospel. God really became man, and Jesus came not with water only (his heavenly nature? his baptism?) but with blood (his human nature? his crucifixion?). Whatever the precise meaning of this difficult phrase, John is saying that in Jesus the divine did become accessible to human touch and sight. And the same continues to be true! The sacraments of the water and the blood (and there must surely be at least an *allusion* to baptism and the Lord's Supper in those words) are used by the Spirit to bear witness to us of the reality of our salvation, and of the fact that we are indeed sons in the heavenly Father's family. More, they are the physical bearers of spiritual blessing, for the Spirit can and does work through the sacraments in the Church, just as he worked through the life of Jesus of Nazareth. But just as one could look at Jesus, listen to him, and touch him in the days of his flesh without gaining any benefit from him or even realising who he was, so it is with the sacraments. They may be bare signs, or they may be vibrant with the life of the Spirit: it depends, not a little, on the receptivity and faith of the recipient. Certainly churchmen are not to sit back confident that they must be all right with God because of their sacraments. 1 Corinthians 10 is written to that situation. The Corinthians seem to have been regarding their sacramental life as a sort of talisman which would allow them to engage in idolatry and fornication with impunity. Paul reminds them that the Israelites of old had their counterpart to the Christian sacraments and relied on them for security—but in vain. They went in for fornication and idolatry like the Corinthians, and "God was not pleased; for they were overthrown in the wilderness". The sacraments in the Church are a means of grace and an objective, palpable ground of assurance. But they are not magic.

The Spirit inaugurates mission

Another mark of the Spirit in the Church is mission. It has been so from the first days of Christianity, as we saw in chapter 5. Outreach to others is the complement to fellowship within the Christian family. The Spirit's activity in the worship and fellowship, the Scriptures, the preaching and the sacraments of the Church must be balanced by driving out its members in mission to a needy world: "*ite, missa est*". There can be nothing exclusive about the Christian gospel. The Church, when it is truly the Church, can never be a cosy club for insiders. It must always see itself as the family of God gathered for mission. Accordingly, we find repeatedly in the early Church that the sequel to worship is evangelism. We will glance briefly at a few examples, since we have already examined the nexus between the Spirit and mission in some detail. But it is noteworthy how in Acts 2, after recording the worship and fellowship of the early believers, we read, "And the Lord added to their number daily those who were being saved" (2: 47). Again, after the prayer meeting in chapter 4 we read that, "they spoke the word of God with boldness . . . and with great power the apostles gave their testimony to the resurrection of the Lord Jesus, and great grace was upon them all". In the passage in 1 Corinthians which we have noted earlier, the expected result of Spirit-filled worship is the conversion of people who come in. In the case of the Antiochene church of Acts 13, it is the same pattern; mission follows hard on the heels of Spirit-led worship. The point is important, because there are few such powerful evangelistic agencies as a Christian fellowship at worship, where the various gifts of the Spirit are being exercised in love and harmony by people who are consciously under the leadership of that same Spirit. And this brings us naturally to a final important mark of the Spirit in the Church, namely interdependence in the body of Christ.

It is a lesson they had not digested at Corinth, and Paul spends three chapters in teaching it to them.

The Spirit builds up the Body—in love

Corinth was a richly gifted church. And they rated very highly among these gifts the ability to speak in tongues. The value they set on it was very understandable from either a Hebrew or a Greek background. One has only to think of the *ruach adonai* coming with supernatural violence upon Saul so that he danced like a dervish, or upon Ezekiel so that he was carried away to another place, to sympathise with the Corinthians in supposing that extraordinary manifestations like this were the sure mark of the Spirit's activity. In the Greek world it was the same. Even that great intellectual Plato could write in the *Phaedrus*, "It is through *mania* (ecstasy due to divine possession) that the greatest blessings come to us" and in the *Timaeus*, "No one in possession of his *nous* (rational mind) has reached divine and true exaltation". The non-rational was the mark of divine inspiration: the more *pneuma*, the less *nous*. The Corinthians would have rated in ascending order of value the teacher (in reliance on his rationality), the prophet (who spoke under divine inspiration but intelligibly), and the man who spoke in tongues (whose inspiration was marked by unintelligibility).

A vital, dynamic church; a highly talented church, with freedom and openness and freshness. But the Corinthian church was in serious danger. To suppose that the more a man loses self-possession the more inspired by God he must be, is to deny God his place in the rational. To suppose that non-personal irruptions of *ruach* are the mark of inspiration is to forget that it is the Spirit of *Jesus* with whom we are dealing. Any such depersonalisation of the Spirit is also disparagement of the ethical, as if it does not much matter how you behave so long as you have this mark of divine inspiration upon you. If this particular gift is prized above all others, it easily leads to a cult of experience, and to excessive individualism (jealousy in those who have not got the gift, pride in those who have). In the midst of all this, Christian love can easily disappear.

How does Paul handle this difficult situation, a situation which could easily wreck all interdependence in the Christian community, and set the various members in jealous competition for spiritual gifts? He faces it head on.

In verses 1–3 he explains the relation of the Holy Spirit to ecstasy. First, he reminds them that not all ecstatic speech is Christian. They knew it in their unregenerate days of worshipping Bacchus or Attis. They had shared in feasts in honour of demons (10: 19f), and had fallen under their influence. Indeed, the force of the word used in the Greek here, *apagomenoi*, indicates that they had actually experienced demon possession: they had been "taken out of themselves" in frenzied speech as they worshipped idols that themselves were dumb and gave no answer to the prayers of suppliants. Justin spoke of pagans being "chased with the scourge of evil demons" (1 *Apology*, 5), and Lucian speaking of the power of love, says, "A sort of god (literally *demon*, the same word that Paul uses) carries us away (*agei*) wherever he wills, and it is impossible to resist him" (*Dialogues of the Dead*, 19: 1). This is the sort of supernatural power which the Corinthians had experienced in their pagan days, driving them on in their worship of idols. It is salutary to remember that Muslim devotees in the Sudan speak in tongues no less than Christians in Guildford or Cleveland!

It is not easy to be sure quite what was happening when people cried out in church, apparently under inspiration from above, that "Jesus is accursed". It seems almost inconceivable to us that any Christians should even count it a possibility to curse Jesus. But we know at least three types of situation where it actually happened. The Roman governor of Bithynia, Pliny, tells the Emperor Trajan of his attempts to stamp out Christianity in the Province about A.D. 112, and of the way in which "some who were or had been Christians . . . invoked the gods and cursed Christ, none of which things, it is said, genuine Christians can be compelled to do" (*Epistles* 10: 96). If some cursed Jesus under the pressure of persecution, others did so through rejecting the historical Jesus who died in agony on a cross of shame; instead, they concentrated their devotion on the heavenly Lord, the risen Christ. Cerinthus made just this division, and was severely taken to task by the Church fathers such as Epiphanius and Irenaeus. Again, there were the Ophites, a heretical Gnostic Christian sect who required their members to curse Jesus (Origen, *Contra Celsum* 5: 1.28). This shows that it was not unheard of for professed followers of Christ to curse Jesus. Probably some of the ecstatic Christians at Corinth, carried away by the champagne of religious experience, separated the historic Jesus from the Spirit-giving Christ: a similar sort of thing seems to have happened in the community to which 1 John was written, where "liars" were saying that Jesus is not the Christ (1 John 2: 22). At all events, Paul used this shocking happening to teach the Corinthians a most important lesson. The really crucial mark of the Spirit's presence is not religious fervour or even speaking in tongues (which can arise from demon possession or psychological conditioning as well as from the Spirit), but the confession that Jesus is Lord. In other words, it is the *content* of the Christian proclamation which matters. The man who walked the streets of Palestine is exalted to the throne of the universe; the Jesus of history cannot be divorced from the Christ of faith. Once again we see as in chapters three and four, that the Spirit of Christ bears witness to the historical Jesus. The one we encounter as Spirit is the Spirit of *Jesus*: there are other spirits, and it is all too easy to be deceived by them (1 John 4: 1ff).

Incidentally, there is good reason to suppose that "Jesus is Lord" was the earliest baptismal confession. It was certainly something every believer could say; it was the irreducible minimum of Christian faith. Paul is concerned to show the Corinthians that genuine Spirit-possession is not marked out by tongues but by the unambiguous confession that Jesus of Nazareth is Lord; Lord of the universe, and Lord of your life. That is the first and foremost criterion of the Spirit's authentic presence. And it was something that was not restricted to certain Corinthian Christians with particular gifts who despised others as not being *pneumatikoi*, "Spirit-filled"; but was rather the basic condition of being a Christian at all, embodied in the baptismal confession! Paul gives another great mark of authentic spirituality, and we shall come to it in verse 7. But this one is fundamental to the whole of the subsequent discussion.

In verses 4–6 Paul goes on to make a most important point. He contrasts the variety of the gifts with the unity of the Giver. Note the repetition in "the same Spirit ... the same Lord ... the same God", compared with the triple "there are varieties ..." in these verses. We have here the oldest trinitarian (or, to be more accurate, triadic) formula in the whole of the New Testament. It is thoroughly Hebraic. St. Paul is not so much thinking in Greek terms of three "persons" in one Godhead. He is thinking, as a true Israelite, of God in action. One and the same God acts in three different ways. It is therefore important to examine the difference between the three words Paul uses to describe the variety of God's action. The answer is simple enough linguistically: *charisma* "gift", *diakonia* "service", and *energēma*, "empowering" are self-explanatory. But the interesting thing is the way the apostle has paired them up. The gifts of grace, *charismata*, are linked with the Spirit; the acts of service with the Lord Jesus; and the requisite power with God the Creator. In other words, the spiritual gifts I have are *gifts* imparted by the supreme gift of grace, the Holy Spirit himself. They are not possessions of my own to use as I please. They are lent by him. And what are they for? Not for personal pride or gratification. Not for showing off, or comparing myself with others who have less or different gifts. No. They are intended for service of others, *diakonia*, after the pattern of the one who was uniquely endued with the Spirit, and supremely the Servant of the Lord. And when this service leads to success, when it helps anyone else, that is not because of my talents or my holiness; it is simply due to the empowering given by God who called all things into being from the beginning of time, and sustains them by his might.

We shall be examining verses 7–11 in some detail in chapter 10. Here it is sufficient to notice that Paul carries his argument a stage further by telling the Corinthians that the Spirit gives gifts to all members of the Church; that these gifts have various and concrete manifestations in the differing endowments of different members; and that it is all for the common good. This brings us to the second and complementary truth about the criteria proper to distinguishing a genuine gift of the Spirit. The first we saw in verse 3. We must ask, "Does it point unmistakably to Jesus as Lord?" The second meets us in verse 7: "Does it benefit and build up the Christian community?" The content of the message and the community of God's people are the two important questions that the apostle bids us ask if we are in doubt about the validity of some spiritual claim or experience.

In these crucial verses, then, Paul has shown us the unity of the Spirit's working through a wide variety of gifts. He grounds his argument in the very nature of God's being and action in history. Because God himself is diversity-in-unity, and has revealed himself that way throughout his saving acts in history, so is the Church where he is active. One God is the source of these various manifestations of the one Spirit in the body of the one Christ, the Church. These manifestations of God at work are called *energēmata* "workings", where the emphasis is on what God does (12: 6, 10), *charismata* where the emphasis is on the gracious gift of his sovereign distribution of these capacities (12: 4, 9, 28), and *diakoniai* to remind his readers that all gifts are intended for service of others (12: 5). Thus there are indeed varieties of gifts, but it is the same Spirit who distributes them. There are indeed varieties of ways of serving the Lord, but it is the same Lord we all serve. There are indeed

varieties in the way the Father is active in us, but every capacity
and the strength to make good use of it are his alone. There is
therefore no room either for boasting or jealousy. These gifts
have no necessary link with holiness of life nor with power in
service: they are gifts of the Spirit, not graces of character.
And they are intended for the building up of the whole
Christian community in service to the common Lord.

From verse 12 to the end of the chapter Paul uses a graphic
illustration to expound the purpose of the Spirit's gifts. He sees
the Church as Christ's body, in which all the Corinthians
(12:27) and indeed all believers throughout the world (1:2)
are members. All are incorporated into this one body of
Christ. It is God the Father who appoints us our place to fill
and give us gifts to do it with (12:18, 24, 28). It is the Holy Spirit
who makes us members of that body. "By one Spirit we were
all baptised into one body—Jews or Greeks, slaves or free—
and were all made to drink of that one Spirit" (12:13). Paul
is insisting that the one Spirit of God baptised all Christians
into this one body, whatever their background, nationality
and gifts. Some of them had impressive gifts like tongues; some
of them did not (12:30). But all alike have been immersed in
the sea of the Spirit; all alike have had his living water
irrigating their parched lives (such seems to be the meaning of
the two metaphors in verse 13). There are particular problems
of detail in this famous verse to which we shall turn in a later
chapter. But it is clear from the context that the apostle is not
referring to a baptism by or in the Spirit which only *some* of
them possess; he is insisting that they *all* have it, just as they
are all members of Christ, and sons of the heavenly Father.
The thought is trinitarian through and through. Indeed, it is
shocking, and is intended to be so. We too easily gloss over the
shattering half-expressed analogy in verse 12, with which he
opens this section of the argument. Had he said, "Just as the
body is one and has many members, and all the members of
the body, though many, are one body, *so it is with the Church*", the
point would have been clear—and unremarkable. There would
even have been parallels in Stoic thought. But he says something quite unparalleled in religious literature anywhere. He
says "*so it is with Christ*". What does he mean by this enigmatic
statement?

He is making the Corinthians sit up and take notice. The
Church is no earthly society. It is the embodiment of Jesus the
Messiah. Whatever the Church is, it is by virtue of the power
and presence and action of its Lord. Christ is the one in whom

all believers are incorporate. Christ is the very air they breathe. It is perhaps significant, as Professor Eduard Schweizer has often remarked, that the title "Christians" only appears in the New Testament upon the lips of pagans! Paul's favourite title for the Church is men who are "in Christ". If they are different, it is because Christ is in them and they are in Christ. That is the important thing about the Church. That is why Paul speaks not about the Church but Christ as being the body to which we all belong. And by their divisive and arrogant spirit, these Corinthians were spoiling the harmony not of the Church, so much as of Christ.

Very well then. All the Corinthians have the Holy Spirit. And the gifts they revel in are gifts of his ordaining. Their individual rôle may be that of ear or eye, hand or foot in that body. The point is that they are there as a result of God's appointment and their equipment is that of the Spirit's giving.

Next, Paul deals with two separate tendencies within the body of Christ. Some members have less outstanding gifts, and they are tempted to feel that they are inferior members in the body. Paul encourages them in verses 14–20. How awful it would be if the body consisted of just one great eye! If all had the same gift, the harmony of "unity-in-diversity" would give way to dreary uniformity (12: 19, 20); moreover they would be tacitly blaspheming God who arranged each of the organs in the body as he saw fit (12: 18). Let them take heart. An inferiority complex is out of place in the household of God. He knows what he is doing with the diverse gifts he imparts. All members of the body are necessary and interdependent.

In the verses which follow, Paul addresses himself to those who suffer from a superiority complex. They are reminded that all members have a part to play, but that God delights to give special honour to the less showy parts; "the parts of the body which seem to be weaker are indispensable, and those parts of the body which we think less honourable we invest with the greater honour" (12: 22f). If those with the less spectacular gifts are slighted, the whole Church is impoverished.

This is the point which Paul labours to bring home to them in his closing words as he applies his analogy directly to them. Once again, he has often been misunderstood. When he says "if one member suffers, all suffer together; if one member is honoured, all rejoice together" he is not saying anything at all about Christian sympathy. His point is altogether more penetrating to Corinthian pride. He wants the more arrogant members of the body there to realise that if any one member, however mean and ordinary his service, is inhibited from making that service, *then the whole body suffers*! If, on the other hand, one member is honoured by being able to render its proper service acceptably, then the whole body is honoured. The truth that the whole Church is the loser if it is not so constituted that all members get the chance to make their God-given contribution to its life and worship was as surprising and unacceptable to the Corinthians as it is to us. But that is what Paul is asserting throughout this chapter. Always for him, the body of Christ is primary, and the individual member secondary. This is the precise opposite of the Corinthian—and our own—atomised way of thinking. The Corinthians had to learn that they were not individually "little Christs" with all the gifts, but rather, members of Christ with some gifts. Nobody was unnecessary, and nobody self-sufficient: they needed each other in the body of Christ.

It is at this point that Paul contributes his masterly chapter on love. We do not know if it was composed before he wrote this letter, by himself or by someone else. At all events it is highly appropriate here. "Seek the greatest gifts", is his final injunction in chapter 12, and the greatest gift the Spirit can impart to us is not tongues or prophecy, healing or the ability to work miracles, but love, *agapē*. The ancient world knew all about *philia*, friendship, and about *erōs*, passionate love; but it did not know anything about the love which is determined not by the worthiness of the recipient but by the goodness of the donor, the love which seeks the good of all men irrespective of their merits and of personal attraction. The world had to wait for Jesus Christ before it saw love like that. And then a new word, *agapē*, was added to the vocabulary of love in order to describe it. And as we have already seen, "Jesus" could without loss be substituted for "love" throughout 1 Corinthians 13. This love, which can never be worked up by human effort, is the supreme gift of the Holy Spirit to his people. "God's own love is poured out into our hearts through the Holy Spirit who is given us" (Romans 5: 5). There can be no higher gift than this, and that is why it is inserted in the middle of this three-chapter discussion of spiritual gifts. Unless men meet the risen, loving Christ mediated through me by the Spirit, it is immaterial that I can speak in tongues, or have prophetic insight, or the gift of wisdom and spiritual understanding, or mountain-moving faith: I may dole out all my possessions and even face the ultimate sacrifice of martyrdom, but unless the loving Jesus is encountered in me through all this, nothing is achieved. What a rebuke to those Corinthians, proud of their various gifts—what a rebuke to us, too. In this marvellous chapter the love of Jesus is set alongside the vices of the Corinthians. It is the opposite of the pride in spiritual experience which "puffed them up" (4). It is the opposite of that emphasis on particular gifts which made the recipients proud and the aspirants jealous (4). It is the opposite of that selfish exercise of special gifts for personal gratification which Paul calls "seeking one's own" (5). The Corinthians were seeking the "higher way" of spiritual experience. Paul sets before them the "lower way", as they might think it, of love; the love of Jesus the Servant, who was never puffed up and never selfish in the exercise of his gifts. All was for others. Thus he returns to the theme at the end of chapter 12, where "the common good" dominated the exercise of gifts, a theme which he will develop in chapter 14. For a loving self-giving for others is the way of Jesus; it is the way of the Spirit; indeed, it is the very life of heaven itself, for in the day when all our earthly gifts are past, when prophecy has found its fulfilment, when tongues are taken up into the song of the redeemed in heaven, when we know even as we are known, faith is turned to sight, and hope fulfilled in ultimate possession by the Beloved—then love remains. The redeemed in heaven will still be united in that glad self-offering to the Lord and to the brethren which marked the highest flights of their spirituality on earth when they were brought by the Spirit most closely into conformity with the love of Jesus the Servant.

Well might Paul therefore implore the Corinthians at the end of this memorable chapter, "Make love your aim" (14: 1). His plea is taken up by John Wesley in *A Plain Account of Christian Perfection*, in a passage which will appropriately close this chapter.

Another ground of these, and a thousand mistakes, is the not considering deeply that love is the highest gift of God—humble, gentle, patient love; that all visions, revelations, manifestations whatever, are little things compared to love; and that all the gifts above mentioned are either the same with it or infinitely inferior to it.

It were well you should be thoroughly sensible of this— the heaven of heavens is love. There is nothing higher in religion—there is, in effect, nothing else; if you look for anything but more love, you are looking wide of the mark, you are getting out of the royal way. And when you are asking others, "Have you received this or that blessing?" if you mean anything but more love, you mean wrong; you are leading them out of the way, and putting them upon a false scent. Settle it in your heart, that . . . you are to aim at nothing more, but more of that love described in the thirteenth of Corinthians. You can go no higher than this till you are carried into Abraham's bosom.

CHAPTER 8

The Spirit's Baptism

1. The Spirit and Baptism in contemporary debate

ONE OF THE most lively debates about contemporary spirituality concerns what is often called baptism "in" or "by" the Holy Spirit. Broadly speaking, there are three attitudes towards it.

Is the Spirit's baptism water baptism?

First, there are those who identify baptism in the Holy Spirit with water baptism *tout simple*. If a person has been baptised with water in the name of the Trinity, then he must be considered as a child of God, an inheritor of the Kingdom of Heaven, a man equipped with the Spirit of God. Those who take this view believe that the sacrament does not merely symbolise but actually effects the change from darkness to light, from the power of Satan to God, from death to life. They rightly stress the objective nature of Christ's incarnation and atonement which are, as it were, made over to us in baptism. They rightly stress that we are saved not because of anything that we do, but because of what has been done for us by Christ independent of any of our efforts and fancied merits, and long prior to any response that we may make. They properly point to the one baptism shared by Christians throughout the world as the really significant way of marking allegiance to Jesus and fellowship with all others who share the baptismal bath. But where this view is weak is in the whole area of personal response, of faith, of allegiance. There are millions of people who have been baptised in infancy without their knowledge or consent; they have been "done" surreptitiously in a parish church on a Sunday afternoon when nobody but the family was present. They neither believe in the

Christian story themselves, nor do those who brought them to baptism, except perhaps in the most general, not to say superstitious terms. They do not practise the Christian religion. They do not go to church. They do not believe the creeds. They do not know anything of the life-changing power of the Holy Spirit. The question is forced sharply upon us: in what sense is it meaningful to speak of such people as Christians despite the fact that they have been baptised with water in the name of the Trinity?

Is the Spirit's baptism conversion?

The second main view is this. Baptism with the Holy Spirit is identical with conversion. When a man repents and believes in Christ, when he makes his life over to the Lordship of Jesus and receives the Spirit of the risen Christ into his personality, he is thereby baptised with the Holy Spirit. This view, common in Protestant and Evangelical churches, is strong where the previous view was weak, and, conversely, weak where the previous view was strong. Its strength lies in its stress on personal response to the grace of God in Christ. Personal repentance and personal faith are crucial in a man if the Holy Spirit is to baptise him into Christ. But what about water baptism, on this view? It is either thought to be largely irrelevant (after all, what does the symbol matter if you have the reality?) or merely the mark of man's repentance and faith. Assuredly, baptism is integrally connected with repentance and faith, but is that all there is to it? Is it entirely something we do, and not at all something that God does to or for us? If so, it is very odd that the New Testament does not talk about a man baptising himself; instead, baptism is always something that is done for him by another. Clearly, we shall have to look a bit closer at the meaning of baptism in the New Testament before we can accept this identification of conversion with baptism in the Spirit. And even if we were convinced, it would still pose problems, this Protestant view. It is too cerebral, too intellectual. How about the children of believing families? Must they remain alienated from the Spirit of God until they make an act of personal faith? Is the Church merely the body of those who can exercise active belief? Has the Church no room for those who are too old, too young, or too mentally ill-equipped to believe the good news and entrust themselves to Christ? Must all such people be cut off from the Holy Spirit?

Is the Spirit's baptism a two-stage initiation?

The third answer to this question "What is baptism in the Holy Spirit?" comes with a divided voice from two very dissimilar backgrounds. On the one hand, some Catholics, seeing the inadequacy of supposing that water baptism of infants must necessarily produce new birth by the Spirit, have argued that it is not baptism alone, but baptism accompanied (normally years later) by the imposition of hands in confirmation, which imparts the Holy Spirit. Distinguished Catholic theologians like Thornton, Mason, and Gregory Dix have taken up this view. They have drawn attention to two passages in the Acts where the Holy Spirit was given through the imposition of apostles' hands on the heads of folk who had been baptised but had not received the Holy Spirit. In Acts 8 the Samaritans receive the Spirit through the hands of John and Peter; in Acts 19 some disciples of John the Baptist receive him through the ministry of the apostle Paul. Accordingly, they believe that through confirmation by a bishop who is (it is hoped) in direct line with the apostles, people receive the Holy Spirit in a full and distinctive way at confirmation. The phrase "baptism in the Holy Spirit" is not normally used by those who think in this way; but they clearly advocate a two-stage Christian initiation. Stage one, baptism, is incomplete; stage two, confirmation, brings the Holy Spirit into a man's life.

Curiously enough, Pentecostal Christians are in the habit of using precisely the same verses to support their claim that Christian initiation is a two-stage affair. Coming, for the most part, from a Protestant background, they are inclined to take a man's conversion as stage one, and a subsequent overpowering experience of the Holy Spirit, which is normally (though not necessarily) accompanied by speaking in tongues, as stage two. It is this second stage which is commonly called by Pentecostals and neo-Pentecostals "the Baptism in the Holy Spirit". It is seen as the indispensable step to spiritual power and a full Christian life. Although Pentecostalism as a denomination dates only from the first decade of this century, and neo-Pentecostalism (the spread of Spirit-baptism teaching and practice through other denominations) has only become prominent since the middle of this century, the roots go back a long way. John Wesley had taught a "second work of grace" in the believer subsequent to justification. The worldwide Holiness Movement which includes the Keswick Convention, and boasts such influential names as Finney, Torrey, Andrew Murray, and Watchman Nee, espoused this two-stage view of what makes a man a Christian. The nomenclature differed, but whether you spoke of "entire sanctification", "the gift", "the blessing", "the second blessing" or "the baptism with the Holy Spirit" made little difference except in detailed description of the contents of the experience. In all cases it meant a new quality of Christian experience distinct from conversion; an experience which for some made Christian living at the previous level look so pale and shoddy that it was hardly worthy of the name Christian at all. And whether the recipients laid special claim to sanctification of life, as the early Methodists did, or to an experience of the Spirit marked by speaking in tongues, as the Pentecostals did, made little difference in practice. For those who possessed the experience inevitably came to think of themselves as an "in" group, the people who had arrived; and those who did not share that experience were, inevitably, regarded as in some sense second-class Christians. After all, they hadn't got the baptism in the Holy Spirit . . .

In the light of these very divergent views, let us go back to the Bible and try to understand the broad sweep of its teaching on baptism.

2. *The Spirit and Baptism in the New Testament*

"Baptism" in the New Testament

The word *baptisma* is specifically Christian. It is not found before its appearance in the New Testament. The main lines of New Testament teaching about baptism are fairly clearly to be seen from the way in which this word is used. It is applied frequently to the baptism of John, which is called a "baptism of repentance" (Luke 3: 3, Acts 13: 24). John's baptism looked forward to the coming Kingdom, which the Greater than John would introduce. Those who were prepared for God's kingly rule to be exercised in their lives "came together in baptism", as Josephus put it, determined to live a life of virtue and piety (*Antiquities*, 18: 116f). It was baptism "with a view to forgiveness of sins" (*eis aphesin hamartiōn*), so the evangelists tell us (Mark 1: 4, Luke 3: 3). It did not confer forgiveness, but it pointed the way, and it was because of this deeply seated link with forgiveness that early Christians were sometimes embarrassed that Jesus should have been baptised. Hence the conversation recorded in Matthew 3: 13ff where John hesitates to baptise Jesus and Jesus says, "Let it be so now; for thus it is fitting for us to fulfil all righteousness". It seems that Jesus identified himself with sinners in the dramatic act of baptism, though he had no sins of his own to repent of. He was later to identify himself far more profoundly with sinners when he took responsibility for them on the cross. Indeed, it is interesting to notice that Jesus on two occasions alludes to his death in the metaphorical terms of "baptism" (Mark 10: 38, Luke 12: 50). It was the cross that would make possible that forgiveness of sins to which repentant Israelites looked forward when they went down to the Jordan to be baptised by John. Repentance, forgiveness, membership of the messianic community—there was a further gift to which the baptism of John looked forward, though it could not confer. John made it abundantly clear that his baptism with water was a preparatory rite; Jesus would baptise with the Holy Spirit. And this promise began to be fulfilled on the day of Pentecost. We get some further idea of the way in which early Christians regarded baptism by noticing the use of *baptisma* in the writings of Paul and Peter. Paul says that we Christians were buried by our baptism into Christ's death, so that just as Christ was raised from the dead by the glory of the Father, so we too might walk in newness of life. In the context he is talking about justification, and the fact that it does not lead to lawlessness in behaviour. He says, in effect, that it cannot do, for they are baptised into Christ's death and resurrection. Baptism (along, of course, with the faith, repentance and allegiance to Jesus) has united Christians with Christ. They share his death to sin; they share his risen life. Baptism is, in fact, the sacrament of justification. The same point is made in Colossians 2: 12. Paul is arguing that the Colossians do not need any additional saviour figures. They have Christ, and not only "in him the whole fulness of the deity dwells bodily" but they themselves "have come to fulness of life in him". How did this come about? "You were buried with him in baptism, in which you were also raised with him through faith in the working of God who raised him from the dead." He goes on to say that "God made us alive with him, forgiving us all our trespasses, having cancelled the bond that stood against us with its legal demands; this he set aside, nailing it to his cross". Now this is no second experience that Paul refers to: it is Christian baptism, the one baptism that they all share as Christians. Baptism is one of the seven constituents of Church unity to which the apostle can confidently refer in Ephesians 4: 5. "One Lord, one faith one baptism . . ." Baptism is *the* mark of Christian belonging, the badge which all God's people have in common whatever their differences. The New Testament knows nothing of believers in Jesus who do not get baptised (though, of course, someone like the penitent thief did not have the opportunity). Neither does it know anything of Christians who get themselves rebaptised. For baptism is the sacramental expression of Christian initiation.

If the use of the word *baptisma* does not support any two-stage idea of Christian initiation, it does not lend any support, either, to the notion that baptism in water inevitably saves a man irrespective of repentance, faith, obedience, and commitment to Christ and his Church. 1 Peter 3: 21 goes out of its way to make this clear. Peter has been using the story of the ark in the flood, through which Noah and his family were saved, as a picture of Christian baptism. "Baptism, which corresponds to this, now saves you", he says. But as if conscious of the misinterpretation to which his words could be liable, he continues, "not the putting away of the body's defilement" (i.e. the physical washing will not achieve anything by itself) "but the pledge of a good conscience towards God, through the resurrection of Jesus Christ . . ." The word translated "pledge" is variously interpreted. It may refer to the "question" asked of those to be baptised; it may mean "appeal" to God for a good conscience; it may even mean "decision" for God arising out of a good conscience. But in any case it speaks of the genuine commitment on man's side. And the allusion to the resurrection of Christ to God's right hand hints at the power released in the life of the baptised when the candidate does not merely go through a ceremonial washing, but turns in obedient repentance and faith to Jesus Christ. That sort of baptism saves us.

This distinctively Christian word *baptisma*, then, is associated with repentance, entry into the Kingdom, forgiveness of sins, reception of the Spirit, and union with Christ in his death and risen life. It does not allow us to suppose that there is a baptism for Christians subsequent to conversion, nor does it permit us to think that a merely external submission to the rite affects anything. Baptism appears to be the expression in an outward ceremony of the new birth, justification, becoming a son of God, call it what you will; it is the mark of the new life, and that new life involves the other crucial constituents of repentance, faith, and reception of the Spirit of Christ who alone can make us new people.

"Baptise" in the New Testament

When we turn to the verb "baptise", a similar picture meets us. Unlike the noun *baptisma*, the verb *baptizō* was used in pre-Christian Greek. It meant to immerse, and was used literally of "scuppering" a ship, "sinking" in the mud, and, in the passive, "to perish", "to be overwhelmed". It would be attractive to suppose that this idea of being immersed and dying was carried over into the theology of Paul in Romans 6 and Colossians 2, but this cannot be proved.

The word was also used in pre-Christian Judaism, and indeed assumed considerable importance. For converts to Judaism, baptism was a significant part of initiation. Sacrifice was also required, along with circumcision for male members of the household; but all proselytes, male and female, adults and children, were baptised. They washed themselves in a bath of water, and saw this as washing away their Gentile impurities; so much so that the rabbis regarded the baptised proselyte as "a newborn child". He had a new status. Moreover, his baptism enabled him to enter symbolically into the event that was crucial in Israel's salvation history — the Exodus. We have an allusion to this in 1 Corinthians 10: 2 where Paul is alluding to the Old Testament prototypes of the Christian sacraments. He reminds the Corinthians, who seem to have been relying on their baptism and the eucharist as if they were of magical efficacy, that the Old Testament folk had their sacraments too, and these did not save them when they became disobedient. "They all baptised themselves into Moses in the cloud and in the sea" — that is to say, at the Exodus; and "they all ate the same spiritual food and drank the same spiritual drink", but nevertheless many of them perished in the desert for their disobedience and idolatry. This strange phrase, "baptised into Moses", is the nearest parallel we find to the prevailing New Testament description of a Christian as someone who is baptised into Christ. The idea is primarily one of commitment to the figure who is active in salvation, Moses in one case and Christ in the other; but with Jesus there is a further connotation, for he is seen as the head of the new humanity in whom believers become incorporated.

Apart from the evangelists, the only New Testament writer who uses the verb "to baptise" is Paul, and it is instructive to see what he makes of it.

First and foremost, baptism derives its meaning from God's saving act in Christ. "Christ loved the Church", we read, "and

5

gave himself up for her in order that he might set her apart for himself, having cleansed her through washing by water with a word" (Ephesians 5: 25f). Though the word "baptise" is not used here, the meaning is plain, and we have clear allusion to the bathing of the candidate in water, his response in the word of confession (cf. 1 Corinthians 12: 3), and both depending upon the self-sacrificing love of Jesus who went to the cross to make our cleansing possible. Again, the discussion of disunity in 1 Corinthians 1 is settled by Paul reminding them that they were baptised into the name (i.e. the ownership, the possession) of Christ who had been crucified for them (verses 12–15). As we have seen, Jesus had looked forward to his sacrificial death as the supreme baptism, and Paul, looking back on the cross, emphasises the link. Baptism brings a man into contact with the saving work of Christ.

Accordingly we are not surprised to find that baptism is linked with justification in Romans 6: 3f and 1 Corinthians 6: 11. Many Evangelical Christians see justification by faith as the very antithesis of the sacrament of baptism. Paul sees them as the outside and the inside of the same thing. Consider these three points. Baptism, like justification, is *done for us*. No man can justify himself. No man can baptise himself. In contrast to the proselyte baptism of the Jews when the candidate washed himself, Christian baptism is always in the passive. It is something done for you by another, as if to remind you that your salvation is entirely a matter of grace, and not something to which you make any active contribution. Secondly, baptism, like justification, is *once for all*. It is unrepeatable. You can no more be rejustified than you can be rebaptised. Both ideas make nonsense. Baptism speaks of Christ's death once and for all on that cross for our forgiveness. Justification speaks of our account settled, of the verdict of the Last Day which we can know here and now—acquitted. Both have finality. Indeed, the sacrament of circumcision had this purpose in the Old Covenant. Abraham "received circumcision as a sign of or seal on the righteousness by faith which he had when he was still uncircumcised" (Romans 4: 11). Abraham is a prototype of the true believer. God met him in undeserved grace, and offered to give him the ends of the earth for his inheritance and seed like the stars of heaven. Abraham responded in faith and obedience, and was given the rite of circumcision as a physical sign of the right standing he now enjoyed with God and as a seal on the whole transaction, to which he could look back with confidence in days when he was tempted to doubt. Baptism is like that: a gracious gift to believers, as a sign of their right standing with God and a seal on the whole transaction between divine grace and human faith.

And thirdly baptism, like justification, speaks of *incorporation into Christ*. That is the whole point of this remarkable phrase we repeatedly meet of "baptism *into* Christ"—the Greek word *eis* is utterly explicit. Through the whole complex of repentance, faith and baptism a man is brought *into* Christ, so that from now on his position can be described by Paul's favourite definition of a Christian, as someone who is *"in* Christ". Yes, baptism speaks of incorporation into Christ. And so does justification. It is quite wrong to imagine that justification is some cold legal status conferred upon us by God reckoning Christ's merits to our account; far from it. Christ acted for us decisively and sufficiently through his cross and resurrection; as a result of that action we can be justified, acquitted, reckoned to be right with God but only as we are incorporated in Christ, united with the Righteous One, accepted in the Beloved. Hence the first half of Romans 5 can be so strong on justification: Christ for us. The second half of that chapter is all about the New Adam and our incorporation in him: us in Christ. The two belong together. For justification has incorporation into Christ as its corollary and rationale. This is made very clear in the concluding words of 2 Corinthians 5, where Paul insists that God made Jesus actually *to be sin* for us, Jesus who knew no sin; in order that we might *be the righteousness of God*—an almost inconceivable exchange. But Paul does not leave it there, for to do so would rightly merit the charges of injustice and legal fiction on God's part. He adds the crucial phrase *"in him"*. It is only in Christ that we are made right. God was in Christ, justifying me: I am in Christ, justified. Justification, like baptism, speaks of incorporation into Christ.

If it were necessary to stress even more emphatically the rôle of baptism as the sacrament of Christian initiation, we could turn to the end of Galatians chapter 3. In successive sentences Paul can say "Christ came that we might be justified by faith", "In Jesus Christ you are all sons of God through faith", and "As many of you as have been baptised into Christ have put on Christ" (verses 24, 26, 27). Being justified by faith, becoming sons of God, and being baptised into Christ are three ways of describing the same thing—the beginning of the Christian life. And to conclude the paragraph, by taking us back to the great paradigm of justification by faith, Paul reminds his readers "If you are Christ's, then you are Abraham's offspring, and heirs according to promise". Just as Abraham believed God's promise, obeyed his call, was justified by faith in God's grace, and received the sign and seal of circumcision—so with the Christian. The parallel is exact. God has had only one way of saving men throughout all the ages. He did not save men by their works in Old Testament days, and by faith in New Testament days. He has been constant throughout history, accepting into close relationship with himself men from every age who were willing to turn from their evil ways, cast themselves on his mercy, and enter a recognisable community through an outward sacrament— circumcision in the old days, and baptism in the Christian era. Indeed, in a remarkable passage in his letter to the Colossians, Paul brings the sacraments of the Old and New Covenant together round the cross of Christ which alone gives them efficacy. "In Christ you were circumcised with a circumcision made without hands . . . and you were buried with him in baptism": and all of this because Christ triumphed over the forces of evil in the cross (Colossians 2: 11–15).

Baptism—one-stage initiation

Baptism then, and not baptism plus a subsequent confirmation or "baptism with the Spirit" is what marks a man as a Christian. It is the unrepeatable sacrament of Christian beginnings, just as the communion is the sacrament of going on with Christ in his Church. Of course, baptism is not to be seen as the bare external rite. The Bible is full of attacks on the merely outward (see Psalm 51: 10, Romans 2: 28, 1 Corinthians 10: 1–11, Mark 7: 14ff, Ezekiel 18: 31, 26: 26, Isaiah 1: 10ff etc.). Baptism includes the idea of sonship, of entry into the kingdom, of incorporation into Christ, of reception of his Spirit, of justification. Sometimes one word is used, sometimes another; but the whole complex belongs together. There are three strands which taken together make a man a Christian. There is the human side—repentance and faith. There is the divine side—reception of the Spirit, adoption into the family of God, forgiveness of sins, justification. There is the churchly side— baptism into the body of believers. And all three belong together and are necessary parts of initiation. If you start asking "Which is the most necessary?", it is a silly question, but I suppose the answer would have to be—the divine side.

If you ask which is the least important, that would be an even more silly question, but I suppose the answer would have to be—the churchly side. But whichever order they come in (and experience shows that, as Augustine realised long ago, baptism sometimes precedes regeneration, sometimes follows it, and sometimes never leads to it for lack of faith on man's side and the gift of the Spirit on God's), the three belong together in the plan of God as surely as loving companionship, sexual relationship, and children belong together in God's plan for marriage.

What, then, of "two-stage" passages?

If this is so, what are we to make of those passages in Acts which speak of a two-stage initiation?

At first sight there are two such passages: Acts 8 where the Samaritan believers did not receive the Holy Spirit immediately, and Acts 19 where a handful of disciples, who had been followers of John the Baptist declared themselves unaware of the existence of the Holy Spirit, but subsequently received him, spoke with tongues and prophesied. In addition we might add the conversion of Saul of Tarsus, where there seems to have been a three day gap between his surrender to Christ on the Damascus road and his baptism and filling with the Holy Spirit. But before we lay too much stress on these passages, it is worth noticing a general point. Luke appears quite uninterested in providing a theology of Christian initiation. Those who have gone to him for tidy theological schemes have been disappointed. Sometimes reception of the Spirit follows baptism (e.g. Acts 2: 38ff); sometimes it precedes baptism (e.g. Acts 10: 44–48); and sometimes a man is baptised who has no part nor lot in the Christian thing, and whose heart is still fast bound in wickedness (Acts 8: 21). Luke is so little concerned to write a handbook on Christian initiation that he does not even tell us whether Apollos received Christian baptism from Aquila and Priscilla, who took him in hand and instructed him when "he knew only the baptism of John". Nevertheless in the very next chapter, Luke gives us this remarkable excursus on the rebaptism of a dozen disciples of the Baptist at the hands of Paul! Dunn would argue, in his *Baptism in the Holy Spirit* that the reason is plain: all that really matters is the possession of the Holy Spirit, and Apollos possessed the Spirit already, so was not rebaptised, whilst the disciples of John at Ephesus had not received the Spirit and so were given full Christian initiation. He may be right; but I doubt it. His claim that Apollos was full of the Holy Spirit is very precariously based in the text. The phrase *zeōn tō pneumati* in Acts 18: 25 could mean "burning hot with the Holy Spirit", but could also mean "fervent in spiritual disposition", which is the probable meaning in the only other place it occurs, Romans 12: 11. It has often been observed that Paul is more interested in the interior work of the Spirit, assuring believers, transforming their lives, and so on; whereas Luke is more interested in the broader picture of the coming of the Spirit on the Church, his external manifestations in prophecy and tongues, and his direction of the Christian mission. It would certainly be a mistake to try to base a doctrine of theological necessity upon passages in Luke's writings which were designed to describe the various stages which seemed to him significant in the spread of a work for God.

With this note of caution in mind, let us examine the three passages in question.

St. Paul's conversion?

It would be very precarious to found a doctrine of two-stage initiation on the three day delay in Paul's conversion experience. As we have seen from his own writings, he was clearly a one-stage man, for whom justification and sonship were symbolised and sealed in baptism and reception of the Spirit. Luke, too, sees the whole three day experience as one. Thus in the account he gives of Paul's conversion before the Jerusalem Jews (Acts 22: 10ff), the Ananias incident is recalled along with Paul's commission and baptism; while in his other account of it, before Agrippa (Acts 26: 12ff) there is no mention of the three day wait, the rôle of Ananias, or even of baptism. The one unified emphasis which confronts us in all three accounts, as well as Paul's allusions in his own letters, is of a radical, life-changing encounter between Saul of Tarsus and the risen Jesus.

The Ephesian dozen?

There is no greater ground for supposing that the events of Acts 19 are meant to advocate a two-stage initiation for Christian people. It is clearly an exceptional instance: only a handful of men are involved, a mere dozen "disciples". The word to be sure, usually denotes Christians, and Paul clearly mistook them for Christians. But he soon found out his mistake.

They seemed to possess none of the marks of the Spirit's indwelling. So he asked them, *not*, as the Authorised Version rather carelessly put it, "Have you received the Holy Ghost *since ye believed?*", as if the Greek warranted some great space between their belief and their reception of the Spirit; but, "Have you believed and received the Holy Spirit?"—the participle "believing" being contemporaneous with their receiving. It is unfortunate that many Pentecostal writings still rely on this simple mistranslation of the Greek original for their teaching on a two-stage experience. I have before me, as I write, a little book by Don Basham, *Ministering the Baptism in the Holy Spirit*. He is associated with the Full Gospel Business Men's Fellowship, a leading Pentecostal agency, and wrote as recently as 1971. He explains Acts 19: 2 as follows. "Have you received the baptism in the Holy Spirit since you accepted Jesus Christ as your Saviour?" Not only is there nothing in the verse about "accepting Jesus Christ as Saviour" nor about "receiving the baptism in the Holy Spirit", but the time reference indicated by the English "since you accepted . . ." has no warrant in the Greek. It is rather ironical to read in his Introduction, after three major errors in the exposition of one verse like this, that "the Holy Spirit led him (i.e. Basham) into presenting almost word for word the message this book contains". This type of slipshod exegesis is not likely to recommend the Pentecostal case.

The passage goes on to make it crystal clear that these disciples were in no sense Christians. They were followers of John the Baptist, baptised by him (v. 3) who had then made their way hundreds of miles north-west to Ephesus. They had clearly not been in touch with John's later testimony to Jesus, for they needed to be informed by Paul that the Coming One whom John predicted was in fact Jesus. They had neither heard of Jesus, nor believed in Jesus, nor been baptised into the name of Jesus, and they were quite uninformed about the Holy Spirit. Once again the old King James' Version is likely to mislead us at this point. According to it, they reply to Paul, "We have not so much as heard whether there be any Holy Ghost" (v. 2). This is certainly a possible way to take the Greek, but it would have been difficult for anyone who listened, however inattentively, to John the Baptist to be in doubt that he was interested in the Holy Spirit! It is much more likely that the original should be translated, "We have not even heard if the Holy Spirit is available". Not only did John the Baptist speak of the Holy Spirit as the future gift of

the Coming One, but as John the Evangelist observed concerning a statement of Jesus, "As yet the Spirit had not been
given, because Jesus was not yet glorified" (John 7: 39). The
followers of John at Ephesus did not know if the age of the
Spirit had broken in yet. It is rather hard to suppose that men
who were disciples of the Baptist, who did not know about
Jesus or the Holy Spirit can be called Christians and made
models for a two-stage initiation! The fact seems to be that
these men were not Christians at all, and their initiation into
Christ followed the preaching by Paul. They were baptised in
the name of the Lord Jesus. They had Paul's hands laid upon
them. They received the Spirit in a very manifest way, for
they spoke in tongues and prophesied. Very much one-
stagers . . .

The Samaritan converts?

Which brings us to the remaining passage, Acts 8. However
you choose to interpret it, it leaves you with problems. Philip
preached the gospel to the Samaritans. Multitudes responded.
Evil spirits were cast out; lame folk were healed; and much joy
marked the city. Simon the magician is then brought before
our eyes. He had set himself up as a great power from God,
but saw himself outclassed, and "even Simon himself believed,
and after being baptised he continued with Philip, and seeing
signs and great miracles performed, he was amazed". At this
point Peter and John came up from Jerusalem to see what was
going on, and they prayed that the Samaritans might receive
the Holy Spirit, "for it had not yet fallen upon any of them,
but they had merely been baptised into the name of the Lord
Jesus". Why the delay?

The Pentecostal answer, and the answer of many Catholics,
is the same. The Samaritan believers needed the laying on of
apostolic hands in confirmation to make them full members
of the Church (on the Catholic view) or to baptise them with
the Holy Spirit (on the Pentecostal view). Quite apart from
the mutually contradictory theologies built by Catholics and
Pentecostals on this passage, it has to be pointed out that
nowhere else in the New Testament is the laying on of hands
seen as the decisive act in Christian initiation. To be sure, it
sometimes has a place, as passages like Acts 19: 6 and Hebrews
6: 2 make clear; but nobody laid hands on the apostles at
Pentecost to confirm them—or to equip them with the Holy
Spirit; nor on Cornelius, nor on the Ethiopian eunuch, nor

the converts on the day of Pentecost nor almost every other recorded conversion! If Acts 8 is taken as justification for regarding either confirmation or baptism with the Spirit through the laying on of hands as the second essential stage in becoming a Christian, then on the showing of the New Testament itself, there are precious few Christians! No, this incident at Samaria was not typical, and Luke records it *because it is not typical*. He has something important that he wants to show us by it, but unfortunately he has failed to make his point abundantly plain!

One view recently propounded by Professor Lampe in *St. Luke and the Church of Jerusalem*, and owing a good deal to the writings of Conzelmann, is that Luke is at great pains to stress the links between the apostolic Church at Jerusalem on the one hand and the spreading circles of Christian outreach on the other. There is a lot of evidence to support this view. In this particular incident, accordingly, Lampe sees Peter and John being sent by the Jerusalem church "not to administer confirmation to the Samaritans, but to confirm their baptism by Philip, and to incorporate them, by the sign of solidarity, the laying on of hands, into the community of the Pentecostal Spirit; so that the Samaritan converts, too, became a sort of extension of the Jerusalem church" (p. 22). This view, though attractive, does not quite fit the evidence. Saul's conversion was, on any showing, a major advance for Christianity, yet it was Ananias, who had no close links with Jerusalem, so far as we know, who laid hands on his head. And in the even more climactic turning to the Gentiles in the first missionary journey (13: 46) we hear of no hands being laid on anyone's heads, but faith, the growth of the word of the Lord, joy and the Holy Spirit.[1]

[1] Professor Lampe comments: "I don't think that my view that the Samaritan mission became a sort of extension of the Jerusalem church through the action of Peter and John is invalidated by what you say. Luke is keen to show that the major developments in the Church's mission were brought about under the wing of Jerusalem, but he knows that this was done in a variety of ways. At Samaria it had to be by this special action by the heads of the Jerusalem apostolate, because Philip's baptisms clearly needed authenticating and ratifying. Paul was given the same sign by Ananias. The presence of Peter and John was not required: no schism had to be bridged in Paul's case. But Luke emphasises that Ananias was an established Jewish-Christian disciple (Acts 22: 12, 9: 10), i.e. a representative of the primitive community; and he brings Paul to Jerusalem and to fellowship with the apostles there as soon as possible after the Ananias episode. There was no need for hands to be laid on Gentiles at 13: 46 or anywhere else in that mission, for Paul and Barnabas were authorised by the Antioch church, which had itself been authenticated by Barnabas as an envoy of Jerusalem (11: 22ff). Paul was

Another view has recently been propounded by Dr. Dunn in his *Baptism in the Holy Spirit*. He thinks that the Samaritans never really believed at all; their attention was fixed on Philip, not on Christ. Simon, though baptised and said to be believing, was clearly not a Christian, as Dr. Dunn rightly observes. He suggests that the rest of the Samaritans were caught up in a wave of emotion and believed Philip rather than Christ, on the basis of the Greek construction *pisteuō* with the dative rather than the more usual *pisteuō eis*. However, there are other cases where *pisteuō* with the dative denotes saving faith (e.g. Acts 16: 34, 18: 8), so we cannot give much weight to that point. And the healings, the joy, the exorcisms which marked their belief at Samaria strongly suggest that it was real Christian faith all right. Why, then, did God withold his Holy Spirit on this unique occasion?

I believe the answer lies in the centuries old split between the Jews and the Samaritans. "The Jews had no dealings with the Samaritans" or perhaps "refused to use vessels in common with the Samaritans", as St. John had remarked (John 4: 9). If the Holy Spirit had been given immediately upon profession of faith and baptism by the Samaritans this ancient schism might have continued, and there would have been two churches, out of fellowship with each other. Acts 15 shows how carefully a decisive split between Jewish and Gentile Christianity was avoided by the early Christians. Acts 8 seems to stress that a similarly disastrous split was avoided at Samaria. God did not give his Holy Spirit (or, perhaps, the supernatural manifestations of that Spirit in tongues and prophecy?) to the Samaritans at once: not until representatives from Jerusalem came down and expressed their solidarity with the converts by praying for them and laying their hands on them. Then they received the Holy Spirit; indeed, the use of the imperfect tense, *elambanon*, may be significant; they received repeated manifestations of the Holy Spirit. It was not so much an authorisation from Jerusalem or an extension of the Jerusalem church, as a divine veto on schism in the infant Church, a schism which could

---

himself, according to Luke, an envoy of Jerusalem, reporting back as often as possible. The only people, after Paul himself, who needed authentication were Apollos, through instruction by Paul's associates, and the Ephesians who were possibly Apollos's converts." As will be seen from the text, I do not share Professor Lampe's view in every detail, and I do not think that Luke was as keen on authentication as he does. Nevertheless the account he gives may be the correct one, and certainly makes sense of the diverse phenomena in Acts.

have slipped almost unnoticed into the Christian fellowship, as
converts from the two sides of the "Samaritan curtain" found
Christ without finding each other. That would have been the
denial of the one baptism and all it stood for. It was for this
reason, I believe, that God made delay on this occasion.
Acts 8 is recorded precisely to show the abnormality of a
baptism which does not lead to reception of the Holy Spirit.
The two, this passage implies (and the rest of the New
Testament states explicitly), belong together. Indeed, Simon
Tugwell puts it very well when he writes, "This does not mean
that the New Testament has no interest in other manifestations
of the Spirit. Obviously it has! All that is being claimed is
that baptism is the appointed locus, the appointed 'visibility'
of reception of the Spirit. We should neither exaggerate this
claim, as sacramentalists have tended to do, nor reduce it, as
Evangelicals and especially Pentecostals have tended to do.
There is a great diversity of ways in which the Spirit works in
us; the one thing that is common to all and is the bond of our
unity, is baptism" (*Did you receive the Spirit?* p. 85f).

New Testament teaching on baptism in the Holy Spirit

It is perhaps surprising that there are so few references in
the New Testament to baptism in or by the Holy Spirit. There
are in fact only seven. Before we look at them, it is worth
clearing up the phrase I have just used, "in or by" the Holy
Spirit. In Greek the word *en* can either mean "in" or can
denote the instrumentality through which something happens,
"by". It is not possible to decide finally whether baptism with
the Holy Spirit refers to the Spirit as the one in whom we are
immersed, or as the one by whom we are baptised into sharing
the fortunes and destiny of Christ. The evidence leans a little
towards the latter interpretation, as we shall see.

There are, as I say, seven places in the New Testament where
this phrase is used. And six of them refer to the baptism which
John the Baptist promised that the Coming One would bring.
In contrast to his own water baptism, Jesus would baptise
with the Spirit. That is the plain meaning of Mark 1: 8, and
its parallels in Luke 3: 16, and Matthew 3: 11. John 1: 33 is
similar, and we have already examined it: "He on whom you
see the Spirit descend and remain, this is he who baptises with
the Holy Spirit." Acts 1: 5 is equally explicit. Jesus reminds
them of John's words, "for John baptised with water, but

before many days you shall be baptised with the Holy Spirit".
This promise of Jesus was fulfilled a few days later, when the
Spirit which had "rested" on Jesus came and "rested" on them,
filling them, and enabling them to speak in other tongues. The
sixth reference comes in Acts 11 : 16. Peter is explaining the
Cornelius incident to his critics at Jerusalem. "As I began to
speak, the Holy Spirit fell on them (i.e., Cornelius and his
household) just as on us at the beginning. And I remembered
the word of the Lord, how he said 'John baptised with water,
but you shall be baptised with the Holy Spirit'. If then God
gave the same gift to them as he gave to us when we believed
on the Lord Jesus Christ, who was I that I could withstand
God?" Peter is referring to an incident as significant for
Christian advance as the conversion of the first Samaritan
believers: the Gentile "godfearer" Cornelius has been grafted
into God's family. And just as God withheld his Spirit from the
Samaritans until the Jewish Christians were willing to heal
the breach with them and make one Church; so now God
gives his Spirit to Cornelius and his family before Peter can
make any appeal for repentance and faith, so as to cleanse all
traces of pride and superiority out of Peter and teach him not
to despise Gentiles and call them common or unclean. It is
one of the high points in Acts, where the Spirit of God breaks
through human apartheid. That is why it is recorded no less
than three times. That is why Peter recognises it as the Gentile
equivalent of Pentecost. Jesus has baptised not only Jews and
Samaritans but Gentiles with the Spirit promised long ago by
John. The same gift is for "them" as for "us". There is no
distinction amongst those who have repented (11 : 18), believed
in the Lord Jesus (11 : 17) and received the same Holy Spirit,
baptising them into union with Christ.

    In these six references so far we have an unambiguous picture
presented. John baptises with water as a mark of repentance;
Jesus will baptise with the Holy Spirit, to bring men into the
blessings of the New Covenant. This became possible on the
day of Pentecost, when the disciples who had already submitted
to John's baptism were baptised by the Holy Spirit. It was the
Holy Spirit who baptised Jews who had companied long and
deeply with the incarnate Christ; it was the same Holy Spirit
who, to the amazement of Peter, baptised Cornelius into
Christ, Cornelius who neither knew about nor knew the
incarnate Christ. In both instances baptism with the Holy
Spirit initiated men into the blessings of the New Covenant.
And exactly the same thing is taught in the seventh and final

reference to baptism in the Holy Spirit in 1 Corinthians 12: 13.
"By one Spirit we were all baptised into one body—Jews or
Greeks, slaves or free—and all were made to drink of one
Spirit." Paul could hardly put it more plainly, nor indeed
more polemically. For many of his Corinthian readers prided
themselves on gifts of healings, tongues, prophecy, faith and so
forth, and despised others, setting themselves apart. How they
would have loved to claim that only the healers, only the
tongues speakers were baptised in, or by, that Spirit. But Paul
demolishes that claim before it is uttered. It is the one Spirit
who enables men to make the baptismal confession, "Jesus is
Lord" (12: 3). And it is the one Spirit who baptises believers
into the one body of Christ—whatever the differences between
them. The one baptism by the one Spirit is as decisive a
unitive factor as the one Father who inspires all his children
alike, and the one Lord Jesus whom they all serve (12: 4f).
It is not certain whether the "*en*" is locative or instrumental.
It could mean that all are immersed in one Spirit, but since it
goes on "into the body" that would be very harsh, and the
instrumental use is highly likely here and in the other references
we have looked at. The Corinthians were all baptised by the
one Spirit into the one body of Christ. And, for good measure,
Paul sees the Spirit not only as the one who plunges them into
Christ, but as the one who comes within them like a draught of
cool water, or irrigation on parched soil: "you were all made
to drink of one Spirit".

What this evidence shows is two facts of considerable
doctrinal importance. First, nowhere are *Christians* subsequent
to the day of Pentecost said to be baptised with the Spirit.
Pentecost was the anointing, the "christing" of the original
disciples. They had had Jesus alongside them. They now had
the Spirit of Jesus within them. And the gift of the Spirit, made
on that first Whit Sunday, has never been withdrawn. The
Spirit is available for all who repent and believe and are
baptised into Christ. The converts on the day of Pentecost
found this: "Repent, and be baptised every one of you . . . for
the forgiveness of sins, and you shall receive the gift of the Holy
Spirit" Peter had promised them. They did repent, and they
found it true. The two distinctive blessings of the New
Covenant were theirs at once. Cornelius found the truth of
this; so did the Corinthians; and so have Christians down the
ages. Indeed, "if any man does not have the Spirit of Christ,
he is no Christian" (Romans 8: 9). So baptism with the Holy
Spirit is not a second-stage experience for some Christians,

but an initiatory experience for all Christians. Without it we are not Christians at all.

The second important thing is this. Christians are never told to wait for or pray for the baptism in the Holy Spirit. Of course not, for they are already baptised by the Spirit. The original disciples were indeed told to wait for the coming of the Spirit, but this was before Pentecost, before the distinctive experience of the Spirit of Jesus, internalised within the believer, was open to men. Ever since Pentecost there has been no need for "waiting meetings" for baptism with the Holy Spirit. This is our Christian starting point, not our goal.

3. False linguistics: genuine experience

The experience of "baptism in the Holy Spirit"

If this is what the New Testament teaches about baptism in the Holy Spirit, how is it that so many zealous Christians use the term in a quite different sense? Why do they refer it to some second experience? It is in that word experience that the answer lies. They have had an overwhelming experience of the Spirit of God; an experience that has changed their Christian lives as decisively as wrestling with God by Jabbok changed Jacob's. They then attach this label to the experience. Graham Pulkingham's experience is a celebrated and not atypical example. In *Gathered for Power* he tells us of the Liberal circles of Episcopalianism in which he had been brought up, of his appointment to The Church of the Redeemer, Houston, of his powerlessness in the face of the depressed condition of the church and the neighbourhood, and of his longing for a deeper experience of God. He tells us how he met David Wilkerson of *Cross and Switchblade* fame, and went with him to a home for rescued prostitutes which David's organisation looked after. "It was here that I received the baptism with the Spirit", says Pulkingham (p. 75). Abruptly Dave Wilkerson told him to kneel down, and Pulkingham recalls "I knelt and they came across the room hurriedly. When their hands touched my head something inside of me leapt with gladness, and even the unusual manner of their prayer was not offensive—it was loudly proclaimed in languages that were entirely foreign to me". Almost immediately "all awareness of the men and their prayers, of the room, and even of myself was obliterated by the immense presence of God's power. He was unmistakably there, and my inner response was like the clatter of a bamboo wind chime in a gale; the very foundations of my soul shook violently." He bowed low before the greatness of God, and wept at his own unworthiness. "We can go now; the Baptiser's here" said Dave to his companion, and they departed, leaving Graham alone with God.

That is how Graham Pulkingham describes the experience of God which revolutionised his Christian life. There followed a new gladness, a new power in ministry, in healing, in preaching, a liberty in prayer and worship, a crossing of denominational backgrounds, and a wonderful experiment (which is still going on) in community living after the apostolic fashion which so struck a commercial Broadcasting Company in the States that they made a documentary of it. How could Pulkingham call the experience which triggered off such mighty revolutions in all he had known as Christianity by a lesser name than "baptism in the Holy Spirit"?

The description "baptism in the Holy Spirit"

It is very understandable for Christians with experiences of God like Graham Pulkingham's to call that experience "baptism in the Holy Spirit", but all the same it is mistaken. This is not how the New Testament relates baptism and the Spirit. Always, as we have seen, the baptism in the Spirit is an initiatory experience. The Spirit of God brings men into the family of God, and it is utterly confusing to speak of the Spirit baptising people who already have the Spirit. It is a confusion which leads to several unfortunate results.

First, it either has to neglect or to distort what the New Testament has to say about the Spirit and baptism. Take Dennis Bennett's *The Holy Spirit and You* as an example. He quotes the "one baptism" of Ephesians 4:5 and continues "yet it is clear that in the New Testament this 'one baptism' divides into three. In 1 Corinthians 12:13 Paul says, 'In one Spirit we were all baptised into one body . . . and were all made to drink into one Spirit'. This refers to the spiritual baptism into Christ which takes place as soon as Jesus is received as Saviour. This was followed by the baptism with the Holy Spirit, in which the now indwelling Holy Spirit poured forth to manifest Jesus to the world through the life of the believer. Either before or after the baptism with the Holy Spirit there was the outward sign of baptism with water." Notice the knots into which he ties himself! Not one baptism, but three. And in order to differentiate them, they require explanatory glosses: *"spiritual* baptism into Christ", "baptism *with the Holy Spirit"* and *"the outward sign of* baptism with water". As we have seen, God has joined these three together in significance, however they may differ in the time at which they are experienced. Baptism in water is the sacramental symbol of repentance and faith on one side and the gift of the Spirit on the other. The whole thing belongs together. We therefore do despite to the New Testament if we use the phrase "baptism with the Holy Spirit" to refer to a second experience for Christians.

Once you do use the phrase in this way, you immediately find yourself in deep theological trouble. Because it is plain from such verses as Romans 8: 9 that all Christians have the Spirit. How is it, then, that they have the Spirit on the one hand, but have not received the baptism with the Spirit on the other? All very confusing and contradictory. In successive sentences Dennis Bennett says, "Because you have received Jesus, you already have the Holy Spirit, so no one needs to 'give' Him to you" and "Jesus is living in you and he is ready to baptise you in the Holy Spirit as soon as you are ready to respond" (p. 56). What he intends is clear enough; he calls "baptism with the Holy Spirit" an experience of God which involves speaking in tongues. "We have shown that speaking in tongues is indeed a common denominator in examples of the baptism in the Holy Spirit given in the Scriptures" (p. 57). In other words, for Bennett, though he is by no means a hard-line neo-Pentecostal, speaking in tongues is an essential part of the baptism with the Spirit. It is surprising to find this being claimed by a moderate charismatic as recently as 1971: I thought we had got past that type of exclusiveness. It was just what the charismatics at Corinth thought; just what necessitated those three chapters 1 Corinthians 12–14, with their stress on the one Spirit although he manifests himself in various ways in the body of Christ into which all Christians are baptised.

A third most unfortunate consequence which follows from regarding this deep experience of God, often marked by the ability to speak in tongues, as "baptism in the Holy Spirit" is divisiveness. The New Testament makes it very plain that a man who has the Spirit of God is very different from one who does not. You are either "in the Spirit" or "in the flesh". But charismatics tend to transfer this strong Christian dualism, this "either/or", to the experience they have labelled "baptism in the Holy Spirit". Those who have had the baptism are

"in", and those who have not had the baptism are "out".
Hence the divisiveness which the charismatic movement has
often brought to churches. There are, of course, various
reasons for this division; the unspirituality of many of the
ordinary members of the congregation and their unwillingness
to be open before God and their brethren; an arrogant sense
of having arrived by some neo-Pentecostals, and so on. But
much of the trouble is due to this use of the phrase "baptism
in the Holy Spirit". For baptism means beginning; it is the
initiatory Christian rite, and it speaks of the initiatory
Christian experience. If believing Christians are told they must
be baptised with the Spirit, it inevitably suggests that they
lack him already, that they have not yet begun. But they *have*
begun! They are in Christ, justified, adopted into God's
family, recipients of his gracious Spirit. The unintended
arrogance of the division of Christians into those who have
been baptised in the Holy Spirit and those who have not
would be lessened if charismatics rejected the unscriptural use
of this term "baptism in the Holy Spirit" to describe a second
experience for those who are already Christians. It is contrary
to the usage of the New Testament, confusing in the extreme,
and contributory to division among the one people of the
Spirit.

It is greatly to the credit of some thoughtful Christians
within the Catholic charismatic movement, that they have
perceived and avoided this danger of taking over uncritically
the Pentecostal description of "baptism in the Holy Spirit" to
describe the renewal they have received. Fr. Killian McDonnell,
O.S.B., writing on the theological basis of the Catholic
charismatic renewal, grasped the nettle which had proved
too prickly for his fellow Roman Catholic, Simon Tugwell, in
chapter 5 of *Did You Receive the Spirit?* He integrates every
experience of the Spirit with the one baptism. "The charismatic renewal has its theological foundations in the celebration
of initiation, and calls for a renewal of baptismal consciousness
broadly conceived, that is, 'that we might understand the gifts
bestowed on us' (1 Corinthians 2: 12). A feature of the
renewal which causes confusion is the use of the phrase
'baptism in the Holy Spirit'. For historical reasons many
Catholics in the renewal have adopted this phrase, already
current among classical Pentecostals, to describe the experience
through which they came into a new awareness of the presence
and power of the Spirit in their lives.

"But there is a problem in the use of this phrase, as it could

be taken to mean that only those who have had a particular
kind of experience of the Spirit have really been baptised in
the Spirit. This is not the case, since every valid and fruitful
Christian initiation confers the 'gift of the Holy Spirit' (Acts
2: 38), and 'to be baptised in the Holy Spirit' is simply another
scriptural way of saying 'to receive the Holy Spirit'.

"Hence, many prefer to use other expressions to describe
what is happening in the charismatic renewal. Among other
alternatives which have been proposed are: 'release of the
Spirit', 'renewal of the sacraments of initiation', 'actualisation
of gifts already received in potentiality', and 'a manifestation
of baptism, whereby the hidden grace given in baptism breaks
through into conscious experience'. These are all ways of
saying that the power of the Holy Spirit, given in Christian
initiation, but hitherto unexperienced, becomes a matter of
personal conscious experience." He goes on to show that this
conscious experience may develop gradually or through a
crisis experience: "both the growth pattern and the crisis
pattern should be looked upon as authentic ways of realising
the grace of initiation at the conscious level." If all those
within the renewal would use language with the same care
as this Roman Catholic theologian, a great deal of confusion
and heartbreak would be avoided.

The reality behind the inaccurate description

On the other hand, if the language which the neo-
Pentecostals use for their experience is unfortunate, the same
need not be the case with the experience itself. It is tragic that
many Christians have robbed themselves of blessing because
they distrusted, feared or despised this movement. They have
been satisfied with a low level of spirituality. They have not
allowed God to release them in prayer and praise and personal
relationships, from the imprisonment of age-long inhibitions.
They have not expected to see God at work in conversions, in
changing tough lives, in healing, in explicit guidance. They
have forgotten that the manifestations of the Spirit in the New
Testament had an uncomfortably concrete nature. Much of
the division in the churches that has come with the Pentecostals, has not been the fault of the Pentecostals themselves,
but of the narrow, fearful, unspiritual Christianity in whose
lukewarm waters many of us have for so long been willing to
stay, terrified to launch out into the deep of experience of God.
In an age when the Spirit of God is breaking up the fallow

ground and the man-made barriers all over the world and irrespective of denomination, it would be ironic indeed if we missed what he has for us because we refused to get below the false linguistics in which the Pentecostals customarily express their living experience of God. Let those who want to retain the New Testament link between baptism in the Spirit and water baptism, justification, adoption—becoming a Christian in fact—make very sure that it is the full New Testament concept of baptism which they espouse; a plunging beneath the waters of the Spirit, an inundation with him, a vitality produced by him that could cause folk to wonder if we were drunk. Have we that power in prayer, that strength over temptation, that growing Christlikeness, which marked the communities of Christ in New Testament days and of which the one baptism was the outward bond?

When in the sixteenth century this tension between tradition and experience, between churchly Christianity and new life in Christ was felt so acutely, the Reformers did not say, "Away with church structures. Down with water baptism, because it clearly does not bring new birth. All that matters is justification." Instead, they spoke of "improving on" their baptism, by which they meant ensuring that they had the reality as well as the symbol. If they lived in our day they would show themselves too good scholars, I fancy, to use the phrase "baptism in the Holy Spirit" in the way many Pentecostals do; they would retain the biblical sense of the word as the divine element in Christian initiation. But they would want to go all the way with the Pentecostals in emphasising the deep experience of God. They would call on us today to "improve on" our baptism, and make sure that we are not merely immersed in the Spirit symbolically through our baptism, but in our lives. It is to this full surrender to the Lord who is Spirit, this openness to his sweeping through our lives, that the Pentecostal movement is recalling the Church of God. If the Church fails to heed, then the new wine may regretfully be found to require new bottles.

CHAPTER 9

The Spirit's Fulness

Two initial surprises about "fulness"

IT HAS BEEN characteristic of holiness movements throughout Church history to claim that the fulness of the Holy Spirit
depends on conformity with their particular shibboleth. The
terminology changes: "perfection", "brokenness", "full surrender", "sanctification" have all been used, but "the fulness
of the Holy Spirit" is perhaps the most contemporary and
explicit in its claim. It is a commonplace in Pentecostal and
neo-Pentecostal literature that while all Christians share to
some extent in the Holy Spirit, only those who have been
"baptised in" the Holy Spirit can know his fulness. The fulness
of the Holy Spirit which comes from his personal, permanent
and full indwelling, is intended to equip us for service, and is
obtained only by this crisis experience of "baptism in the Holy
Spirit". Indeed "Spirit-filled" is often used by charismatic
people to describe someone who shares their experience, in
contra-distinction to run-of-the-mill Christians. What does the
New Testament say about the fulness of the Holy Spirit?

Surprisingly, it says nothing at all. The Greek word for
fulness, *plērōma*, is applied to many things in the New
Testament, notably to both Christ and the Church; but never
to the Holy Spirit. This is not an important point, because the
idea may be present without the word; but it does show how
ill-based in Scripture is any attempt to make the "fulness of
the Holy Spirit" into a doctrinal war cry, as if it were a most
important and neglected biblical emphasis.

The second noteworthy point is that the verb "to be filled
with", *pimplēsthai*, is almost exclusively Lucan. Apart from two
occasions in Matthew, all its other twenty-two occurrences are
in Luke's Gospel or Acts. The adjective "full" has a wider
spread, but of its sixteen appearances eleven are in Luke or
Acts. It is clear that this is a favourite word of Luke's. In

addition we ought perhaps to mention the normal word for "to fill", *plēroun*, but this is only twice used of the Holy Spirit (Acts 13: 52, Ephesians 5: 18) and twice loosely associated with him (Romans 15: 13f, Colossians 1: 8, 9).

Two main uses of "fulness"

The words are used in two main ways. One is to denote the general characteristic of a man, "full of the Spirit". The supreme exemplar for this use is, of course, Jesus (Luke 4: 1), but after Pentecost it is occasionally applied to Christians by Luke. The qualifications sought in the Seven of Acts 6 were that they should be "full of wisdom and the Holy Spirit". Among them Stephen is described as "a man full of faith and the Holy Spirit", and the point is re-emphasised at his martyrdom (7: 55). Barnabas is the only other man so described (11: 24) "He was a good man, full of the Holy Spirit and of faith". Luke seems to be using this phrase of a man's governing characteristic, his controlling disposition. Thus we read of a man "full of leprosy" (Luke 5: 12), that is to say gripped by the disease. We read that Elymas was "full of all deceit and villainy" (13: 10) and understand that he was controlled by these evil impulses. The meaning of "full of the Holy Spirit" is therefore not hard to fathom. It signifies someone who is habitually governed and controlled by the Lord the Spirit, just as Jesus was. There is no suggestion that this state is due to any particular ritual or experience.

The second way in which the notion of being filled with the Spirit meets us in the Scriptures is quite different. It does not refer to the settled characteristics of a lifetime but to the sudden inspiration of a moment. The instances where it occurs are as follows, and they are most interesting because sometimes they bear what we might call a "charismatic" character, and sometimes a "non-charismatic" one. But the strangest of all is the first, John the Baptist. For the promise to Zacharias is that "he shall be filled with the Holy Spirit even from his mother's womb" (Luke 1: 15). Now a statement like that does not chime in with anybody's ready-made theological pattern, and what a healthy thing that it does not! For God is God. He is free to act in accordance with his sovereign will and purposes. If he determines to fill the Baptist with his Spirit from his mother's womb, who are we to cavil? However, it is worth remembering that here and in the two references which follow, we are not dealing with the full Christian experience of the

Holy Spirit, made possible only after the death and glorification of Jesus, but something much more akin to the *ruach adonai* of Old Testament days. Great though John the Baptist was, he pointed forward to the Kingdom but was not a member of it, and did not enjoy the distinctive blessing of the Kingdom, the presence of the Spirit of Jesus within him (Matthew 11: 11).

Perhaps the emphasis on John's being filled with the Spirit from his mother's womb was due to the fact that the New Testament sees him as "the voice of one crying in the wilderness 'Prepare the way of the Lord' ". His was a prophetic function, and prophets were equipped with the Spirit of the Lord so that they could proclaim the Lord's word. This is what is meant when Elizabeth (1: 41) and Zacharias (1: 67) are said to be filled with the Holy Spirit. In both cases the purpose is made explicit: it is so that they may prophesy. The Spirit comes upon them, fills them, and enables them to give inspired utterance.

But it is the passages subsequent to Pentecost that primarily concern us. Can we discern from what is said about people who are filled with the Spirit in the Acts any clear guidelines for our day?

There are just five instances. The first is on the day of Pentecost, where the "tongues as of fire" came upon the disciples and "they were all filled with the Holy Spirit". What was the result of this first, crucial filling? They spoke in other tongues, they burst out in praise to God, and they preached the gospel boldly and effectively through their spokesman, Peter. The Spirit equipped them with power for service, loosened their tongues in praise, and enabled them to speak in tongues. In emphasising these characteristics of the filling with the Holy Spirit, the Pentecostals are perfectly correct. When they extrapolate from this incident and assume that filling with the Holy Spirit must always have the same results, they make a serious mistake. When they assume that the filling with the Spirit is a single unrepeatable experience which puts a man on a plateau from which he never thereafter descends, they make an equally serious mistake—though not as serious as those earth-bound Christians who do not believe that there is any plateau of spirituality to be scaled. For what do we find in the second reference to being filled with the Spirit?

It comes in 4: 8, and concerns Peter. Already filled though he was on the day of Pentecost, he is again filled with the Holy Spirit, and for the very important purpose of bearing witness to Jesus. No tongues, no praise, no never-to-be-repeated experience, but bold preaching. Jesus had told them to expect the Spirit to equip them for impromptu witness of this sort (Matthew 10: 19f) and Peter was experiencing the fulfilment of it, as countless Christian witnesses have ever since. It was a special infilling to meet a special opportunity.

The same holds good of 4: 31. The infant Church was deeply engaged in intercession. They cast themselves in utter dependence upon God. The result was that "they spoke the word of God with boldness". It is this emphasis on witness which characterises the next reference to a man being filled with the Holy Spirit. This time it is Saul of Tarsus. Ananias comes to him, at the Lord's behest, to enable those blind eyes to be filled with light and that empty life to be filled with the Holy Spirit (9: 17). We read that he received his sight, was baptised, took food and was strengthened, and then that he went out in courageous testimony to Jesus in the very city where he had planned to arrest all the followers of Jesus he could find.

The fifth reference is in 13: 9. Elymas, relying on magical powers, is contesting with the apostle Paul for the soul of the Roman proconsul of the island of Cyprus, Sergius Paulus, over whom he seems to have exercised considerable ascendancy. As if he wants to contrast the power of the Spirit of God with the power of magic, Luke records that Saul was filled with the Holy Spirit, that Elymas suddenly found himself blind—the one who had set out to lead others had to be led by the hand—and the proconsul came to faith. No doubt the miraculous blinding of Elymas had a lot to do with persuading him of the power of God, but what we are told really astonished him was "the teaching of the Lord". Once again, the filling with the Holy Spirit is directly related to witness-bearing.

There is one further occasion in Acts where, as I mentioned earlier, a different word is used for being filled. In 13: 52 we read that the disciples in Pisidian Antioch were filled with joy and with the Holy Spirit. The context is illuminating. It is one of witness-bearing and persecution. They are fulfilling the rôle of the Servant in being a light to the Gentiles to bring salvation to the ends of the earth (13: 47). They are suffering the fate of the Servant in widespread rejection and opposition. Appropriately, they enjoy the equipment of the Servant, the Spirit himself.

If we look back over these references to being filled with the Spirit, what may we conclude? Surely that Christians should be full of the Spirit, as Jesus was (Luke 4: 1), as Stephen was (Acts 6: 5), as Barnabas was (11: 24), as the Seven were (6: 3).

This should be the continual state of the Christian, but he can look for special fillings of the Spirit in special circumstances, particularly when he has opportunity to witness for Christ. It is right to stress that on the day of Pentecost being filled with the Spirit showed itself in speaking in tongues, and that in the Elymas incident it showed itself in a miracle. These things have too often been forgotten by "non-charismatics". But it is also important to remember that bold witness, a united prayer meeting, humble administration, and courageous joyful testimony in the face of persecution are no less marks of men who are filled with the Spirit of God.

"Be filled with the Spirit"

In the light of all this, what are we to make of the command in Ephesians 5: 18 that we should not get drunk, but should be filled with the Holy Spirit? One could plausibly give a Pentecostal interpretation to this injunction. The comparison of the Spirit's effects with those of drunkenness take us naturally back to what was being suspected at Pentecost; and the references to singing to the Lord, giving thanks always, and understanding his will, which figure in the immediate context, could all refer to charismatic gifts of the Spirit. However, a more careful examination of the context suggests otherwise. Paul is giving here instructions for Christian behaviour. The light of the gospel shines in dark places, and therefore Christians must be careful of their behaviour, quick to snap up opportunities of service, anxious to discern and follow the Lord's leading. They must not derive their stimulation from drink; excess of that can bring a hang-over. But no amount of the Holy Spirit can have that effect! Men filled with him are full of joy, full of thanks to the Lord, and ready to submit in love to other members of the Christian body. He then goes on to give examples—husband and wife, master and servant. While not excluding the possibility that Paul may be thinking of some particular spiritual gift, it is pretty plain that his command is for all Christians irrespective of their gifts. All are commanded to be filled with the Spirit so that they may fulfil their light-bearing function in society. Once again we see, sketched out in the broadest terms, the essential New Testament conviction that the Spirit is for mission. The correctness of this interpretation of Ephesians 5: 18 is supported, it seems to me, by the two loosely related passages which I alluded to earlier. In Romans 15: 13 in a context exclusively concerned with mission to the Gentiles, Paul prays that they may have God's full measure of hope, joy and peace in believing, as they are empowered by the Holy Spirit. It is clearly the ethical qualities of the Spirit which he associates with the filling. Similarly in Colossians 1 : 8, 9, where Paul gives thanks for their love in the Spirit and prays that they may be filled with the knowledge of God's will in all wisdom and spiritual understanding—it is in order that their lives may bring credit on the Lord, that they may be fruitful, increase in knowing God, and be strengthened to endure hardship patiently as they bear witness to God's delivering them out of darkness and putting them in the kingdom of the Son of his love. In so far as this is an allusion to any filling with the Spirit, the distinctively charismatic connotations of the term are notably absent and the ethical implications of the Spirit of Jesus very much to the fore. To be filled with the Spirit means to allow Jesus to have the fullest control in our lives that we are conscious of. In so far as we do that, we will always be finding new areas of self-centredness to surrender as the Lord who is Spirit possesses us more and more fully. To such submission all Christians are called. And it is no once and for all transaction: "go on being filled with the Spirit" is the meaning of the original.

Thus, while baptism in the Spirit is the initial experience of Christ brought about by the Spirit in response to repentance, faith and baptism, the fulness of the Holy Spirit is intended to be the continual state of the Christian. It is not a plateau on to which you are ushered by some second stage in initiation, a plateau which separates you from other Christians who have not had the same experience. The New Testament gives no support to that view whatsoever. In plain language, we are meant to be progressively filled with the Spirit of our Saviour Jesus Christ. That position can be lost, through disobedience (e.g., Acts 5: 3, 9, 7: 51). It can also be regained, through repentance and asking God to fill us afresh. God gives his Spirit to those that obey him (Acts 5: 32) and to those who ask him (Luke 11: 13). I discovered this shortly after my conversion when I surrendered to his Lordship a prized area of disobedient selfishness: after the battle and the surrender I was flooded with joy and peace and a sense of his power. Call that a second blessing if you will. But do not let it rest there. I have had many a similar experience since then as I have grown in knowledge of the Lord and living in the Spirit. A second blessing becomes ossified if it is overstressed. Let us look for a third, and a hundred and third as we press on along the upward path for the purpose for which Christ has laid his hand on us.

Any doctrine of a special spiritual state defined as "the fulness of the Holy Spirit" is very hazardous indeed, and has little to support it in the New Testament. It may be worth enquiring why this should be so.

Danger in exclusive claims to "fulness"

In the first place, any exclusivist doctrine of a fulness of the Holy Spirit subsequent to conversion, and deemed to be essential to high quality Christian living, has to face the strictures of Paul against similar positions in his letters to the Galatians and the Colossians. Certain teachers in Galatia were maintaining that unless you kept the Jewish law and got yourself circumcised you were either a very second-rate Christian or no Christian at all. The whole burden of his passionate letter to them is that Christ and Christ alone is the way of salvation. It was through faith in Christ, "placarded before them as crucified", that the Galatians entered into the realm of the Spirit: and now, by adding a further requirement to Christ (namely law-keeping) they were implying that Jesus was insufficient. The whole thrust of his letter is a repudiation of that calumny on Christ. Savagely, he wishes they would go and mutilate themselves (5 : 12).

At Colossae, it was not legalism but a syncretistic philosophy that was causing the trouble. It was being urged that Jesus is merely one of the mediatorial beings who bring men to God, that he offers men part of the fulness of the Godhead, that he is an effective though not an exclusive agent in redemption. Paul's answer to this is sharp and decisive. Christ alone, who is both the agent in creation, and the one who sustains it, can redeem men in virtue of his death on the cross (Colossians 1 : 14–20). Far from thinking of Jesus as a partial intermediary between God and man, they must realise that in Christ dwells all the fulness of the Godhead in bodily form, and that they are complete in him (2 : 9). That claim is very precise and very exclusive. The locus of God's fulness is "in him" and in him alone. It is not disseminated among various celestial figures, as the Colossian heretics taught: "all the fulness" is to be found in him. Moreover, there is a strong and a weak word for "Godhead" in Greek, and it is the former that Paul uses; there is a word which denotes permanent residence and another which means temporary stay, and it is, once again, the former that he uses. As a final fling he adds "in bodily form", that is to say, in the historical Jesus who lived and died and rose and was presented to them as the one meeting place of God and man. It is plain that Paul will have no truck with any doctrine which makes Jesus merely the precursor of some further spiritual blessing. The man who said so emphatic a "no" to the cry of "Jesus *and* circumcision" or "Jesus *and* philosophical knowledge" or "Jesus *and* angelic mediators", would assuredly find no place for a doctrine which says, in effect, "You must have Jesus *and* the fulness of the Holy Spirit for a high-octane Christian life". Indeed, he goes on to remind the Colossians that so far from needing to be initiated into further mysteries and spiritual visions (2: 18ff), so far from needing further spiritual resources (1: 15–20) they have everything they need in Christ, who embodies the divine fulness: "and you have come to fulness of life in him" (2: 9). In the face of this, it is difficult to maintain that Paul would give any support to a second blessing doctrine which advocated a fulness additional to Christ.

Furthermore, if we make exclusive individual claims to possess the fulness of the Holy Spirit, we run into the dangers so evident at Corinth. These are, I suppose, five-fold.

In the first place, their whole attitude was Gnostic. It claimed a form of knowledge which made them superior to ordinary Christians. Knowledge, Paul had to remind them, puffs up; love builds up (1 Corinthians 8: 1).

Secondly, like the Gnostics, the Corinthians were not interested in any future resurrection or kingdom; they had their fulness now, they had already entered upon their reign (1 Corinthians 15 and 4: 8ff). "I wish you had entered on your reign", replied the apostle tartly; then perhaps I could share it with you! He then reminds them that apostle though he is, he shares the suffering, the rejection and the costliness of discipleship which marked his Lord. They need to remember that the truly Christian life is marked by the cross as well as by the resurrection. The ultimate fulfilment lies with Christ in heaven, and any claim to fulness now is an illicit anticipation of God's future.

Thirdly, the Corinthians, with all their claim to fulness and to having entered on their heavenly reign, were distressingly defective in Christian behaviour. Party strife, litigiousness, immorality of a dimension unheard of in paganism, coupled with greed and disorder in the assemblies, marked their lives. No wonder Paul has to castigate them as carnal Christians.

And yet here were the very people who possessed these gifts of tongues, miracles, faith, healing and the like which convinced them that they were the favoured children of heaven and had already become full! It is still an observable fact that those who speak most about being full of the Holy Spirit are often governed by other spirits, such as arrogance, divisiveness and party spirit, disorder, lack of love and criticism. It is hard to see how a man can be full of the Spirit if these glaring failures of character persist.

Fourthly, the Corinthians were extremely experience-orientated. They were fascinated above all with the supernatural gifts of the Spirit. It was tongues and miracles that thrilled them most. And part of the thrust of Paul's reply is to demolish the division between "natural" and "supernatural" which they delighted in. I have just been reading Harold Horton's book, *The Gifts of the Spirit*. He maintains the usual Pentecostal position that there are nine gifts of the Spirit, no more and no less (1 Corinthians 12: 8ff), and as he says of his book, "stress is laid throughout on the hundred-per-cent supernatural character of each and all of the Gifts" (p. 8). However, neither Paul nor the rest of the biblical writers countenance this disastrous dichotomy between "natural" and "supernatural". Just as the Bible will not allow any disjunction between creation and redemption (they both hang together as complementary aspects of God's self-disclosure) so it simply does not know any disjunction between the natural and the supernatural. All truth is God's truth; all gifts are his gifts; nature and grace both stem from one Author. The notion of the natural and the supernatural is Greek and not Christian, and to prize the so-called supernatural gifts of the Spirit above the natural is to affront the God who became incarnate in Christ. Yet that is precisely the mistake the Corinthians were making, and it is often enough repeated today among Christians who discount the "helpers, the administrators, the teachers" of 1 Corinthians 12; 28ff, in favour of the "workers of miracles, healers, speakers in tongues". They have yet to learn interdependence in the body of Christ, and it is to this that Paul calls them in chapter 12 of the Epistle.

This leads naturally into the fifth danger in the Corinthian position. It was excessively individualistic. So is much of the talk these days about the fulness of the Holy Spirit. It is implied that this is a personal quality which can be had in independence of the rest of the Christian community. Now while it is true that there need to be Christians of outstanding leadership and dedication to God who will draw others after them, it is significant that whenever the New Testament uses the word "fulness" it is in a corporate, not an individualistic sense. We have noted Colossians 2: 9 where "the fulness" is attributed to Christ; it continues "and you (plural) are complete (or 'filled full') in him". Similarly in Ephesians 1: 23 the Church with all its variety-in-unity, is said to be Christ's *plērōma*, his "fulness" or "complement". Similarly in Ephesians 3: 17ff, when Paul prays for the growth of his Ephesian friends, he asks that they *together with all Christians*, may be rooted and grounded in love and be filled with all the fulness of God. In the classic verse, Ephesians 5: 18, it is to be remembered that the command to be filled with the Spirit is in the plural. In other words, it is not very meaningful, and certainly, not very biblical, to speak of the fulness of the Spirit in a merely individualistic sense. God is concerned for the variety-in-unity of the body of Christ indwelt by the Spirit. The fulness of the Holy Spirit, like salvation itself, is corporate no less than individual.

For all these reasons we should do well to be cautious of claiming to have the fulness of the Holy Spirit. Such a claim is often immature and individualistic, sometimes almost Gnostic in its exclusiveness towards other Christians, dangerously liable to add something to the sufficiency of Christ, often disproved by ethical failings, and resting upon the non-Christian disjunction between the natural and the supernatural. But we should be in a far worse case if, in reaction against the imprecise phraseology and indifferent theology of some Pentecostals, we failed to emulate their real dedication to Christ, their sacrificial living, and their faith in the reality of God and his willingness to speak, to empower, to heal and to deliver men from bondage to evil spirits. So long as twentieth-century Christianity remains powerless, earthbound, sceptical and oblivious of the spiritual battle and the need to watch and pray, so long the Pentecostal emphasis will continue to challenge and reprove those whose theology is perhaps better based, but whose knowledge and experience of the living God is so much less.

A church full of the Spirit?

I want to finish this chapter with a brief sketch of a church I visited recently where I was sensitive as rarely before of the fulness of the Holy Spirit. It belonged to none of the recognised denominations. People had flocked into it from a variety of other churches where they had been neither warmed nor fed; the spectrum included liturgical churches like the Roman Catholic, the Anglican and the Lutheran; and also Mennonites, Methodists, Baptists, Brethren and Pentecostals. But most of them had come from no church; they had been converted here. The building was packed, as it is three times a Sunday. Five hundred or so assembled, overflowing from the seats on to the floor. The welcome as people came in was remarkable — warmth and embraces everywhere. "Greet one another with a holy kiss", was literally carried out. The service took some two hours, and passed like a few minutes. The people really sensed what it was to be one body in Christ. The minister and his assistant took a part in the service, but not a dominant one. They sat inconspicuously with others, and were dressed in ordinary clothes. Street people and tramps, professors and housewives mixed joyfully and naturally in the worship. All age groups, both men and women, were represented, with the majority under thirty rather than over it. There was no choir: the congregation sang from its heart to the Lord. It was an unforgettable experience to sing the praises of God with this congregation. We were lifted out of ourselves in the worship of the Lord. There was a period of singing in tongues, and the variety in the sound was matched only by its harmony and the unanimity with which it began and ended, almost as if at the signal of a conductor; but there was no conductor — at least, not a human one. One person sang in a tongue, and then interpreted in song. The interpretation exactly fitted the tune she had just sung in tongues, and the sound of her voice was simply out of this world. I gathered later that her ordinary singing voice is quite unremarkable. The content of the interpretation was a call to the congregation to pray for the Jehovah's Witnesses who were meeting in a big convention in the city at that time. The whole thing was inspired by love, not by a censorious spirit, and the congregation began to pray for the Jehovah's Witnesses in response. Despite the heat and congestion in the building, the congregation listened with rapt attention to a forty-five minute sermon, and clearly wanted more. The minister then invited people to question the preacher and raise difficulties or suggestions, so that the communication should not be one-way. Another twenty minutes of dialogue ensued, and this was obviously appreciated. More singing, more worship, most generous giving in the offering, and the service came to an end. But people did not rush away. In one part of the church a Christian in tears sought counsel; in another, a believer who had been healed rejoiced with his friends. Outside, the people enjoyed each other's fellowship for nearly an hour before departing. They felt that God was in the whole place, and they were right. I met some of the people who had given up their homes and were living in extended families. About 100 of the congregation do this; they have all things in common like the early Church; their whole lives are bathed in prayer and service to one another and to others who drop in. They know from experience how hard this is, and how easily they can give way to self-centredness and division. But still the households grow in number and in quality of life. Children as well as parents, young people as well as older ones, live together in this way. They do not form a household on mere human affinity, but as they sense themselves moved by the Lord who is Spirit. Sometimes there is a re-grouping. Sometimes the family splits, amoeba-like, so as to add new members. It is perhaps too soon properly to assess this radical departure from the nuclear family pattern which has dominated the West for so long. So far as I could see the children did not suffer; the mothers had more help; the rough edges in character were smoothed away in the intimacy of common life; and the warmth of fellowship could only be sustained by a depth and intensity of prayer which is unknown among most of us, coupled with an honesty in confessing faults to one another to which most of our Christian fellowships are complete strangers. If there was one place where, it seemed to me, the patterns of Christian communal living and worship as indicated in the New Testament were being carried out, it was here. I have rarely experienced such depth of fellowship, and never such unity, dedication and joy in corporate worship. Here, if anywhere, was a church which could claim to be full of the Holy Spirit.

But that was not so. They would not have claimed it for themselves. They were too honest to suppose they had arrived, and, surprisingly, too ecumenically concerned to be self-satisfied or self-sufficient. They had a great sense of the Church Catholic, and were struggling to find a means of expressing it. Witness the fact that when there was a big movement of the Spirit among the counter culture and large numbers of flower people came to faith in Christ, they alone of all the churches in the city made room for these bare-footed, unwashed brothers in Christ and made them so much at home that they are now indistinguishable from other members of the congregation.

Yes, they would not claim for their church or for themselves individually that they were full of the Spirit, and in that they would be right. For they still have a long way to go: there is, for instance, considerable tension and awkwardness in personal relationships among the leadership of that church. As at Corinth, sharp personal differences went hand in hand with a remarkable richness in gifts and worship. If God waited until a church or an individual was perfect before filling them with his Spirit, he would wait for ever. For the plain truth is that we are citizens of two worlds, children of two families; we are both in Christ and in Adam, and so we remain until we die. God's fulness awaits the last day, when the salvation of man is complete, and we are delivered for ever from the evil which haunts us and twines its tendrils among the very roots of our being. Not until then shall we be totally free of evil, totally full of the Filler. The Christian path until then is plain; it is also difficult. It does not consist in making great claims for our state of fulness, nor of vying in the evaluation of our gifts. It means that with St. Paul we shall say, "Not that I have already arrived, or am already perfect. But I press on towards the goal for the prize of the upward call of God in Christ Jesus" (Philippians 3: 12, 14). The mature Christian might well covet the simple inscription found on the grave of a Swiss mountain guide: "Died climbing".

CHAPTER 10

The Spirit's Gifts

IN CHAPTER 7 we examined some of the ways in which the Spirit manifests himself in the Church, and we ended in the troubled waters of 1 Corinthians 12 where Paul was urging this richly talented church to use their gifts for the benefit of the whole body of Christ, rather than vie with one another in selfish indulgence of their gifts. This prompts the question, what were these *charismata* on which the Corinthians laid such stress?

For many centuries these chapters have been passed over in comparative silence by the churches, but since the rise of the Pentecostal movement in this century, and its spread into the main denominations in the past twenty years, the subject has come into great prominence wherever the Holy Spirit is discussed. Since the Pentecostal movement in all its varieties, lays such stress on the *charismata*, let us follow a well known and representative writer of that school, Dennis Bennett, in examining them one by one. He maintains the usual Pentecostal position that there are nine such gifts, set out for us in 1 Corinthians 12: 8–10. They are "a word of wisdom, a word of knowledge, faith, healings, prophecy, discernment of spirits, different kinds of tongues, and interpretation of tongues". They can conveniently be grouped into three areas, the gifts to *say* (prophecy, tongues, and interpretation); the gifts to *do* (healings, miracles, faith); and the gifts to *know* (discerning of spirits, knowledge and wisdom).

1. *Gifts of utterance*

The gift of tongues

First, the gift of tongues. This is the ability to speak in language that the speaker has not learnt, that he does not understand, and that is incomprehensible to the hearer. I say "language" with some hesitation, for whilst some charismatics claim that they speak in a definite human language, others do not, but regard the gift as a "Holy Spirit language" designed to enable them to worship God in greater depth and with greater release in their inner being—rather like the love language of a happily married couple, which may not *mean* anything, when the words are analysed; but which *denotes* the intimacy and trust of the couple concerned. The latter view would chime in well with Paul's hints in 1 Corinthians 14: 7–11. He gives three analogies.

First, from inanimate musical instruments. If the flute or the harp give no meaningful variation in notes, nobody will understand, and nobody will do anything about it. Uninterpreted tongues are like these musical instruments played at random in contrast to prophecy, which is both intelligible, and rouses men to action.

Second, he turns to the human tongue itself, and makes the same two points. If I do not enunciate clear words, I am not understood, and I achieve nothing. Paul in this analogy is making a play on the word "tongue"; the Greek word can mean either the part of the body, or the "language" of "tongues". And he is gently rebuking the Corinthians for their cult of the unintelligible. For to them "speaking in a tongue" spelt unintelligibility; to Paul the tongue, as part of the body, was essentially associated with intelligibility, or else it achieved nothing at all.

Third, he gives an illustration from other languages, making the same two points as before. If I speak in a foreign tongue people will not be able to understand me or respond to my communication—unless it is interpreted. I shall sound like a barbarian to them. That was a particularly wounding shaft to the Corinthians, who, as Greeks, despised the foreigners whose languages sounded like a meaningless jabber of "bar-bar-bar"— hence the pejorative name they gave them of "barbarians". Each of these three points made by the apostle to discourage the uninterpreted use of tongues in church seems to indicate that the phenomenon of tongues was not a language but rather the deeply felt love-language of the Corinthians to their Lord.

However, there are so many well-attested examples of "tongues" being understood by someone present who happens to belong to another language group and knows the tongue in question, that it is probably best to give the fullest possible breadth to Paul's phrase "different kinds of tongues" and to conclude that whereas some glossolalia may be speaking in a language unknown to the speaker but intelligible to somebody who knows the particular language employed, other "tongues" may not be a particular language at all but will rather be the effusion of the deepest longings of the heart released by the Spirit of God in prayer, praise or song.

Tongues, then, may be a language, or it may not, depending on circumstances and the particular gift of God to the individual. Incidentally, it is wrongly translated "tongues of ecstasy" in some of the modern translations of the Bible, notably the *New English Bible*. There is nothing necessarily compulsive or ecstatic about it. It is (as those who have the gift well know) under the control of the speaker—otherwise it would have been pointless for Paul to bid the tongues-speakers to control themselves in church if an interpreter is not present.

What, then, is the purpose of this gift? St. Paul gives several. Firstly, it enables a man to speak to God in prayer: "he speaks not to men but to God; nobody understands him, but he speaks mysteries in his spirit (or perhaps, 'in the Spirit')". Thus the apostle in 1 Corinthians 14: 2. He is maintaining that the gift of tongues opens a new dimension to a man's prayer life. He actually longs to pray whereas before it had been an effort. Time seems unimportant, and it will be nothing out of the way for him to spend an hour or two in communion with his Lord. Today, the gift of tongues produces precisely the same effect; a genuine liberty in prayer.

Secondly, tongues enables a man to praise God at a depth unknown previously. This is certainly a major emphasis in the Acts of the Apostles. In the house of Cornelius the new converts "spoke with tongues and glorified God" (Acts 10: 46). On the day of Pentecost this was very much the same. The crowd realised clearly enough that these men were praising God for his wonderful works, even though they suspected that drink might be the cause (Acts 2: 11–13). Perhaps Paul's references to singing spiritual songs to the Lord (Ephesians 5: 19, Colossians 3: 16) allude to singing in tongues; certainly this is a most beautiful and harmonious phenomenon, and elates the soul in worship to a remarkable degree. But whether the singing is in tongues or no, it is an undeniable fact that when men receive this gift of tongues they find themselves free to praise and thank and adore and glorify their heavenly Father as never before. In charismatic prayer meetings praise is usually the dominant element; in the run-of-the-mill evangelical prayer meeting this is not normally the case.

We should not be surprised by this. Every religious revival throughout the history of the Church has been accompanied by singing. When God's Spirit is at work within, men must give vent to their emotions in songs of praise. The lovely, spiritual, scriptural songs of, for instance, "The Fisherfolk" are the natural outworking of what the Lord the Spirit has worked within.

Thirdly, tongues edifies the individual (1 Corinthians 14: 4). This is not surprising, if it releases the inhibitions which keep us from prayer and praise of God. To be sure, Paul in this chapter is concerned to contrast speaking in tongues, which only edifies the speaker, with prophecy, which also builds up the church. But it is illicit for that reason to deny that tongues-speaking does edify the individual, as many commentators infer. No, it is one of the ways of growth in the Christian life for those who have been given this gift. Tongues is given, like the other manifestations of the Spirit, for our profit (1 Corinthians 12: 7).

Perhaps one of the areas of profit that we may need to be reminded of in an over-cerebral age is this: it allows the human spirit to pray, even when the mind is unfruitful because it cannot understand (1 Corinthians 14: 14). Many people pray in tongues while driving a car or washing up—their mind can be employed elsewhere. Clearly, therefore, tongues is a valuable gift for private edification. The apostle makes it clear that it is of no value in congregational worship, but is rather a menace, unless someone is present who has the gift of interpretation. For it simply will not be understood. "I thank God that I speak in tongues more than you all; nevertheless in church I would rather speak five words with my mind in order to instruct others, than ten thousand words in a tongue" (1 Corinthians 14: 19).

If tongues is of no value for the edification of the church unless it is interpreted, it is even more useless in evangelism. It will cause the outsider who happens to be in the assembly to think the Christians are mad (1 Corinthians 14: 23). It would be quite wrong to suppose that tongues was used evangelistically on the day of Pentecost. It is sometimes imagined by non-charismatics that Pentecostals believe this, but such is not the case. Harold Horton explains succinctly, in his *The Gifts of the Spirit* (p. 152).

The notion that the Gift of Tongues was a miraculous bestowal of foreign languages to the early apostles that they might preach the gospel to every creature is an error that could only be held by those who have never taken care to examine all the Scriptures on the subject. Peter was the only one, according to the record, who preached the gospel on the day of Pentecost, and he employed not other tongues but the universally understood Aramaic, or the equally universally understood Greek.

The "other tongues" was the praise of God by the disciples, not their preaching of the gospel. The varied language groups present were, it would seem, given the gift of interpretation on this occasion, so that they heard the praises of God in their own languages.

Indeed, not only are uninterpreted tongues disastrous in evangelism; they may even denote the judgment of God upon the Christian community. Such seems to be the thrust of 1 Corinthians 14: 20ff. After pointing out the futility of uninterpreted tongues in Church, Paul continues; "Brethren, do not be children in your thinking; be babes in evil, but in your thinking be mature. In the law it is written 'By men of strange tongues and by the lips of foreigners will I speak to this people, and even then they will not listen to me, says the Lord'. Thus, tongues are a sign not for believers but for unbelievers." The reference is to Isaiah 28: 11, 12. The point is that Israel spurned the message of the prophets, delivered as it was in clear unambiguous speech. And so God, by way of punishment, had to speak to them through the strange, unwelcome tongues of the Assyrians. These tongues came to them because they were "unbelieving". They did not believe what the prophets had said, and they did not obey. The tongues of the Assyrians were, therefore, "a sign to those who did not believe". The tongues bespoke God's separation from his people, not his presence; they denoted his judgment, not his pleasure. When God speaks intelligibly it is to reveal himself to his people. When he speaks unintelligibly, it is to hide himself. So in their preference for the unintelligible tongues over the straightforward prophecy the Corinthians were sailing dangerously near to the judgment of God. So far from boasting, they should beware of an unrestricted use of this medium in public worship, and especially when pagans were present.[1] Even here, however, men's mistakes can be

---

[1] It is sometimes suggested that this reference to Isaiah 28: 11f merely indicates that tongues are a sign of God's rejection of unbelievers, i.e. outsiders; pagans approaching the assembly and hearing only tongues do not hear the gospel, but only receive a sign that God rejects them, confirming them in unbelief; whereas

mercifully overruled by God. There are on record several
examples of people coming to faith in Christ through hearing
their own tongue spoken by someone in a Christian assembly
who had never learnt it.

The gift of interpretation

So much for tongues. Interpretation of tongues is a gift which
can be dealt with much more briefly. It is the ability to give
the sense of what has been said in an unknown tongue, when
this has been exercised in the congregation. Just as the Spirit
leads one person to speak in a tongue he does not understand,
so the same Spirit leads either him or someone else present to
interpret what has been said or sung. It is not an exact translation. The interpreter does not normally understand the
tongue that has been used any better than the rest of the
congregation. But he feels the Spirit impelling him to speak,
not a translation but an interpretation. This is very much an
exercise in faith. When he gets up to speak he does not know
more than the very first words of what he is going to say.
He must trust the leading of the Lord the Spirit. Indeed, the
whole subject of interpreting tongues is most obscure and open

---

through the use of prophecy they may be converted. This is attractive, but it
forces "this people" from the prophecy to refer not to God's disobedient people but
to pagans, and makes no sense of "and *even then* they will not listen to me, says
the Lord". Perhaps a more probable suggestion is that of J. P. M. Sweet in *J.T.S.*
1966, pp. 240–57. He thinks it probable that the "spiritual men" at Corinth, the
teleioi of verse 20, were arguing that "tongues is a sign for believers"; it was a
slogan to denote their spiritual superiority. Paul retorts by asking them to listen
to Scripture (verse 21). He quotes a text from Isaiah 28 which looks as if it may
well have been used by Christians in anti-Jewish apologetic. Laughed at by the
Jews for glossolalia (cf Acts 2: 13), Christians had turned to this text for vindication.
But in verse 22 Paul turns the tables on the Corinthian advocates of Isaiah
28: 11, 12. The verse does nothing to substantiate their claims to spiritual
superiority because they could speak in tongues; it is no "sign for believers". It is
rather a sign against (the dative being taken as a dative of disadvantage, which
is possible) unbelievers. It hardens unbelievers in their rejection of the gospel,
giving colour to their view that the Christians are mad. By way of contrast, a
word of prophecy pierces to the very soul of the visitor.
    This is ingenious, it seems to me, but has one fatal weakness, which brings me
back to the interpretation I have advanced above: Sweet's view makes no sense
of "prophecy is not for unbelievers but for believers". So he has to maintain
that the phrase, "not for unbelievers" is put in merely "for rhetorical balance". It
is hard to evade the plain meaning of the passage, particularly in its context here
and in Isaiah; that if the Corinthians insist on the unrestrained use of tongues in
evangelistic meetings they not only drive away those who are enquiring about the
faith but risk falling under the judgment of God.

to abuse. It is not possible for others to have any objective criteria for checking that the interpretation is genuine, and it is not possible to ensure beforehand that the apostolic injunction will be obeyed, that nobody is to speak in tongues in church unless someone is present who can interpret. Of course, it may be that a particular person in the congregation regularly has the gift of interpretation and can be relied on; in other circumstances the gift is given to a particular person for a particular occasion.

Those who have the gift of speaking in tongues are exhorted by Paul to pray for the gift of interpretation (14: 13). Though some men have the gift of interpretation who cannot themselves speak in tongues, this is unusual; for the most part it is those who already have tongues who gain this further gift of interpretation. And it is obviously highly desirable, for the edification of the church, when tongues are used in worship; and also for the edification of the mind of the individual Christian when praying in tongues—for as we have seen, his mind remains unfruitful although his spirit is lifted up in prayer to God.

It seems clear from 1 Corinthians 14: 5 that although tongues is an inferior gift to prophecy (the ability to speak direct from God to a situation) because it edifies only the individual and not the church; nevertheless tongues and interpretation together are the equivalent of prophecy. Like prophecy they are a divinely inspired message; and like prophecy the two gifts, taken together, are intelligible and therefore touch the minds as well as the spirits of those present. Even so, Paul's preferences in the matter are plain. "Desire to prophesy" is his conclusion of the matter, "and do not forbid speaking in tongues" (1 Corinthians 14: 39)!

If, then, we are to take 1 Corinthians as our guide, we must recognise that tongues, along with interpretation, can be a genuine gift of the Spirit of God to certain people, and Paul expected the gift to be used in private devotions for the edification of the believer, and in public when the two gifts could be employed together. He is careful to regulate this latter practice, however, in his concern for greater order in the disarray of Corinthian worship: women should not speak in tongues (almost certainly the meaning of *lalein* in 1 Corinthians 14: 35) in church; the ancient world had enough crazy females professing divination and bringing their various cults into disrepute! As for the men, "two or at most three, and that in turn; and let one interpret" is his injunction. It is difficult not to detect a note of distaste in Paul's advice. He is not happy at the way in which things are going at Corinth, with their infatuation with tongues. He knows it can be a real gift of the Spirit of God, and therefore while regulating it carefully he does not forbid it. But he also knows, I fancy, that glossolalia could be psychologically induced (as it certainly can: I know of more than one person who can get anyone to speak in tongues). He also realised, as many Pentecostals do, that there is a demonic counterfeit to tongues-speaking. In the Corinthian assembly men were saying "a curse on Jesus" and were using the tongues of their old pagan days which they had learnt in idol worship. Tongues, in fact, is a phenomenon which is widely disseminated and is observable in many cultures, ancient and modern. It is no exclusive mark of the possession of the Holy Spirit; but the Holy Spirit can take it and use it. But because of its very ambivalence, because of its incomprehensibility, because of its selfishness, because of its liability to abuse, and because of its non-ethical and sub-personal character the apostle was most unwilling to concur with the Corinthians' estimate of it as the best and most valuable of the gifts of the Spirit. It is perhaps not accidental that every time he mentions tongues and their interpretation, they come last on his list, not first, as the Corinthians would undoubtedly have rated them.

The gift of prophecy

The third of the gifts of speech is prophecy. Prophecy had been dead in Israel for centuries, but blazed into life again with the coming of Jesus, the prophet of Nazareth, the prophet like Moses (Matthew 21: 11, Acts 3: 22, 7: 37). Jesus came to fulfil not only the Torah but the prophets (Matthew 5: 19), and his fulfilment did not only show itself in a burst of prophecy round his birth and in John the Baptist but continued among his people after his death. Indeed one would not be far wrong in asserting that Christian prophecy was born on the day of Pentecost, when the remarkable invasion of the Spirit of God convinced the disciples that they were witnessing the fulfilment of Joel's prophecy, "and upon my servants and my hand-maidens in those days I will pour out a portion of my Spirit, and they shall prophesy" (Acts 2: 18). The last phrase, "and they shall prophesy" is not in the original of Joel; it is a Christian gloss. But it shows very clearly that they were conscious of the prophetic Spirit among them, and saw this as a direct overflow of the Spirit which had indwelt their

Master and a fulfilment of the hopes of the Old Testament that all God's people should prophesy (Numbers 11: 29). Christian prophecy could be delivered by men or women (Acts 21: 9, Revelation 2: 20, 1 Corinthians 11: 5). The four prophesying daughters of Philip the Evangelist made a tremendous impact on the Church at large and were a model well into the second century; indeed, even in 1 Corinthians where Paul is very concerned to regulate glossolalia and avoid any excesses which could bring the Christian cause into disrepute, he does nothing to discourage the woman prophet from speaking in the assembly; rather the reverse (11: 1ff).

Prophecy was very widely disseminated. There were prophets not only in Jerusalem and Caesarea, but in Antioch (Acts 11: 27, 13: 1), Rome (Romans 12: 6), Corinth, Thessalonica (1 Thessalonians 5: 19, 20) and the churches of Asia Minor (Revelation 1: 3). Both Luke and Matthew indicate that Jesus anticipated a continuation of prophecy among his followers (Matthew 10: 41f, Luke 11: 49). It was a gift very highly valued, whether it was exercised by a single individual, or, as certain passages suggest, by a prophetic group of believers (Acts 13: 1, Ephesians 2: 20, 3: 5, 4: 11, Revelation 10: 7, 22: 6, 9). It is easy to see why it was so prized: for prophecy meant domination by the Lord the Spirit. In prophecy God was communicating directly with men through men. The prophet shared with the apostle in being an agent of revelation; but prophets were inferior to apostles because they did not and could not go behind or beyond the apostolic testimony to Jesus—after all, they were not, as the apostles were, eyewitnesses of the final revelation of God, Jesus, come in the flesh.

Prophecy, then, was valued, because through it God spoke directly to his people. He had done so through the prophets and prophetesses of the Old Testament days; he had done so through "the prophet of Nazareth", that "prophet like Moses", Jesus himself; and he continued to do it through inspired individuals or groups bearing testimony in words not of their own contriving to Jesus, the risen fount of all wisdom and knowledge.

It is not easy to be clear precisely what early Christian prophecy was. It could vary from the predictions of a man like Agabus, the mysteries of the Book of Revelation (a remarkable example of early prophecy, see Revelation 1: 3), to the indication of a Christian for a particular office (1 Timothy 4: 14), testimony to Jesus (Revelation 19: 10), and use in evangelism, edification, consolation, or teaching (1 Corinthians 14: 3f, 24f, 29f). It was certainly very varied, but of two things we can be sure.

First, it was a direct word from God for the situation on hand, through the mouth of one of his people (and on occasion, this could apparently be any Christian, including those not reckoned to be "prophets", Revelation 10: 7, 11: 10). The other thing about it is that it was clear speech, which did not need any interpretation. Herein lay its great advantage over tongues. Because of its intelligibility, it used the mind of the speaker (that mind which lies fallow while he is speaking in tongues, 1 Corinthians 14: 14); it contributed to the edification of the whole Christian body assembled for worship; it struck to the heart of unbelievers present who were amazed at the directness and relevance of what was said; it showed that God was indeed present in the congregation (1 Corinthians 14: 4, 24f). Therefore it was a gift to be sought and prized by Christians. Not all Christians have it (1 Corinthians 12: 29), but all are encouraged to pray for it, because it is so useful for other members of the body of Christ (1 Corinthians 14: 1).

Several misunderstandings commonly crop up at this point. The first is to call prophecy "ecstatic speech". It is much the same mistake as we saw in examining the use of the term "ecstasy" for tongues. It is an accurate description if it means that the gift comes from a direct leading of the Spirit. It is inaccurate if it suggests a compulsive, excitable urge which cannot be resisted. For there is no indication in the New Testament that prophecy is the product of spiritual excitement. And there is no indication that it is compulsive. Quite the reverse.[1] Paul can instruct some prophets to keep quiet, while others have their chance to speak. He can also restrict the use of prophecy in any one church gathering to two or three speakers (1 Corinthians 14: 29). This would be quite impossible if the gift were used independently of the will of the user: but

[1] Interestingly enough, in the hey-day of the Montanist movement, the claim was made that prophecy was something compulsive that could not be evaded. Montanus claimed that "Man is like a lyre and I (i.e. the Spirit) rush upon it like a plectrum" (Epiphanius, *Haer.* 48: 4. 1). Maximilla is said to have put it still more emphatically: "The Lord has sent me as an adherent, preacher and interpreter of this affliction and this covenant and this promise; he has compelled me, willingly or unwillingly, to learn the knowledge of God" (*ibid.* 48: 13. 1). This undue emphasis on compulsion gives full force, to be sure, to the inner sense of conviction that every prophet has; but fails to make room for the co-operation with God which is implicit in authentic prophecy. The balance of the New Testament teaching has been slightly but decisively altered.

it is not. It involves the use of his mind. It is subservient to his rational decision.

Second, one commonly hears it said that prophecy is the same as preaching or teaching. This could only be maintained in defiance of the whole weight of New Testament evidence. The men of the first century knew preaching and teaching when they heard it, and they knew prophecy as well. The two were quite different. Prophets and teachers are distinguished in passages such as Acts 13: 1, 1 Corinthians 12: 29. It is one thing to prepare one's address in dependence on the Spirit, and to preach it in the power of that same Spirit; it is quite another thing to find the Spirit taking over and speaking directly from Christ through you, in words that you had never intended to use at all. In *Evangelism in the Early Church* I pointed to a fascinating passage in the second-century Bishop Melito of Sardis that has only recently come to light among the Bodmer Papyri. In it this distinguished Christian teacher suddenly breaks out into prophecy, and Christ speaks through him directly. The change is startling. Melito is preaching: "The Lord, having put on human nature, and having suffered for him who suffered, having been bound for him who was bound, and having been buried for him who was buried (i.e., in sin) is risen from the dead, and loudly proclaims this message". Then comes the prophecy:

Who will contend against me? Let him stand before me.
It is I who delivered the condemned. It is I who gave life to the dead.
It is I who raised up the buried. Who will argue with me?
It is I, says Christ, who destroyed death. It is I who triumphed over the enemy,
And trod down Hades, and bound the Strong Man,
And snatched mankind up to the heights of heaven. It is I, says Christ.
So then, come here all you families of men, weighed down by your sins
And receive pardon for your misdeeds. For I am your pardon.
I am the Passover which brings salvation. I am your life, your resurrection.
I am your light, I am your salvation, I am your King.
It is I who bring you up to the heights of heaven.
It is I who will give you the resurrection there.
I will show you the Eternal Father. I will raise you up with my own right hand.

By no stretch of the imagination could that be described as simply preaching or teaching. The Spirit has taken over, and addresses the hearers directly through Melito. That is the essence of Christian prophecy.

A third misunderstanding is to suppose that prophecy came to an end at the conclusion of the apostolic age. It certainly became less important for the churches as the New Testament Scriptures gained in circulation and became recognised as authoritative teaching about Jesus. Clearly, there was nothing one could add to God's last word to mankind, Jesus the Word of God incarnate; and there was nothing fresh about him that could be added by men of the second and subsequent generation except through the medium of the apostolic testimony. So the sphere of prophecy became more restricted as the canon of Scripture became more clear; indeed, the need for it diminished, in so far as general teaching of the faithful was concerned. But to suppose that prophecy was no longer needed for the encouragement of the faithful, for the conviction of unbelievers, and for the guidance of the Church on specific issues, would be very wrong. For example, it was in response to a piece of Christian prophecy that the Jerusalem church escaped from the city prior to the fall of Jerusalem in A.D. 70 and took up residence in Pella (Eusebius *Hist. Eccl.* 3: 5, 3). In the subapostolic age, we find wandering prophets circulating round the Christian churches exercising a charismatic ministry, and complementing the work of the resident presbyters. Famous names like Ammia and Quadratus meet us among the prophets of the second century; and authors like Ignatius (*Trallians* 5, *Ephesians* 20), Polycarp (*Epistle* 5:2, and *Martyr. Polyc.* 16), Hermas (*Mand.* 11) are well aware of the continuance of prophets in their day. The unknown writer against the Montanists speaks for main line Christianity of the second century when he writes, "the apostle believes that the prophetic charisma should continue until the end of the age throughout the church" (Eusebius *H.E.* 5: 17). As late as the fourth century Cyril of Jerusalem clearly thinks it possible (if unlikely!) that his candidates for baptism may receive the gift of prophecy (*Catechetical lectures* 16: 12, 17: 37).

Although, therefore, prophecy continued, it became increasingly suspect and liable to abuse. The *Didache*, dating from perhaps the second quarter of the second century, has some sharp things to say about bogus and self-seeking prophets, as we shall see when we come to examine the gift of discernment. It is sufficient to note that prophecy was intended to continue in the Church, but that because of the dangers of abuse and subjectivism, and supremely because of the Montanist movement at the end of the second century, it died out. Only a few years previously, Justin had been maintaining that there was no difference in degree of inspiration between the Old Testament and the New Testament prophets. Both bore witness to Jesus. That is why, he argues, the Jews have had no more prophets since the days of Christ, whereas the prophetic office has been much in evidence in the Church (*Dialogue* 51 and 82). Prophets were for the benefit of the people of God at large, and that is why Hermas wrote his *Shepherd* to the whole Church, just as John wrote his Apocalypse to the seven churches of Asia, symbolising the Church catholic. But with the Montanist movement, all that came to an end. Already there had been a tendency to identify the prophetic function with the office of the bishop (aided by the fact that some distinguished bishops like Melito and Polycarp were also prophets in their own right), but after the Montanist troubles this identification became absolute, and the bishop became regarded as the authoritative mouthpiece of divine teaching for his diocese. This swallowing up of the prophet in the bishop was disastrous for the Church, but in the circumstances it was understandable. For Montanus, an Asian bishop, claimed that he and his female associates, Maximilla and Prisca, were descendants of the prophetic tradition of early Christianity. So far so good. But when they taught (professing to be the mouthpiece of the Spirit) that the Heavenly Jerusalem would immediately appear near Pepuza; when they claimed that they personally embodied the Holy Spirit; when they wrote off other Christians as carnal and proclaimed themselves alone as "Spirit-filled"; when they refused to have their teaching tested by the Scriptures but regarded it as every bit as authoritative as the New Testament records—then the Church had to take action. That action was to reject the Montanists emphatically, and at the same time, to quench the prophetic Spirit in the Church. How much better it would have been for the Church at large if the Montanists had determined to submit to the authority of Scripture, and to resist the temptation to be exclusive and write off other Christians. How much better if the Catholics had stressed tests for the genuineness of prophecy rather than writing off the whole movement, good and bad, together. Apparently the Catholic leadership regarded the existence of prophets as a threat to the regular ministry of the Church. But this need not have been the case at all, when one remembers that men like Jude and Silas, Saul and Barnabas were both prophets and presbyters; and when some of the leading bishops in the second century, Ignatius, Polycarp and Melito among them, combined the office of a bishop with the gift of prophecy. If prophecy unregulated by order could dissipate in individualism and end in sectarianism and heresy; order without prophecy could so easily turn a deaf ear to the leading of God and relapse into the peace of the graveyard. To "charismatic" and to "non-charismatic" alike, the total failure of communication over the Montanist affair is a tragedy that must not be repeated, if the Church values on the one hand her unity and on the other hand her vitality.

2. Gifts of action

So much for tongues, interpretation and prophecy, the gifts of speaking. Now for the gifts of doing: healings, miracles, faith.

The gifts of healing

Jesus healed men; and he commissioned his disciples to do the same. It is interesting to recall that the word "save" means in the original "to heal" just as much as it does "to rescue". Undeniably, many of the needy people whom Jesus met in the days of his flesh were both spiritually put right with God and physically healed. Equally undeniably, there is less and less stress on healing as the ministry of Jesus runs its course. He deprecated men's quest for miracles and mighty works; and he was limited in performing them by lack of faith in the recipients. Moreover, on occasion he withdrew from promising healing situations, in order to concentrate on preaching (Mark 1: 38, Luke 4: 4).

When we consider the healing activity of the early Christians, there is similar need for caution. On the one hand the apostles are once commanded to heal during the course of the ministry of Jesus (Matthew 10: 8 cf. the Seventy in Luke 10: 9) but those who wish to take this as an all-embracing command for Christians today should recall the next phrase "raise the dead". Does this mark Christian healing today? It will not do to turn such a question aside by reference to some very doubtfully attested raisings from the dead reported at third and fourth hand from Indonesia.

Both Peter and Paul exercise gifts of healing in Acts, and healing is given a place in the list of spiritual gifts in 1 Corinthians 12: 9, 28, 30. It is, therefore, a real gift of God to be exercised in and for the body of Christ. But one does not get the impression that it played a major part in the spread of the gospel in early times. It is not mentioned in the lists of workers in the Church in Ephesians 4: 11, or in the fuller list in Romans 12: 6–8. In the Pastoral Epistles the tasks of Christian ministry are fully described, but there is no hint that healing is seen as one of them. James 5: 14 certainly speaks of the healing power of God in answer to believing prayer and the anointing with oil (ceremonial or medical?) on the part of the Christian leadership. But quite clearly the healing is contingent, not universal. The apostles themselves were not always able to heal. God was not at their disposal to be manipulated as they willed. Paul himself had to leave his friend Trophimus sick at Miletus (2 Timothy 4: 20). He could not, apparently, do anything about the illness of Epaphroditus (Philippians 2: 25–7). He advised Timothy, when suffering from a gastric complaint, to use wine in its medicinal sense, not to ask for a supernatural healing (1 Timothy 5: 23). He himself was racked with a thorn in the flesh which God in his wisdom did not see fit to remove. The Lord gave, not healing, but the strength to bear the affliction (2 Corinthians 12: 7–9). It is important to remember this side of the biblical material when excessive claims are made by "charismatic" Christians that it is never God's will for us to be ill. Dennis Bennett, once again, tends to be very misleading in this direction. "God has made it perfectly clear in His Word that it *is* His will to heal the sick—period!", he writes, in *The Holy Spirit and You* p. 114. He is attacking the faith-destroying habit, as he regards it, of praying "if it be Thy Will", which often concludes prayer for the sick. He is quite right in inveighing against lack of faith: he is quite wrong in supposing that physical healing is always the direct will of God for us. In a world where sin is not excluded from the permissive will of God (though it is obviously not his direct will for us), why should we think that we have the right to be rid of suffering? Paul had no such exemption. Neither have we. Suffering, sin, disease and death are all part of the fallen lot of mankind, and they will be with us until heaven. It is cruel to see the mental anguish that has been induced by well-meaning "charismatic" people who have raised the hopes of the sick that they would be physically healed, and then no such healing has come; the rejoinder has then been that the patient either had some unconfessed sin in the way,[1] or else that his faith was inadequate. The ensuing agonised heart-searchings are not hard to imagine. I do not know whether such therapists do more or less harm than the materialistically minded Christians of small vision, who do not believe that God could possibly heal without medical means. Of course he can. And of course he does. It happens all over the world. It happens with organic illnesses, such as tuberculosis and cancer, blindness and limb deformity, as well as with inorganic ailments. The point is that all healing is God's work. He is able to heal with or without medical means. It is no more "spiritual" if the healing comes through the laying on of hands and prayer than if it comes through the hospital and drugs. But God does not always choose to heal us physically, and perhaps it is as well that he does not. How people would rush to Christianity (and for all the wrong motives) if it carried with it automatic exemption from sickness! What a nonsense it would make of Christian virtues like longsuffering, patience and endurance if instant wholeness were available for all the Christian sick! What a wrong impression it would give of salvation if physical wholeness were perfectly realised on earth whilst spiritual wholeness were partly reserved for heaven! What a very curious thing it would be if God were to decree death for all his children whilst not allowing illness for any of them! No, those who claim Christian immunity from illness not only fly in the face of facts and conjure up false hopes; they are guilty of the same basic theological error as those who preach the possibility of sinless perfection in this life. Both are wanting to have here and now what God has kept for the life to come, where perfect wholeness and perfect freedom from indwelling sin will go hand-in-hand.

Healing, then, is a gift that God has given to some members of the body of Christ, to enable them to act as channels of his love and compassion to others. "Have all the gift of healing?" asks the apostle. The answer, clearly is "No". But those who have this gift are to use it for the benefit of others. It seems to be one of the good gifts of the Spirit which is increasingly being realised today, and Christians who had no idea that they

[1] Sometimes, of course, illness is due to sin. In Luke 13: 10–17 Jesus specifically attributes the woman's condition to Satan (in contrast to the first five verses of that chapter where Jesus denies that Pilate's slaughter of some Galileans is in any way to be interpreted as a punishment for their sins). Paul believed that some of the illness and even deaths at Corinth stemmed from their sins against the fellowship. On the links between healing and salvation, see my *The Meaning of Salvation*, Hodder, p. 218ff.

possessed it are finding that they are being used in this ministry of healing. There have recently been large outbreaks of healings in two cathedrals, one in Africa and one in Asia, where I have personal friends who were present and witnessed them. They tell me of thousands who came, and many who were healed of blindness, cancer, lameness and other diseases, whilst many more came to a living faith in the Saviour. The reality of this gift can only be doubted by those who are not prepared to examine the evidence. Equally, those who maintain that Christians should never, if they are living close to God, suffer illness, and who maintain that healing and salvation are always and properly inseparable, do not match up to the evidence of Scripture, history or experience.

The gift of miracles

The next of the gifts of doing, namely "the working of miracles", is very widely attested in the Bible. Miracles were common in the Old Testament, in the life of Jesus, and in the Acts of the Apostles. One thinks of prison doors opening to release a Peter or a Paul; of Elymas the sorcerer being struck with blindness, and so forth. If it is correct to read the plural *dunameōn* after *energēmata* in 1 Corinthians 12: 10, then it can only mean that Paul reckoned the ability to work miracles as one of the gifts of the Spirit. However, the genitive singular (*dunameōs*) is read by several of the best MSS: the meaning would then be not "the working of miracles" but "the effects of power"—the outworking in Christian ministry of the divine power as believers accept and use the gift of the Spirit. Whichever is the right reading of that disputed text, the emphasis is clearly on power. Some men in apostolic days, and since, have been given particular endowments of God's power within them, enabling them to do what they would otherwise never have been able to contemplate. One need only think of the effects of Christ's power in men like Martin Luther in the sixteenth century or Martin Luther King in the twentieth to take the point.

Not a great deal is written about the gift of doing miracles, in current Pentecostal literature. It gets nothing like the coverage of tongues, prophecy and healing. Such references as there are generally concern the current revival in Indonesia, where some two millions of Moslems and animists have turned to the Christian faith and from where there are remarkable stories of miraculous happenings to parallel anything that is

recorded in the Acts of the Apostles. John 14: 12 is adduced
to indicate that Jesus expected his followers to do greater
things than he had himself accomplished, and the matter is
generally left there, apart from some more or less impressive
personal anecdotes.

To glance at these in turn, there are strong political factors
which have affected the undoubted spiritual movement
towards Christianity in Indonesia; and personal acquaintances
of mine who have visited the country there more than once
tell me that reports of miracles have been greatly exaggerated.
Distance, as ever, lends enchantment. John 14: 12 need not
necessarily refer to miraculous works at all; merely to the
undoubted fact that Jesus during the course of his ministry
had deliberately restricted himself to working in Israel. After
his return to the Father (which is the whole thrust of the
context) the disciples would achieve far more than he had
himself done, because the Spirit of Jesus, now no longer limited
by a human body, but resident within their personalities,
would empower them to be Christ's witnesses in word and
deed throughout the whole known world. This power may
well have been intended to include the miraculous, but the
verse does not say so.

Dennis Bennett takes "the working of miracles" to mean the
suspension of what are normally understood as the laws of
nature. He not only maintains that Philip the Evangelist was
"*physically* and *bodily* picked up by the Holy Spirit and carried
from Gaza to Azotus, a distance of 24 miles" (Acts 8: 39), but
tells us of a case when the well-known Pentecostal leader,
David duPlessis had just the same experience, and was
immediately carried a mile to the home of a very ill friend for
whom he and some friends had been engaged in praying: the
friends, who had to travel by foot, arrived puffing and blowing
later on, and were amazed that he had got there so soon! Of
the duPlessis story I can say nothing: but the Acts passage
does not necessarily mean that the Holy Spirit whisked Philip
away in a miraculous fashion. It may simply mean that under
the impelling constraint of the Spirit Philip was snatched away
from the encounter with the Ethiopan eunuch and turned up at
Azotus. He may well have travelled on foot: and probably did.

I do not think that this sort of incident was in Paul's mind
when he spoke of the gift of *energēmata dunameōs* or *dunameōn.*
I believe he may have been pointing to the singular effective-
ness God gives to some Christians to impress men by their
words and deeds. That is what Jesus was meaning in the

passage in John 14. He tells the disciples that the demonstration available to them of the reality of a Father they cannot see, is the words (14: 10) and the deeds (14: 11) of Jesus. Similarly, he promises them that they will do greater works than this when he returns to his Father and sends them the Spirit. Their words and their deeds will be the evidence to men of all nations (not Israel only) of the reality of the Jesus who is preached to them, but whom they cannot see. It was this *dunamis*, this powerful impact, which struck men about the teaching of Jesus and his behaviour. Hearing his teaching in the Nazareth synagogue, his fellow countrymen were amazed and asked, "Where does this man get his wisdom from, and his *dunameis*, his acts of power?"

I do not for one moment wish to minimise the supernatural power of which Paul is speaking. The word is certainly used in the Gospels to indicate the miraculous healings of Jesus and indeed the splendour of his Advent, as well as the impact of his words and deeds. I, for one, do not believe that Almighty is shackled by "laws of nature" (which are nothing more—nor less—than a massive series of observed uniformities). If levitation, for instance, to return to Bennett's interpretation of the Philip incident, can be practised in occultism and Eastern meditation, I see no reason why it should not be available to Christians through the Spirit. It is simply a question of exegesis. Does Paul mean that the Spirit enables some Christians to break what are normally taken to be physical laws? Or does it mean that the Spirit so takes control of the personalities of some Christians that their words and deeds have a particularly powerful impact for God?

If the singular, *dunameōs*, is the correct reading in 1 Corinthians 12: 10, it is probable that we should accept the second of the above alternatives. This would accord well with Paul's claim that the Spirit empowers his words (1 Thessalonians 1: 5, Romans 15: 19, 1 Corinthians 2: 4, 2 Corinthians 6: 7) and shines powerfully through his life (Philippians 3: 10, Colossians 1: 11, Ephesians 1: 19f, 2 Corinthians 12: 9f). This is the true *imitatio Christi*, the impact made by Christ's Spirit when active in the believer's words and deeds.

If, however, the plural *dunameōn*, is correct, this swings the balance back towards the interpretation, "working of miracles"; particularly in the light of the plural in 1 Corinthians 12: 28, 29, and of the unambiguous miraculous meaning of the word in Romans 15: 18 and 2 Corinthians 12: 12 where it is joined with "signs and wonders". If this is the case, we have to ask ourselves whether there was a well-attested supernatural demonstration of power notable both in the life of Jesus and of the later apostolic age? Immediately one comes to mind: exorcism. The power of Jesus was signally demonstrated in the casting out of evil spirits: "with authority and power he commands the unclean spirits, and they come out" (Luke 4: 36). Exorcism was regularly practised in the sub-apostolic Church, and was highly prized. The early, though unauthentic, Longer Ending of St. Mark lists exorcism among the signs which would follow the preaching of the gospel. It continued to be a major weapon in the Christian armoury in the sub-apostolic period. Justin, for instance, writes, "And now you may learn this from what goes on under your own eyes. Many of our Christian men have exorcised (in the name of Jesus Christ who was crucified under Pontius Pilate) numberless demoniacs throughout the whole world, and in your city. When all other exorcists and specialists in incantations and drugs have failed, they have healed them and still do heal, rendering the demons impotent and driving them out" (2 *Apology* 6). This is not the place to examine exorcism in depth. As with healing, it is a gift long disused, whose value is being recognised afresh in the Church. Particularly in view of its immediate juxtaposition to "healings" in Paul's lists of spiritual gifts exorcism is probably the meaning uppermost in his mind if it is "miracles" rather than the special impact of Christian word and life to which he is referring.

The gift of faith

The third of this group of gifts of action is the gift of faith. All commentators are agreed that Paul is not speaking of the saving faith by which a man believes in Christ. True, this is a gift of God, if only in the sense that without the God-given capacity to trust, faith in Christ would be impossible for any one of us. Clearly, Paul is not thinking of that here. He is referring to the special ability to trust God in the dark when all the odds are against you: the ability to hold on to God in prayer over many years for the conversion of some loved one: the sure perception of the will of God on a particular matter in the future which enables you to act as though it had already happened. Noah had this gift of faith, in believing God, against all the odds, that there would be a flood, and acting on that belief by building an ark, despite the laughter of his fellows. Abraham had this gift of faith, in believing that God was calling him out of Ur even though it was economic madness to leave his expensive home in that prosperous city and entrust himself to God and to the desert. Hudson Taylor had this gift of faith in founding and maintaining one of the world's biggest missionary societies on a complete absence of financial backing, a refusal to ask for funds, and an unshakeable conviction about the will of God. I remember as a boy having the orphanages bordering the County Cricket Ground at Bristol pointed out to me by a schoolmaster who was scarcely celebrated for his Christian allegiance: "Don't laugh at prayer", he used to tell us. "You can see answers to prayer in bricks and mortar when you look at those orphanages. George Müller built them on prayer and kept them going on prayer." It was perfectly true; Müller was another of these men who had been given by God this exceptional gift of faith. The gift is not extinct!

It is obvious why this gift is mentioned alongside healing and miracles (?or "power"). You cannot heal in the name of the Lord without having faith that the great Healer himself will act. You cannot exorcise in Christ's name without a deep exercise of faith. The faith that moves mountains is a gift of the Spirit, and it is closely allied to action in the power of the Spirit. It is not the same as that fruit of the Spirit which includes love, joy, peace, faith and others. These qualities should increasingly be seen in every Christian life. The gift of faith seems rather to be this clear insight into the will of God, this staking all upon it, this unwavering conviction that God will provide even in the most impossible circumstances, that has marked some Christians in every age who have received that particular gift from the Spirit.

3. Gifts of Knowledge

The last trio of gifts mentioned in this crucial passage, 1 Corinthians 12: 6–10, are gifts not of speech, not of action, but of knowledge. They are all God-given disclosures. It remains part of the work of the Spirit to reveal the things of God to those whom he indwells. And this is of the utmost importance. When praying for the Colossians whom he had never yet seen, Paul's first request for them was that they may be filled with a deep knowledge of God's will, along with all wisdom and spiritual understanding: only so would they be able to live lives obedient, pleasing to the Lord (Colossians 1; 9–11).

The gift of knowledge

Let us examine first what Paul means by knowledge. *Gnōsis* is the Greek word employed, and it is used very sparingly in the New Testament, probably because of incipient Gnosticism. This was a movement which sought salvation by knowledge. "Knowledge" might be anything from magic, ranging through the revelations to the initiate in the Mystery Religions, to philosophy. This pagan idea of salvation by knowledge was a particular problem at Corinth, and formed a dangerous antithesis to Christian knowledge in three ways.

First, in the sphere of religious practice, it led to compromise. It is clear from 1 Corinthians 8: 1ff that Christians tarred with this Gnostic brush were making their "knowledge" a substitute for obedience. They were too sophisticated to believe in the reality of idols, and therefore were prepared to compromise their Christian position by eating meals in an idol's temple. No wonder they were castigated as carnal Christians in chapter three of the Epistle. Keen on knowledge, they were one with the pagans in supposing that salvation was a matter of this knowledge, which they, fortunately possessed.

Second, in the physical sphere, emphasis on "knowledge" led to the twin, though opposite results, of asceticism and licence. An important strand in Greek thought, which seems to have affected the Corinthians, held that the body was a tomb, in which the eternal soul lay imprisoned. The important thing was the illumination of that soul and its eventual rescue from the confines of the body; what happened to the body did not matter. Therefore one could run to the extreme of asceticism, mortifying the body by harsh discomforts; or one could indulge the body by rampant sensuality. It simply did not matter. What mattered was the soul. It is against this background that we can understand the rebukes of Paul to the libertines in chapter six and the ascetics in chapter seven. Both operated from the same false view of the body as evil (or at best indifferent) and the soul as good (especially when illuminated with knowledge).

Third, their emphasis on knowledge produced a most unhealthy divisiveness. If salvation is primarily a matter of knowledge, those who have it are in a position to look down on others, despise them, and boast over them. That is what happened at Corinth. It accounts for the party strife which we read of in the first three chapters. It accounts for the litigousness of chapter six, and for the troubles at the Lord's table in chapter eleven when some would eat and drink to excess whilst others had none. It accounts for the need Paul felt to insert that superb chapter thirteen on love, the gift without which all others were of no avail.

Knowledge, therefore, as understood at Corinth, facilitated religious compromise, emancipated you from the claims of normal morality, and enabled you to look down on brother Christians who lacked your gift. This background perhaps puts us in a better position to understand what Paul means by the spiritual gift of knowledge. It is important to realise that none of us can be quite sure what Paul meant by the gift of knowledge in this list, although some people think they know! However, an examination of some of his other uses of the word may give us some clue.

First, this is knowledge of God himself, as made manifest in Jesus Christ (2 Corinthians 2: 14, 4: 6). It is not knowledge of heavenly mysteries or recondite intellectual methods of salvation, but knowledge of God. Paul sometimes uses the intensified form of the word, *epignōsis*, which has the nuance of deep or personal knowledge. This knowledge of God is not arrived at by human endeavour; 1 Corinthians 2 is insistent on that. Finite, sinful man cannot possibly arrive by intellectual processes and spiritual striving at God who is both infinite and holy. All knowledge of God must be mediated to us by the Spirit, who searches the deep things of God and reveals them to believers, so that they can be said to have the mind of Christ (1 Corinthians 2: 9–16).

Second, this knowledge is incompatible with an unholy life. The Pastoral Epistles lay an enormous stress on the link between soundness in doctrine and holiness of life, and Paul does the same in his letters to the Corinthians. He claims that he is richly gifted in knowledge, but in the very same verse opens his life up to inspection by the Corinthians (2 Corinthians 11: 6). As we have seen, he denounces the "knowledge" which thinks nothing of compromise with idolatry. True knowledge of a holy God must be inextricably linked with holiness of life.

Third, this knowledge is incompatible with a selfish or arrogant attitude towards other people. Hence the emphasis in 1 Corinthians 8 on respect for the other man's conscience even when you reckon it is misguided, for this is the way of love. The same goes for chapter thirteen, of course, and also for chapter 6, where Paul points out that the way of love should encourage Christians even to be defrauded rather than to go

to law against each other (6: 7). Interestingly enough knowledge is placed between "pureness" and "long-suffering" in
2 Corinthians 6: 6, as if it were partly at least determined by
holiness in personal life, and by patience towards others.
Certainly in 2 Corinthians 8: 7 loving contribution to others
in need is seen as the outcome of "knowledge". Indeed, the
outward thrust to others implicit in this gift is stressed by
the form in which it occurs in the list we are examining, "the
word of knowledge": what marks it out as coming from God is
not merely its content but its communication. The man who
has knowledge of God will not be able to keep it to himself.
He must pass it on.

Such is Christian knowledge. It centres on Jesus Christ, in
whom are hid all the treasures of wisdom and knowledge
(Colossians 2: 3). And it is something which all the Corinthians
were expected to have and to grow in (1 Corinthians 1: 5).
But in all probability Paul means something further by the
inclusion of knowledge in this list of spiritual gifts. If we
compare the passage here with 1 Corinthians 13: 2 and 14: 6
it becomes apparent that Paul is speaking of some revelatory
word from God for the benefit of others. Jesus clearly had this
gift when he knew that the woman of Samaria had already
had five husbands. Peter had it, when he knew that the heart
of Ananias and Sapphira was not right with God. This seems
to be the gift of which the apostle is speaking. It is a God-given
disclosure of knowledge that could not normally be available
to the recipient. It is intended not for the gratification of the
individual who receives it, but for the benefit of the congregation
or some member of it. It is a particularly precious gift for the
Christian counsellor, who needs to know the heart of the man
to whom he is speaking.

The gift of wisdom

Much that has been said of the gift of knowledge is applicable
to the closely allied gift of wisdom. The Greeks were always
inclined to think of God in terms of wisdom, and there was a
strong tendency to do the same in later Judaism where Wisdom
was personified and even seen as the consort of Yahweh.
Clearly something of the sort had caught on at Corinth.
Christianity was seen as the new wisdom. Its teachers were
viewed as purveyors of the new wisdom. And they, the
Corinthians, were in the position of judges between an Apollos,
a Paul, a Peter: they could discriminate between teachers, for

they were wise! This utterly misconstrues the nature of the gospel, of Christians, and of their Christian teachers: so Paul, in his First Epistle, has first to destroy, and then to build up.

First, he destroys their idea that Christianity is wisdom. It is radically different from the wisdom of this world. The world in all its wisdom never arrived at a knowledge of God: had not God declared in Scripture that he "will destroy the wisdom of the wise, and will bring to nothing the understanding of the prudent"? (1:19) No, the Christian message is sheer folly, for it centres round a crucified Jesus. Scarcely any wisdom there! A crucified man is a failure, on any showing. And even had he been the most glowing success, ultimate wisdom could not have been found in a particular — every educated man since the day of Plato knew that it reposed in general maxims, ideas, and the like, of universal significance. That is how a Greek would have reacted to the preaching of the cross. But precisely because of this misplaced Corinthian reliance on wisdom, Paul determined to preach nothing but the cross: folly, indeed, to men, but to those who had tasted its saving power, the wisdom of God (1:18).

Second, Christian teachers are not teachers of wisdom, as the Corinthians thought. That is to give them at once too high a place, as though they were anything at all in independence of God (3:7ff), and too low a place, as though they were accountable to the Corinthians for what they taught and did (4:1–13). It is to forget that the cross is not something merely to be taught about but to be lived; it is not just the content of apostolic doctrine but the pattern of apostolic life. What arrogance for the Corinthians to assume that the heavenly powers had so come upon them that they had entered on their reign, and could sidestep the way of the cross in the exuberance of an experience of resurrection. The scorn of Paul's rebuke cannot be missed even in translation. "You have come into your fortune already. You have come into your kingdom — and left us out. How I wish you had indeed won your kingdom; then you might share it with us! . . . We apostles are fools for Christ's sake, while you are such sensible Christians. We are weak; you are so powerful. We are in disgrace; you are honoured" (3:8ff). In other words, the apostles live the way of the cross, and the Corinthians, for all their spiritual gifts, do not.

So Paul turns to their third mistake, to suppose that they could sit as judges on their ministers, just as they would on any wandering sophist who came to initiate them into his

particular brand of Greek wisdom. They had no right to judge
their leaders, overconfident as they were in the richness of
their own spiritual gifts. Paul's biggest problem at Corinth
was a band of lawless, charismatic Christians who regarded
spiritual gifts as a substitute for the way of the cross, for
obedience to Christian leaders, for holiness of life, and for love
of the brethren. Is it surprising, therefore, that Paul should
dub these gifted charismatics "carnal", "babes in Christ"?
They regarded others who lacked their gifts as "psychic" or
unspiritual; it was they themselves who demonstrated all the
characteristics of men whose behaviour was not governed by
the Spirit, despite the amount they talked about him. They
were still psychic Christians (3: 3), whose daily behaviour was
governed by the natural appetites of their fallen nature, not
by the unity, humility, love, holiness and teachings of Christ.
Therefore Paul tells them that it makes little difference to him
how they account of him. It is not their judgment now that
he has to face, but Christ's judgment at the last day: and they
will have to face it too. They are not the judges, but the judged.
And the Lord who knows every man through and through
will apportion praise in the last day. In the meantime, they
would be wise to do less boasting about wisdom, and more
copying of the apostolic way of living and suffering and dying
along the way of the cross, after Jesus.

Any attempt, then, to claim wisdom as a spiritual endowment
is a mark of unspirituality. God has not called the men who
reckon themselves wise, and who as spiritual people, regard
"psychic" (i.e. ordinary, second-class) Christians as fools
(3: 18, 2: 14). On the contrary, he has called those who know
they are fools, to confound the wise (1: 26f). For the only
source of wisdom is God. He will not have anybody boast in
his presence. It was entirely his work that these Corinthians
were in Christ at all, and in Christ alone could they find
wisdom, right standing, holiness, and redemption (1: 30).
Any boasting, therefore, was rigorously excluded.

Paul thus goes out of his way to attack Corinthian pride and
misconceptions about wisdom. There is indeed a Christian
wisdom. But they lacked as yet the maturity to take it in
(2: 7f). In the verses which follow, Paul goes on to show that
it centres on Christ, it embraces the cross, and it is imparted by
the Spirit. It is a broad word, this wisdom. In Ephesians, for
instance, Paul applies it to the whole mystery of our redemption,
our acceptance in Christ, and the riches of God's grace (1: 8).
He prays that God would give them the spirit (Spirit?) of

wisdom in revealing to them more of the Lord, the hope to which he calls them, the wealth and glory of the share he offers them among his people in their heritage, and how vast are the resources of his power open to those who trust him (Ephesians 1: 17f). Wisdom, this gift of the Spirit, would seem to be, therefore, a many-splendoured thing (Ephesians 3: 10): it springs from Christ in whom all wisdom is hidden (Colossians 2: 3), is nourished by the word of Christ learnt and relied on (Colossians 3: 16) and includes practical wisdom in behaving in a Christian way to those who are not Christians (Colossians 4: 5).

James also speaks of the practical, peaceful way in which divine wisdom will show itself (3: 13). It is a gift that God promises to the believer who asks in faith (James 1: 5). And James writes to his readers about it in a way that Paul could easily have echoed towards the Corinthians.

> Who among you is wise and clever? Let his right conduct give proof of it, with the modesty that comes of wisdom. But if you are harbouring bitter jealousy and selfish ambition in your hearts, consider whether your claims are not false. This is not the wisdom that comes from above; it is earth-bound, sensual, demonic. For with jealousy and ambition come disorder and evil of every kind. But the wisdom from above is in the first place pure; then peace loving, considerate, and open to reason; it is straightforward and sincere, rich in mercy and in the kindly deeds that are its fruit (James 3: 13–18).

This seems to be the nature of the wisdom to which Paul is inviting the Corinthians once they have renounced their claims to man-made wisdom and the arrogance to which it gives rise.

There seems to be little to justify the neo-Pentecostal claim that the wisdom to which Paul refers in his list of spiritual gifts is "the sudden and miraculous giving of wisdom to meet a particular situation, answer a particular question, or utilise a particular piece of knowledge, natural or supernatural" (Bennett, op. cit. p. 163). In the first place, there is no suggestion in 1 Corinthians that this word of wisdom is supernatural and miraculous. Paul was not dogged by any division between natural and supernatural: he saw God as the author of both. All true wisdom comes from him. Second, there is little enough in the New Testament usage to suggest that the gift is sudden. The one verse that could properly be adduced to the contrary is Luke 21 : 15. Here Jesus promises to give his followers "a mouth and wisdom" when they have to bear testimony for him in unexpected circumstances. But rather than suppose that this is a sudden gift of wisdom, in contrast to the normal usage of the New Testament, it is surely more likely to mean that our Lord will give us when a crisis is upon us, the ability to enunciate the broadly based understanding of his salvation which has been growing in us for years. Certainly other references in Luke do not suggest that wisdom is a sudden gift. On the contrary, Jesus and John the Baptist are both said to have grown in wisdom as they grew in years (Luke 2 : 40, 52). We are therefore likely to be on the right track if we interpret the gift of wisdom as a settled disposition of mind, illuminated by the Lord the Spirit, which has a broad understanding of the purposes of God, the Scriptures, and supremely of Jesus himself and his cross.

The gift of discernment

There is one final gift in the Pauline list, the abilities (plural) to distinguish between spirits. This is not just spiritual discernment in the broad sense of the term, but the varied abilities that are needed to discern whether a spirit is from God or not. In a church as charismatically alive as Corinth it was a gift of crucial importance.

Take the matter of tongues, for instance. Tongues, as we have seen, can be a vehicle for the Spirit of God. It can also be psychologically induced, and was a perfectly well-known phenomenon in paganism. The Corinthians had probably engaged in it in their pagan days, so we read in 1 Corinthians 12 : 2. And the hang-over from those days remained in church; some people who laid claim to be speaking in tongues inspired by the Spirit were actually calling down a curse on Jesus (12 : 3). The gift of discernment was needed here.

Or take the question of exorcism. In Acts 16 : 17 the evangelists Paul and Silas were pestered by a girl who kept on shouting, "These men are servants of the Supreme God, and are declaring to you a way of salvation". Perfectly true, they were doing just that. But Paul had the spirit of discernment. He realised that this testimony came from a demonic spirit in the girl, and he exorcised her: "I command you in the name of Jesus Christ, to come out of her", and it went out there and then. Jesus also showed the same gift of discerning spirits when he refused to accept testimony to who he was from demons, even though they spoke the truth (Mark 1: 23ff, 5: 7f). This is the gift of discernment which Paul has in mind.

Or take the gift of prophecy. How are you to know if the man who claims to be a prophet is really speaking from God or making it up? David Watson, in his excellent book *One in the Spirit*, gives us three tests to go with this capacity to discern between spirits, three tests, indeed, which inform that capacity of spiritual discernment.

The tests are clear. (a) Is Jesus Lord of that person's life? "No one can say that Jesus is Lord except by the Holy Spirit" (1 Corinthians 12: 3); (b) Is Jesus Christ acknowledged as Perfect Man and Perfect God? "By this you know the Spirit of God: every spirit which confesses that Jesus Christ has come in the flesh is of God" (1 John 4: 2). (c) Is there a measure of true godliness and holiness about the person? "Every sound tree bears good fruit, but the bad tree bears evil fruit . . . Thus you will know them by their fruits" (Matthew 7: 15–20).

There are other criteria that were applied in the early Church. One was, it seems, the length of discourse. 1 Corinthians 14: 29, 30 imagines a situation in church where one prophet is in full flow while another is sitting by, anxious to have a word. Paul urges "the others" (perhaps other church leaders, perhaps others with the gift of discernment between spirits) to use their faculty of discernment. And then he goes on, "But if someone else, sitting in his place, receives a revelation, let the first speaker stop. You can all prophesy one at a time, so that the whole congregation may receive instruction and encouragement." Presumably, the longer the prophet goes on, the more likely he is to be talking from his own ideas rather than from the Lord! He is to sit down and keep quiet, so that the brother with a fresh message direct from the Lord can make it known.

A further test which came to be applied, as we saw earlier, in Montanist days, was the willingness to submit to Church leadership, and to allow Scripture to be decisive. God is not the author of confusion, and he is not the source of any teaching through a so-called prophet which conflicts with the apostolic testimony about Jesus, nor with duly appointed leadership loyal to that standard. Paul anticipates this test in a piece of biting satire at the end of 1 Corinthians 14. "Did the word of God originate with you? Or are you the only people to whom it came?" he asks, as he upbraids them for their individualism and arrogance. "If anyone claims to be spiritual or a prophet, let him know that what I write to you is a command from the Lord. If any one does not recognise this, he himself is not recognised (i.e. by God). In short, my friends, be eager to prophesy; do not forbid tongues; but let everything be done decently and in order." Notice here the supreme place he accords to his own apostolic testimony to Jesus. If a man is truly spiritual, if he is a prophet speaking from God, he will know and respect and abide by the apostolic testimony. The prophet does not add new items of revelation to "the faith once delivered to the saints". His is a gift of direct speech from God to console, teach, or evangelise by taking some element in that apostolic revelation and applying it with power to the situation in hand. At the same time, Paul is rebuking them for their unwillingness to abide by his authority as their spiritual leader: charismatic revelations sometimes make it hard for the recipients to abide by church order!

One of the most interesting passages we possess on the discerning of spirits comes in the *Didache*, chapter 11. "Not everyone who speaks in a spirit is a prophet, but only if he has the behaviour of the Lord. From his behaviour, then, the true prophet and the false prophet shall be known. And every prophet who teaches the truth, if he does not do what he teaches, is a false prophet." The emphasis on godly living is very strong, and it is also very specific. "Concerning apostles and prophets, act thus according to the ordinance of the gospel. Let every apostle who comes to you be received as the Lord (Matthew 12: 31 seems to be indicated). But let him not stay more than one day, or if need be a second as well; but if he stay three days he is a false prophet." Clearly, there were wandering Christian teachers claiming to be apostles (not, presumably, apostles of Jesus Christ in the sense that the twelve were, but apostles sent out by the churches, cf 2 Corinthians 8: 23, Philippians 2: 25) or prophets, who were on the make for themselves. They got free accommodation and respect, and even tithes from the congregation (*Didache*, 13). But if they stayed on longer than they were needed, it was a clear mark of their self-centredness. The same applied to food. "No prophet who orders a meal in the spirit shall eat of it. Otherwise he is a false prophet," is the wise advice which the unknown Christian writer of the *Didache* offers, in order to guard against the abuse of hospitality. The same shrewdness is applied to finance. "Whosoever shall say in a spirit, 'Give

me money or something else', you shall not listen to him; but
if he tell you to give on behalf of others in want, let none
judge him."

We find much the same shrewd ethical appraisal of those
who claimed the prophetic gift in the writings of Hermas.
"Try the man who has the Spirit of God by his life. First, he
who has the Spirit of God which proceeds from above is meek,
and peaceable, and humble and refrains from all iniquity and
the vain desire of this world, and contents himself with fewer
wants than those of other men; he does not speak privately
(Hermas means, as he goes on to explain, that the true prophet
speaks during the meeting of the church, when men offer up
prayer to God; then the Spirit fills him, and he speaks to the
multitude as the Lord wills) and the Holy Spirit does not
speak at the whim of man, but only when God wishes." On
the other hand, "Hear in regard to the spirit which is earthly,
empty, powerless and foolish. First, the man who seems to
have the Spirit exalts himself, and wishes to have the first seat,
and is bold and impudent and talkative and lives in the midst
of many luxuries and many other delusions, and takes rewards
for his prophecy." The conclusion is short and to the point:
"Try by his deeds and his life the man who says he is inspired"
(*Mand.* 11).

This is precisely the criterion which Jesus himself had laid
down long before. "Beware of false prophets who come to you
in sheep's clothing but inwardly are ravening wolves. You will
know them by their fruits . . . Not every one who says to me,
'Lord, Lord', shall enter the kingdom of heaven, but he who
does the will of my Father who is in heaven. On that day
many will say to me, 'Lord, Lord, did we not prophesy in
your name, and cast out demons in your name, and do many
works mighty in your name?' And then I will declare to
them, 'I never knew you; depart from me, you evildoers' "
(Matthew 7: 15–23).

It is interesting to notice that in its early days, at any rate,
Montanism recognised this criterion. Epiphanius tells us that
Montanus said, "Behold, man is like a lyre, and I rush upon
it like a plectrum. Man sleeps and I awake. Behold, the Lord
is he who throws the hearts of men into ecstasy, and gives to
men a new heart" (*Haer.* 48: 4, 1). In other words, the Spirit
is not only the author of ecstasy but of ethics; he arouses the
heart, and he gives a new heart. No doubt there is an allusion
to those words of Jesus on the true and the false prophet in
Matthew 7 when Maximilla, one of Montanus' prophetesses

claimed plaintively, "I am chased like a wolf from sheep; I am not a wolf; I am word, and spirit, and power" (Eusebius, *H.E.* 5: 16. 17). Nevertheless Maximilla was a wolf after all. One of the criteria for true prophecy was, as we have seen, the difficult one of fulfilment. "After me," says Maximilla, "there will be no more prophets, but only the consummation" (Epiphanius, *Haer.* 48: 2. 4). The Church used the gift of discernment, recognised that Maximilla was not speaking from the Spirit of God, and decisively (perhaps too decisively) rejected the Montanist movement.

There are few gifts of the Spirit more necessary to the Church than this gift of discernment. The Catholic charismatic Fr. Kilian McDonnell writes of this as the greatest problem in the whole movement:

> There is some uncritical acceptance of prophecy and tongues without sufficient discernment as to what comes from the Holy Spirit and what comes from the human psyche. Discernment of spirits is one of the major on-going problems of the renewal. It should be remembered that the final judgment as to the authenticity of the charisms belongs to those who preside over the Church, and to whose special competence it belongs not indeed to extinguish the Spirit, but to test all things, and hold fast to that which is good.

These, then, are the nine gifts of the Holy Spirit which are commonly held among Pentecostal Christians to be the supernatural endowments open to all believers who have been baptised with the Holy Spirit. We have already seen that the category of "Spirit-baptised Christians" over against ordinary Christians is not one which we can reconcile with the New Testament. We have also seen that the New Testament writers do not distinguish between natural and supernatural gifts by the Spirit. What remains to be done is to examine whether there is any justification for restricting the gifts to nine.

4. *Charismatic gifts*

The number of the gifts

There seem to me to be two important reasons why it is impossible to treat these nine gifts as exhaustive in number and quality. The first is that Paul gives various lists of spiritual gifts or functions, and the lists differ. They oscillate between spiritual gifts and spiritual functions, but this should not surprise us if we remember that the various types of ministry in the Church are all called God's gift to his people (Ephesians 4: 11). Ministers are just as much God's gift to us as are spiritual gifts. The two belong together, for spiritual gifts are meaningless unless exercised by spiritual people, intent on serving the Lord with their gifts.

Paul gives three lists of gifts in chapter 12 of 1 Corinthians: the first in verses 8–10, the second in verse 28 and the third in verses 29, 30. The first list contains the nine gifts we have already considered: a word of wisdom, a word of knowledge, faith, gifts of healing, miracles, prophecy, the ability to discern between spirits, tongues and interpretation.

There is a second list in 1 Corinthians 12: 28. Here Paul gives a special order of importance to the first three, which are apostles, prophets, teachers, possibly because all three involve the use of the mind as well as the other aspects of the personality (and we know that he felt this was very important from the whole argument in 1 Corinthians 14), and certainly because all three are concerned with building up the whole Church in the gospel. Then follow miracle workers, healers, helpers, administrators, and speakers in various kinds of tongues. Apostles, teachers, helpers, administrators have come into the list; interpretation of tongues, faith, discerning of spirits, the word of knowledge and the word of wisdom have dropped out.

In the next two verses Paul gives a slightly different list. Once again he combines people, i.e., apostles, prophets, teachers, with qualities, i.e., miracles, gifts of healing, speaking with tongues and interpretation. Once again the gifts of wisdom and knowledge, faith and discernment have dropped out, as compared with the first list; so have helpers and administrators (rôles not highly prized in Corinth!) as compared with the second; whilst interpretation of tongues has found its way back. It is beginning to appear very precarious to argue that any one of the three lists is exhaustive and definitive of the gifts the Spirit can bestow.

This impression is confirmed by the other lists in the Pauline letters. In Romans 12: 6–8 he mentions prophecy, service, teaching, exhortation, contribution, giving help and doing acts of mercy. Only prophecy remains from the original list of 1 Corinthians 12: 8–10.

In Ephesians 4: 11 the emphasis is all on teaching. The gifts of the ascended Christ to his Church are apostles, prophets,

7

evangelists, pastors and teachers, all of whom are called to equip the Christians for service.

One might add the famous passage in Galatians 5: 22f, where Paul enumerates nine characteristic aspects of the fruit of the Spirit in the Christian's life: love, joy, peace, patience, kindness, goodness, faith (or fidelity), gentleness and self-control. Peter, too, refers to two typical Christian *charismata* in 1 Peter 4: 10f, namely rendering service and speaking the oracles of God; another list comes in 2 Peter 1: 5ff, where to initial Christian faith are added virtue, knowledge, self-control, fortitude, piety, brotherly kindness and love.

It is by now quite evident that all these lists are seeking to give samples of what the Spirit will do in the life of the believer, not to make exhaustive lists of gifts, some of which are to be labelled natural and some supernatural. It is of course true that some of these gifts are striking and exciting, such as prophecy, tongues and healing compared with more ordinary and dull gifts like administration, helping people, or teaching. But the same Spirit is active in both. And Paul's estimate of the relative value in the church of the several gifts of the Spirit is made pretty clear by the fact that in each of the three lists in 1 Corinthians 12 he places tongues and their interpretation at the bottom of the list, whereas the Corinthians would have put them at the top! Moreover, gifted though he was in this direction himself, he preferred to play down the more obviously showy and "supernatural" gift of tongues in worship and to speak, however briefly, as a Christian teacher so that he could edify not merely himself but others. "I thank God that I speak in tongues more than you all. Nevertheless, in church I would rather speak five words with my mind, in order to instruct others, than ten thousand words in a tongue" (1 Corinthians 14: 18f) — a proportion of one to two thousand!

The meaning of "charisma"

There is another reason for supposing that we would be wrong to imagine that the nine gifts of 1 Corinthians 12: 8–10 are the only or even the typical *charismata* which the Spirit bestows. The word *charisma*, which has become common coin among Pentecostals and neo-Pentecostals to denote the gifts of 1 Corinthians 12: 8–10 (with particular emphasis on tongues, interpretation, prophecy and healing), literally means a gift of *charis*. And *charis* in Greek denotes God's unmerited love to us. It is instructive to see how the word is used in the

New Testament. Do we find it applied to these nine gifts and them alone? Do we find it restricted to a special class of Christian?

The word is exclusively Pauline apart from 1 Peter 4: 10, which encourages us to use the gifts that have been given us by God, notably speaking his oracles and engaging in his service (neither precisely to be found in 1 Corinthians 12: 8–10). Paul uses it some 16 times, and in a variety of ways. Above all, he uses it of the gracious forgiveness of God in contrast to Adam's disastrous rebellion (Romans 5: 15, 16). To put it another way, men deserve to be paid death for their actions; God, however, makes us a gracious gift, *charisma*, of eternal life (Romans 6: 23). He uses it of the gracious deliverance God gave him from some terrible but unspecified peril (2 Corinthians 1: 11); of the results of the mutual fellowship he expected with the Christians at Rome (Romans 1: 11); of Timothy's ordination (1 Timothy 4: 14, 2 Timothy 1: 6); of God's faithfulness towards his rebellious people Israel (Romans 11: 29); and of marriage (or, alternatively, celibacy) as being a gracious *charisma* of God (1 Corinthians 7: 7). To cap it all, he encourages the Corinthians to long for the best gifts, and in the very next verse begins his hymn to love, thus indicating unmistakably that the greatest of all God's gracious gifts to Christian people is the gift of love, God's very own nature, imparted to us through the Spirit (1 Corinthians 12: 31, 13: 1ff). The charismatic gifts are nothing other than the gifts of God's love. They begin with our redemption. They include the heightening of qualities already present or latent within us, such as gifts of administration, leadership, teaching, marriage, or celibacy. These natural qualities can be *charismata* if, and so long as, they are dedicated to the service of the Lord and the building up of his people in the strength that he gives. If they are used selfishly they can be disastrous. The same is true of the gifts which are beyond normal ken, such as prophecy, tongues, discernment of spirits, healing and exorcism. They too can be a blessing or a curse, depending on whether they are used for the common good or the gratification of the member who possesses them. But all these gifts, inherent and acquired alike, are brought to their head in love, the greatest of them all,[1] and the one which is available to all.

---

[1] It is sometimes argued in neo-Pentecostal circles that love is nowhere said in the New Testament to be a *charisma*. It stands, therefore, apart from the gifts we have been considering. I do not think that this argument will stand. For one thing, 1 Corinthians 13, the great hymn on love, follows immediately upon Paul's

To be a Christian is to be a charismatic. There is no division between charismatics and non-charismatics, between "haves" and "have-nots" in the one-class community of Christ. All alike are charismatics; for all alike are eternally in debt to the sheer *charis* of God who sought us, rescued us, equipped us with varying gifts, and shared his own loving nature with us through the Spirit which he has lavished upon every one of us who are in Christ.

injunction, "be very anxious for the greater (or greatest?) gifts (*charismata*). And moreover I show you the way in abundance (*kath huperbolēn*)". He then proceeds to show the primacy of love, the very life of God. It is supremely apposite to bring love forward at this point, particularly after having refused, in verses 21–6, to countenance any ranking in gifts. For love means self-giving, not self-assertion: it is the way of service, the way Jesus himself adopted. Paradoxically, therefore, love is the greatest of the gifts which permit of no priorities! A second passage which seems to make plain that love is one of the *charismata* is Romans 12. In verse 6 he recalls that we have *charismata* differing according to the grace given to us by God; and after teaching, leading, giving, acting mercifully, he moves naturally on to love. Irrespective, therefore, of the etymology which suggests love is a *charisma*, Romans 12 and 1 Corinthians 12 assert it.

CHAPTER II

What are we to make of the Charismatic Movement?

IT IS IMPOSSIBLE to write on the subject of the Holy Spirit these days without taking full account of the charismatic movement, which is affecting churches throughout the world and right across the theological and ecclesiastical spectrum. Consideration of the *charismata* in the previous chapter leads naturally on to the three questions which will occupy us in this chapter. Should we expect to see the charismatic gifts in the Church today? What are the strengths and the weaknesses of the movement which promotes their use? And is it possible for "charismatics" and "non-charismatics" to live together unitedly and effectively in the same church?

1. *Should we expect to see the charismatic gifts in the Church today?*

Have the gifts died out?

Christians in the main line of both Catholic and Protestant traditions have for a long time been very scared of allowing that these gifts of the Spirit of which we read in the New Testament might be expected to occur today. They are supposed to have died out in the apostolic era.

It is much more comfortable to suppose that this is the case, and to look for the contemporary manifestations of the Holy Spirit in the peace and order of the Church of today rather than in the violent irruptions of earlier days. Both Catholic and Protestant camps have been heavily infected by the rationalism of the Enlightenment, and our Christianity has been unduly cerebral (hence its appeal to the educated only). If the Corinthians were inclined to identify the work of the

Spirit with the abnormal, we tend to make the opposite mistake, and suppose that he can only manifest himself in moral renewal, spiritual illumination, and through either Bible or sacraments according to our theological reference! This attitude, however, is mere escapism from exposing ourselves to the Spirit's powerful life. He remains the Spirit of wind and fire; he remains sovereign in the Church, and is not to be boxed up in any ecclesiastical compartment. It is simply not the case that healing, prophecy, exorcism and speaking in tongues died out with the last apostle. Still less can a passage like 1 Corinthians 13:8 ("as for prophecies, they will pass away; as for tongues, they will cease . . .") be adduced to attest the supposed demise of these gifts. They will pass away only when "the perfect comes", i.e. at the Parousia—not at the end of the apostolic age or the formation of the New Testament canon! There is in fact plenty of evidence in the sub-apostolic days, and periodically throughout Church history, to show that these gifts did not die out, though they were often viewed with great suspicion by Church authorities. I have gathered together some of the sub-apostolic material in my *Evangelism in the Early Church*. And it is perfectly evident from the widespread growth of the Pentecostal Church and the neo-Pentecostal movement in the last fifty years that God has poured out these gifts in rich measure on his people, rationalistic and sceptical though we have been about them.

A place for tongues?

We should, therefore, expect the Spirit of God to show himself as God. We should neither reject speaking in tongues, nor regard it as the be-all and end-all of spirituality. A Catholic charismatic evaluation is valuable at this point: "It is clear that the issue of the renewal is not tongues, nor an insistence that praying in tongues is in any necessary way tied to the spiritual realities received in initiation. Many outside the renewal attribute a centrality to tongues which is not reflected in most sectors of the renewal. On the other hand, those involved in the renewal rightly point out that this *charisma* was quite common in the New Testament communities. It should neither be given undue attention nor despised. Since it is the lowest of the *charismata*, it should not be a matter of surprise that it is so common!"

That is a wise and balanced statement of the truth as the New Testament confronts us with it. We should, therefore, rejoice when a member of the congregation discovers that he has the gift of tongues. Of course, we should be wary. The gift of tongues does not edify anyone else unless it be interpreted; otherwise it is for private use in a man's own devotions. It is clear that not all Christians have this gift, that it is no mark of the signal blessing of the Holy Spirit, and that it may well not be given us even if we ask for it (1 Corinthians 12: 10, 30). I have myself asked God for it, and have not received it: instead he has given me other gifts, and these it is my duty to exercise to the full. I am glad, therefore, that tongues is no more indispensable a part of true Christian living for us than it seems to have been for Jesus. But I rejoice when one of my friends receives this gift. It is a way in which the deep sub-conscious parts of our being can be caught up to praise the Lord; and this brings release, deep joy, peace, and the longing to spend time with God in prayer which nobody who has experienced the gift will deny.

Of course, there are counterfeits. The Corinthians were reminded at the outset of 1 Corinthians, chapter 12, that speaking in tongues is no more exclusively Christian than circumcision was exclusively Jewish. But God takes over, in the case of circumcision, a rite that was widely practised among pagan tribes; in the case of tongues, a psychological phenom-enon that was and is widely experienced: and he uses both as media for his Word, his love, his assuring of believers. If you have this gift, therefore, praise God in ordinary words, and praise him in tongues; sing to him in ordinary words, and sing to him in tongues. Do not be embarrassed to dance before the Lord in the joy the Spirit gives. Allow him to rid you of the inhibitions that may for too long have kept you over-cerebral and sub-personal. Be careful not to regard this gift as the mark of super-spirituality on your own part, something that sets you apart. It is nothing of the sort. Moslem mystics speak in tongues; and, as William Sargent has shown in his *Battle for the Mind*, tongues can be psychologically induced in men who have no faith at all. There is a fascinating story from the charismatic movement of the last century among the Irvingites, of how a young sceptic went to criticise one of their meetings, and found himself speaking in tongues—to his great surprise. In consequence he underwent a conversion from the philo-sophical position of Hegel and became a Zoroastrian! No, tongues is not an exclusively Christian or even religious phenomenon, so there is no ground for pride among those who possess it.

But if you don't possess it, and if after prayer you still do not receive it, do not let that worry you. God has some other gift or gifts for you. It may well be that you do not need tongues. It may be that you need the gift of administrative ability, or of being prepared to act in a subordinate position under someone else's leadership. And, believe me, those gifts to the Church (and they are nothing less than priceless gifts) need just as great an effusion of the Spirit's enabling as does speaking in tongues. Only you will be very careful not to denigrate the gift of tongues which you do not possess. You will neither write off those who have it as extremists nor be secretly jealous of them. For you know that there is one Spirit who gives gifts as he chooses for the building up of the body of Christ, and you will be grateful for the rôle he has chosen for you, and the gifts with which he has equipped you.

A place for healing?

It may be that God has given you a gift of healing. Perhaps you will be used to heal regularly in this way, as a man like Oral Roberts is in America. Perhaps God will use you only once; as happened in the case of a vicar I knew intimately, who was once impelled by a deep inner urge to lay hands on his paralysed son – and the boy recovered: but never afterwards did the gift come back to him. If healing is your gift, rejoice, and use it for the good of those to whom God leads you. But remember the dangers which beset the use of such a gift: the danger of showing off; the danger of supposing that to heal without means is more spiritual than to heal with means – as if God were not the author of all healing, whether through orthodox medicine, acupuncture, hypnosis, psychotherapy, or spiritual healing. You will be tempted to think there is some special property in oil or hands imposed upon the patient. You will be in danger of playing God, and assuring men that they will recover when they will in fact die. You will be in danger of supposing that suffering may not even form part of the permissive will of God, and thereby perhaps underestimate the rôle which suffering has in keeping us dependent on the Lord's strength which comes to fruition in weakness (2 Corinthians 12: 9). You will be tempted to think that God is using you because of some special virtue of your own. The Israelites of old had to learn that God had not chosen them because they were great or holy, but in order to show something of his love in them (Deuteronomy 7: 7) and the same is true of the election and the gifts of God today. So remember the dangers, while you rejoice in the gift for the good of others. And wise is the church that does not restrict its rôle in healing to spiritual solace, but allows scope for those of its members who are gifted in this way to exercise their gift with love and humility alongside the more usual medical methods.

A place for exorcism?

Increasing numbers of Christians are finding that they are called upon to perform exorcism these days. This is perhaps because when, as is so common in our own society, God is driven out of the front door, demonic forces crowd into the house by the back door. Did Jesus not warn us of precisely this danger (Luke 11: 24f)? At all events, there is a most notable increase in black and white magic and in demon possession. Sometimes this comes about by deliberate surrender to the power of evil, as long ago Faust is reputed to have sold his soul to the devil. Sometimes it comes by mere physical contact with, for instance, a charm brought back from an animistic country where it was offered in worship to demons. Sometimes it may be that a house is troubled by an evil spirit, or a group of youngsters start toying with spiritism. We in the West have too long pooh-poohed the idea of demon possession, and we are paying for our arrogance by a marked increase in demonic activity. Why otherwise should a leading intellectual bishop head a report on exorcism? It is a real gift of the Spirit of God, and it certainly did not die out in the apostolic era—fortunately for us. If God gives you the gift of exorcism, thank him, and use it humbly and believingly, knowing that this is often how the Spirit worked in the early Church when the gospel was spreading so fast. Tertullian, for instance, could say to pagans who mocked at Christ:

Mock as you will, but get the demons to mock with you! Let them deny that Christ is coming to judge every human soul. . . . Let them deny that, condemned for their wickedness, they are kept for that judgment day. . . . Why, all the power and authority we have over them is from our naming the name of Christ, the Judge. Fearing God in Christ and Christ in God, they become subject to the servants of God and Christ. At our command they leave, distressed and unwillingly, the bodies they have entered (*Apology* 23).

I do not pretend to understand demon-possession. But I know that it is real, and have on occasion been instrumental in exorcism. But let nobody who has this gift sniff out demons under every bush or in every common cold. Very often there are medical, psychological and spiritual maladies all inter-twined in a person who is demon-possessed, and it is naïve in the extreme to think the case can be cured by pills or E.C.T. alone, by psychotherapy alone, or by spiritual ministry alone. All three may well be needed. Perhaps the surest test of whether a person is demon-possessed or not is to see if he reacts violently at the name of Jesus. This was a characteristic of demoniacs in the days of Jesus' life on earth; and it still is Christ's name which causes profound disturbance to a person who is demon-possessed or dabbling in the occult. "Every spirit that confesses that Jesus Christ has come (or 'is coming') in the flesh is of God, and every spirit which does not confess Jesus is not of God. This is the spirit of antichrist, of which you have heard that it was coming, and now it is in the world already," declares John (1 John 4: 3f). He continues, "Little children, you are of God, and have overcome them; for greater is he that is in you than he who is in the world". The power of the Spirit is greater than the demonic forces that oppress and sometimes possess mankind. And we are right to claim his power in casting out evil forces that remain impervious to medical and psychological treatment. The local church should expect some of its members to be equipped by the Spirit to deal with exorcism, and they should be supported by the prayers of the congregation, for theirs is a perilous work, as those who have engaged in it know.

Prophecy for today?

Nor is there any reason to suppose that prophecy died with the apostolic era. As we have seen in the previous chapter, prophets were alive and well in the second century, and it was only the less acceptable face of Montanism which drove prophecy into disrepute and assumption under the rôle of the bishop. It is encouraging that this gift has been recovered in our day, and that men and women do, as the Spirit leads them, give a word direct from God to their congregation, provided that the local church as a whole recognises the validity of the gift, and encourages them to use it. To be sure the man so gifted needs to remember that it is all too easy for him to be mistaken and confuse his own message with that of the Spirit of God. Much of what is put out as prophecy is banal in content and couched in Elizabethan English! He needs to be clear that God has no further revelation to offer outside Jesus Christ, and therefore that if his prophecy is genuine it will not be dissonant from the prophetic Scriptures of the Old and New Testaments with their focus in Christ. He will not be averse from having his prophecy tested and verified. Quite apart from the assessment of those gifted in discernment, the Old Testament criterion of a true prophet is demanding enough in all conscience:

> When a prophet speaks in the name of the Lord, if the word does not come to pass or come true, that is a word which the Lord has not spoken (Deuteronomy 18: 22).

He will not be bemused by the divine source of his gift into supposing that he is more spiritual than the lady who provides the tea after the meeting at which he has spoken.

But just as the man with this gift needs to beware of these dangers, so does the local church. Let them beware of supposing that only the man with the dog-collar can speak from God in their midst. Let them beware of despising a direct word from God, or fearing to enter into the depth of fellowship where such things could take place. There is in many churches still a terrible famine of hearing the Word of the Lord; and that does not merely mean that the preaching is of an indifferent standard, and the Bible largely misunderstood or little used. The really shocking thing is that congregations are expected (by themselves as much as by the clergy) to keep quiet, and be passive apart from the singing of the hymns. In the Church of the New Testament, and in many churches to-day where charismatic gifts are made welcome, there is an orderly but real opportunity for those who have a message from the Lord to share it simply and directly with the rest of the congregation. Those who speak and those who hear alike are edified.

In a word, just as the "charismatic" Christians need to remain humble and not feel that they are on a higher spiritual level, so the "non-charismatic" Christians, if I may so mis-call them, need to heed Paul's injunction, in a context where he has been talking about the exercise of spiritual gifts, "Do not quench the Spirit. Do not despise prophesyings. Test all things. Hold fast that which is good" (1 Thessalonians 5: 19ff).

2. *What are the strengths and weaknesses of the charismatic movement?*

It is a truism that our weaknesses are very closely allied with our strengths. This is certainly true of the neo-Pentecostal surge in the world Church these days.

In the realm of vitality

It is a movement of life, dynamic spiritual life, in the midst of a Church that has looked very dead in many areas. Vibrant, youthful, unco-ordinated life easily leads to excesses in the spiritual realm just as it does in the physical. Yet where would we be without youth? The church that is determined "not to have any of this charismatic stuff round these parts" may well be putting up a "Keep Out" notice to the Spirit of life in Christ Jesus. The church at Corinth could certainly be taken to task for its many failings, but thank God for the life and rich spirituality of such a church that made possible such failings! To how many modern churches would 1 Corinthians need to be written at all?

It is a movement of faith, deep and real faith in God. Belief that with God all things are possible; belief that the promises of God are meant to be claimed today and not regarded as historical by-gones to be dissected by theologians. It is a revolt against the strait jacket of Protestantism, confining the Spirit to an article in the creed, and of Catholicism, confining the Spirit to predetermined persons and sacraments. It is a revolt against the dead hand of theology which can publish endless dreary (if technically correct) books about the Spirit without ever suggesting that the authors know the power of the Spirit in their lives. What an encouraging sign of life this is. But it lays itself open to various dangers. The danger of spiritual *naïveté*. The danger of anti-intellectualism. The danger of overvaluing the more showy gifts. And the charismatic movement has fallen into all these dangers; but mercifully its leaders have learnt fast, and the intense vitality of the movement is being channelled into healthy growth in these areas where they have been weak.

It is a movement of the gospel, the full-blooded call to repentance, new life, and a new life style through conversion to Jesus and reception of his Spirit. To their credit, the charismatics have refused to remain content with the traditional Catholic tendency to equate water baptism, *tout simple*, with

Christian initiation; or with the traditional Protestant tendency to identify it with intellectual belief in the preached word; or with the typical Evangelical insistence on personal reception of Christ into the life at conversion. They have made it quite clear that you can have all these things, but still remain a pauper in the palace of the King. Unless the Spirit is welcomed as Lord of the life in all his love and power, it is a very sorry Christian life that you will have. And this is a much needed stress. Christianity had become practically binitarian and the Holy Spirit a respected and respectable stranger. But with the proper God-centred emphasis of the charismatic movement went an unbalanced rejection of the earthbound, social gospel which has been characteristic of much Christianity in this century. In consequence its record for social concern and political involvement has been very poor, as friendly critiques, like d'Epinay's *Haven of the Masses* and Hollenweger's *The Pentecostals*, have pointed out and documented.

In the realm of holiness

It is a holiness movement, and sprang from a tradition of such movements. To my observation, many but by no means all of the people who have claimed a "charismatic experience" have in fact become more loving, more unselfish, more dedicated, more reliable and more prayerful than they were before. But this very fact can give rise to the very same danger that there was at Corinth; of the recipients of certain spiritual gifts (particularly tongues) regarding other Christians as second-raters, and even maintaining that the gift is the gateway to spiritual power and character. Quite apart from the fact that Paul is careful to distinguish the fruit of the Spirit in terms of character from the *charismata* of the Spirit in terms of gifts, even a superficial glance at the Corinthian correspondence makes it abundantly plain that these highly charismatic folk were notoriously weak in holiness of life: party strife, gross immorality, disbelief in the resurrection, disorder at the eucharist, chaos in church, criticism of leaders, and so forth, were all too evident. The arrogance that one finds sometimes among immature charismatic people today is no less distressing. Claiming to be superior and to have arrived, they are often cruelly condemning in their attitude to others and refuse to take advice from anyone who is not of their own type of spirituality. This often springs not from any particularly vicious spiritual pride, but from false teaching to which they have been introduced on the subject of initiation, seeing it as a two-stage affair; other Christians may have reached stage one, but they have, through a "baptism in the Holy Spirit" attained *ipso facto* to stage two—a mountain ridge from which they are unable to descend whatever they do (for they are the Spirit-filled folk; they have arrived), a mountain ridge which relieves them of any further necessity to go on climbing. This two-stage initiation theory has already been examined and found wanting. Here it is enough to point to the tragic irony of one of the most loving and effective Christian ministers I know being written off as unspiritual by his son simply because that unstable youth, as he was then, had received the gift of tongues, and his father had not. So long as this arrogance remains among charismatic people they will get and will deserve opposition from within the Church.

In the realm of fellowship

The charismatic movement is a corporate movement, designed to let the different limbs in the body of Christ express their several gifts in harmony. It is the very antithesis of the ministerial exclusivism which afflicts churches of all denominations, where nothing can be done without the minister, and where the conduct of worship is a responsibility shared (or fought over) between him and the organist! It aims to allow room for every member to play his part; the hymns may not be the ones the organist would have chosen; the prayers may come from many lips, not those of the priest; the most powerful word of exhortation may come from a bank clerk, not from the preacher. It is a revolutionary, corporate conception of "body-life". This partly accounts for its appeal. The congregation are no longer an audience, but participants. The priesthood of all believers, so long assented to as a doctrine, has become a reality. And when this happens it can cause tremendous problems. Some ministers try to clamp down on it, because they feel threatened with unemployment, instead of realising that if all the congregation came alive in this way, the pastoral work of the minister would be multiplied ten times over! But there are failures on the side of the charismatics too. They may tend to take little notice of the duly constituted ministry in the local church. They either bow to the dictates of the fashionable charismatic guru of the hour, or to their own ideas; have they not arrived? Does God not speak directly through them in prophecy and heal through them? What need have they for

the stuffy old minister? It is back to the Corinthian situation
once again. Back to the problems which gave rise to the
Epistle of Jude or 2 Peter, where arrogant charismatics, who
thought they had arrived spiritually, were taking no notice of
God's gift to his people, in the shape of the local ministry. It is
interesting that 1 Thessalonians 5 does not only need to say
(to the cautious "non-charismatics") "Do not quench the
Spirit. Do not despise prophesyings", but also (to the pushful
"charismatics") "Respect those who labour among you and
are over you in the Lord and admonish you, and esteem them
very highly in love because of their work." Both injunctions
are still needed.

Then again, the charismatic movement has made fellowship
in the Spirit a reality for many to whom the word "fellowship"
had been almost meaningless. The life-giving Spirit of Christ
has brought the love of Christ into personal relations for
countless modern Christians. Members really do care for one
another and are not ashamed to express their love in embraces,
their joy in dancing, their concern in praying openly for one
another, their trust in open confession and costly reparation
to one another. The depth of the fellowship at local level is one
of the most moving characteristics of the whole movement.
It results in a very high level of sacrificial service, boundless
hospitality, and that caring love for brothers in Christ that
finds nothing too hard to do or bear for them.

On a wider canvas, at a time when the Ecumenical Movement after more than sixty years is showing some signs of
effeteness, the charismatic movement draws its members from
every denomination under the sun, and bids fair to become the
new ecumenism, but with this difference. It derives its vitality
not from the big bosses at the top, but from the common life
in the Spirit experienced at local level among believers, be
they Catholics or Lutherans, Pentecostals or Methodists,
Baptists, Dutch Reformed, Orthodox or Moravian. It is
fellowship at grass roots level and in great depth; therein lies
its power.

The Spirit gives unity, and the charismatics show it in a
degree of love and commitment to one another which is
probably unrivalled in any other strand of contemporary
Christianity. But in this unity lurks its own special temptation.
Fellowship at depth is sometimes restricted to the like-minded,
those Christians who have had a similar experience of the
Spirit. In many a local congregation the coming of the
charismatic movement has spelt an incalculable deepening of

fellowship: but in many others the very reverse has occurred. Instead of enriching the fellowship, it has rent the congregation in two. Similarly, on the ecumenical front, it is true that the charismatic movement binds together men and women from all the different denominations in a way the Ecumenical Movement never began to approach, but it does so at a price. The price paid can sometimes be the virtual exclusion of Christians who do not share the "charismatic experience", and a tendency to dub doctrine unimportant because it divides, whilst emphasis on experience in the Spirit unites. If great care is not taken, therefore, experience becomes the criterion of truth, not truth of experience. And the church which failed because it was too cerebral will give place to the church that fails because it is too non-rational.

The minus . . .

There is plenty more that could be said. F. D. Bruner in his *Theology of the Holy Spirit* has pointed out, from models in the Corinthian correspondence, three striking contrasts.

The charismatics were always out for *more*, and Paul was always insisting that Christ and Christ alone was the blessing for Christians. Any doctrine that adds something to Christ, as some charismatics do in their cry, "Christ, yes, but beyond Christ you need the Spirit", stands self-condemned.

The charismatics were always out for *power*; they were elated by spiritual power, and were always seeking short cuts to power. It is the same today. Paul's reply is to boast not of his power but of his weakness, through which alone the power of Christ can shine. Paul knew all about the marks of an apostle, in signs, wonders and mighty deeds (2 Corinthians 12: 12) but he knew that the power of an apostle, or of any other Christian, came from the patient endurance of suffering, such as he had with his thorn in the flesh, or the patient endurance of reviling and hardship such as he was submitted to in the course of his missionary work (1 Corinthians 4). The charismatics had a theology of the resurrection and its power; they needed to learn afresh the secret of the cross and its shame . . . which yet produced the power of God (1 Corinthians 1: 18).

The charismatics were always out for *evidence*. That is why tongues and healings and miracles were so highly esteemed among them. But Paul knows that we walk by faith while we are in this life, not by sight. There are many times when God

calls on us to trust him in the dark, without any supporting
evidences.

...and the plus

But it would be churlish to end this brief evaluation of the
charismatic movement on a negative note. I believe it has
done much more good than harm. I believe that it has
emphases which the modern churches will neglect at their
peril. It has taught us to believe in God's reality and his ability
to break into the even tenor of our lives with the invading
power of his Spirit. It has taken the doctrine of the Spirit off
the dusty shelf and put the person of the Spirit right in the
heart of the living-room. It has taken the formality, the
stuffiness, the professional domination, the dreary predicta-
bility out of worship, and made it living, corporate, uplifting
and joyful. It has recognised the variety of gifts God has given
to his people, discovered some which had been forgotten for a
long time, and increasingly insists on a structure of church life
where these gifts can be exercised. It has brought together in
intimate fellowship men and women of the most diverse backgrounds. It has driven the silent Christians into bearing joyous
and courageous witness to their Lord. It has taken seriously the
dark element of Satan and the demonic, and has revived among
Christians the sense of spiritual battle. It has opened the flood
gates to prayer and praise in many a heart that had run dry.
In every generation, God raises up some counterpoise to the
current weakness and abuses in his Church. In our own day
he has raised up this remarkable movement which we call
charismatic. It would be tragic if the Church did not learn
from it what God wants us to learn.

This leads directly to our third question.

3. Can order and freedom be reconciled in today's Church?

The tension between order and freedom...

The traditional churchman is highly suspicious of any
pretensions by members of the congregation to direct leading
by the Holy Spirit. Such a claim seems a very horrid thing to
him, just as it did to the Bishop of London when Wesley made
it in the eighteenth century. Order cannot risk allowing the
responsibility of freedom to the Spirit. On the other hand, the
man who is drunk with his experience of the liberating Spirit

of God is tempted to lose patience with the institutional church and pull out into "free" worship among like-minded friends. The charismatic distrusts order, and the tradionalist fears freedom.

It will prove to be a great tragedy if charismatics and non-charismatics cannot live together in peace and harmony in the same church; tragic if we have learnt nothing in the centuries since Paul wrote to the Corinthians. Paul prized order in the Church, for order was a mark of the faithfulness of the Lord the Spirit. Paul equally loved freedom in the Church, for freedom was what the Spirit came to bring us. He knew that order could degenerate into the peace of the graveyard, and freedom turn into the chaos of the revel. The enthusiasts must remember not to do for the Spirit what he does not do for himself, and that is to seek the limelight. The traditionalists must remember that they do not control the Spirit, but that the Spirit creates, indwells and leads the community of the Church. That is why they need not fear to trust him. For the Spirit, at once free and orderly, will not lead the prophets all to speak at once, or the tongues-speakers to hold forth when there is nobody present who will interpret. The charismatics must not make the mistake of always identifying the Spirit's activity with the abnormal; nor of supposing that they have a monopoly of the Spirit, for he is no less present through other gifts and other members of the one body. The more institutionally-minded must for their part be patient if the new wine of the charismatics sometimes breaks the old wine-skins of traditional Church deportment; be understanding if some aspects of the Spirit's work are for a while given a false perspective; and be prepared to learn from the charismatics renewed zeal, deeper devotion to our Lord, and a willingness to take risks for God and be fools for Christ's sake, if need be, whilst committing themselves afresh to the preaching of the gospel and prayer.

In practice it will mean making room within the worshipping life of the congregation for those who have special gifts to exercise them. It is not good enough to approve of the charismatic movement in a benevolent way without making room for the gifts of tongues, prophecy and healing to be used in the mainstream of the Church's life for the benefit of its members. It will not do to restrict these activities to a somewhat secretive mid-week meeting for those who like that kind of thing. If they are gifts at all, they are gifts for the body of Christ, and should be exercised when the congregation meets.

How this will be done needs to be worked out locally. Perhaps the most appropriate occasion would be in the context of the Holy Communion. In churches which have a liturgy, there is already room for freedom and flexibility within that liturgy. Generally speaking, much more participation from a variety of members of the congregation is possible than is in fact practised. Naturally, care must be taken not to make too many innovations too fast. It is impossible to overestimate the conservatism of most congregations. But given patient teaching, love, and a gradual introduction of new features, a congregation can be prepared to welcome hitherto unused and unrecognised gifts; the fellowship can be maintained; and order and freedom can fertilise one another. It really should not be beyond the capabilities of men dependent on the Spirit of God to combine freedom and order, provided that both sides realise that they have complementary and partial insights into the nature and operation of the Spirit, who is so much bigger than our apprehension of him. Alone, both emphases distort the gospel; together, they build up the one body of Christ infused by the Spirit, the one temple of God in which, for all their different emphases, he is pleased to dwell (Ephesians 2: 22). It will certainly not be easy: but then, who ever promised Christians an easy life?

The tension between the order and renewal arises most acutely in three particular areas, the ministry, the church and Christian initiation.

. . . in the Ministry

Charismatics often distrust the settled institutional ministry. It was so in the first century, as 2 Peter and Jude show us; it was a pressing problem in the second century, as the *Didache* makes plain. It still is. And the problem has two main roots.

In the first place, charismatics distrust the institutional ministry for a very proper reason; namely that many priests identify ministry with office, and suppose that no effective ministry can be carried out within the church apart from their own official ministrations. In a word, the official ministry, so far from fulfilling its God-given function of building up the saints for their work of service to the Lord (Ephesians 4: 12) in fact prevents the body acting as the body, with all members taking their proper part. Ministry gets concentrated in the hands of the official; and then not only the official but every part of the body is harmed, because the various members are not allowed to make their contribution. How often have loyal but heartbroken Christians with a special gift for the local congregation told me that they are not allowed to exercise it "because the vicar does not like it". Charismatics are right to distrust the ordained ministry when it misuses its role in this way.

But there is another cause for their unrest, which is not so worthy, though it is readily comprehensible. Charismatics tend to distrust the ordained ministry because often the clergy do not seem to share the intense experience of the Holy Spirit which they themselves enjoy. The ministers concerned feel the hurt of being mistrusted, reckon that the charismatics are immature, and perhaps resent the influence they may have in the church. This again is the tragedy of the half truth. The Spirit does not restrict himself to the charismatic, nor to the official. Office is not the enemy of *charisma*: Paul can speak of ordination as a *charisma* of the Holy Spirit imparted to Timothy by the laying on of his hands and those of his fellow presbyters (1 Timothy 4: 14, 2 Timothy 1: 8). The Holy Spirit can be as really present at (or absent from) a Catholic ordination as a Pentecostal praise meeting. There need be no antipathy between charismatic gift and catholic order so long as the charismatic does not repudiate the function of oversight to which the ordained minister is called by the Lord, and the latter does not presume to think that he and he alone is the "spiritual" man in the congregation, and that none of them can possibly have, or be allowed to exercise, a spiritual gift which he lacks. The way of Jesus, the way of love, the way of building up the body, will refuse to allow a wedge to be driven between order and *charisma*.

... in the Church

The second area where this tension between freedom and order is becoming very pressing is the matter of schism. Since the church down the road is so manifestly unspiritual, we "spiritual people" had better get out, and found one of our own. Alas for the presumption in claiming to obey the Spirit's leading when specifically disobeying the Spirit's commands in Scripture to maintain unity. Alas for the arrogance of supposing that the ensuing church will be any more spiritual than the one from which we have seceded. Charles Spurgeon is reputed once to have answered one such "spiritual" woman who was in search of the perfect church, "You will not find it, madam, this side of heaven; and if you do find it, don't go near it: you will only spoil it". Secession is not God's way: throughout the long history of the Bible, God shows himself as the one who revives, reforms, and remakes vessels which have disappointed. He is the one whose Spirit does not scrap the valley of dry bones, but breathes new life into them. Not even in the Letters to the Seven Churches in Revelation is there any suggestion that one should secede from a "dead" church. It would be ludicrous, were it not so pathetic and damaging, to imagine that any company of sinful human beings could exorcise unspirituality from their midst by the simple expedient of seceding from those they could not easily get on with. What, then, would become of the new humanity, embracing Jew and Gentile, male and female, barbarian and educated, slave and free man—that fellowship of love and unity which was, as we have seen, the Spirit's home in New Testament days? It is through renewal, not secession, that God has purified his people from Abraham's day to our own. When individuals or groups separate, they show that they are not the men of the Spirit which they take themselves to be (1 Corinthians 3: 3). It is wrong, therefore, for charismatics to secede from a church because of its lack of spirituality. It is right for the leadership in the church to exercise control over individual charismatics. But this does not mean that in a properly ordered church they will cease to exercise their gifts. Far from it. The Lord who gave a settled ministry to his Church stemming from the Twelve, also gave prophets to his Church who owned no succession. It was the function of the prophets to prevent the Church from identifying her tradition with the will of God without further question. They were, and still can be, God's gad-fly, his stinging pointers to the truth, when his Church is in danger of sleeping and growing complacent. They must not be silenced.

Of course, just as the official ministry is in danger of identifying the Spirit with traditional ways of doing things, or with traditionally sacred symbols; so the prophet can fall into the trap of identifying the Spirit with his own interpretation of events and even with his own prejudices. Paul was well aware of that, and he appealed not to any legalistic sanctions but rather to the prophet's own sense of discrimination, and that of his fellows, to curb arrogance and wordiness (1 Corinthians 14: 29–32). The prophet is no more immune from the temptations of the world, the flesh and the devil than is presbyter or bishop. Sometimes the word of God will come through the prophetic man; sometimes through the bishop. As Haddon Willmer put it in a most penetrating article on *The Holy Spirit in the Church*, "The bishop may himself be the prophet, and in him the institution itself may become prophetic — or it may not. It follows that no lines can be drawn in advance beyond which the prophet may not go for fear of disturbing the unity of the church." Often, indeed, the tension in church circles will be great. I imagine that there was tension enough at the Council of Jerusalem in the days of the Acts. The mark of the Spirit's presence, Willmer continues, is "not the absence of argument, but its quality. Love that is patient, enduring all things, hoping all things, keeps in check that frustration and despairing touchiness which drives the controversialist to the bitter, boastful and rude extravagances which deprive divisions of the hopefulness characteristic of the Spirit. Love keeps the prophetic spirit from gloating over other men's sins and leads them to delight in the truth, by which alone controversy can be made fruitful" (*Church Quarterly*, April 1971, p. 292f).

. . . in Christian initiation

The third area of tension between *charisma* and order in the Church concerns the whole subject of what makes a man a Christian. There has long been tension, even within the same church, between those who have placed the main emphasis in Christian initiation on the sacraments and those who have placed the main stress on belief in Jesus and conversion. Into this tension has come a further complication. The charismatic movement has made a habit of speaking of the overwhelming experience of God which characterises it as "baptism in the Holy Spirit". This has been both perplexing and distressing to sincere Catholics and Protestants alike, but it should prove to be a most healthy disturbance. For it reminds us that there are three ways, not two, of defining the nature of the Church.

One may think of the Church as an extension of the Old Testament people of God. The Catholic church at large has tended to do this. And there is excellent biblical evidence to support such a view. In the Acts of the Apostles Jerusalem is the centre of the visible Church throughout the world; the Jerusalem church embodies and continues the history of salvation from the days of Abraham onwards. That note is struck on the day of Pentecost when Peter appeals to his hearers to repent and save themselves from "the crooked generation". This is an allusion to Deuteronomy 32: 5 where the true members of Israel are called upon to show themselves distinct from the crooked generation of apostate Israelites around them. The inference is plain. The Church is the true Israel; unbelieving Israel is the crooked generation; to be baptised and join the Church is to show oneself within the true historic Israel of God. The same point is made in Acts 3: 25, 26. Believers in Jesus must show themselves to be the true Israel, in genuine succession to Abraham, by joining this community, entered no longer by circumcision but by baptism. It is instructive to see how the Old Testament name for the people of God, *hoi hagioi*, "the saints", is ransacked by the New Testament writers and applied to the Church (Acts 9: 13, 32, 41 etc.). The Church is the true Israel, and it is entered by baptism. That is the Catholic case in a nutshell. And it is part of the truth.

Another way of defining the Church is to see it as the fellowship of believers. Protestants at large have tended to do this. Once again, there is excellent biblical evidence that can be adduced in support, and from the very same quarry, the Book of Acts. One might turn to the description of Christians as "the believers" which comes so frequently throughout the book (2: 44, 4: 32, 5: 14 etc.). This company was entered by repentance and faith (2: 38, 16: 31). Baptism is the mark and the badge of the believer, for only believers have the right to claim personally what Christ achieved for all men. That is the prevailing Protestant understanding of the Church. And it is part of the truth.

But a third way of looking at the Church has been staring us in the face all down the centuries, and we have been blind to it. The great characteristic of the New Testament Church is that it consisted of men and women who had received a living experience of the Spirit in their own lives. That is what turned the first disciples from a company of disappointed men whose leader had died, risen, and left them, into a Church— reception of the Spirit. That is what marked out those Christians at Samaria once their initiation was complete—a manifest reception of the Holy Spirit. That is how Peter saw that he must swallow his principles and baptise Cornelius— the man had clearly become a Christian, because anyone could see as clear as a pikestaff that his life was radiant with the Spirit. It is one of the merits of J. D. Dunn's *Baptism in the Holy Spirit* that he recognises the centrality of receiving the

Spirit in the New Testament definition of the Church. "What is the distinguishing hallmark of the Christian?", he asks at the conclusion of his book, and continues, "Our study has given us the N.T. answer to this question with some precision; with remarkable consistency the answer came: That man is a Christian who has received the gift of the Holy Spirit by committing himself to the risen Jesus as Lord, and who lives accordingly." It is the Pentecostal movement we have to thank for drawing attention to this crucial New Testament definition. It is perfectly possible to be baptised and to be a believer but not to have the Spirit of the Lord in your life.

It is easy to see the abuses in any one of the three ways of defining the Church that we have just considered, when taken in isolation. The important thing is to see that they all belong together in the purposes of God for his people. It was possible for the author of Acts to embody in his account these three quite different ways of looking at the Church, and yet he would have been amazed had he been told that in later centuries these three would have been set in competition against each other. In a truly biblical theology Christian initiation consists quite simply of three actions which belong together, though they may be widely separated in time and may be received in any order. They are repentance and faith by the individual, water-baptism by the Church, and the giving of the Holy Spirit by God. There is no room in a biblical theology for any further initiation into the Christian community, whether it be through confirmation by the bishop (as some "two-stage Catholics" might argue), or by a "baptism in the Holy Spirit" (as some "two-stage Pentecostals" might maintain). By the same token it will not do for a man simply to say "I am baptised: therefore I am a Christian", or "I have believed in Christ; therefore I am a Christian". The charismatic would very properly point such people to the New Testament where there are clear signs of being a Christian, signs brought about in the life of the individual by the Spirit once he has been welcomed in. They may (or may not) be notable gifts such as prophecy and tongues, but the fruit of the Spirit may be expected in every Christian life. If there is no love, no joy, no peace, no gentleness and goodness, no faith, no self-control then there is no evidence that the Spirit is planted in such a life, no evidence that the man is initiated into Christ, however valid his baptism and however loud his protestations of faith. If there is no sense of wonder and joy at being sons of God, if there is no compassion and concern for other brothers and sisters in the same family, if there is no prayer, no praise, no love of the Scriptures, no desire to reach others with the good news, then—let us face it—it is not New Testament Christianity that we are talking about any more. And the charismatic movement has drawn attention to this fact in no uncertain way.

Marks of the Spirit

To return, then, to our quest for order and freedom within the Church, what marks of the Spirit's work shall we expect to see? We should ask ourselves where reconciliation is being effected; where unity is being guarded without crushing spontaneity; where fellowship is deep and honest; where worship is live and real, shared in by the whole body. We shall look to the place where evangelism has a high place among the priorities of the individual and the congregation alike—for the Lord the Spirit is no less present in the conversion of the penitent than in the tongues of the charismatic. We shall expect to see the work of the Spirit in the interdependence of the church membership, where love controls attitudes, and where gifts are used for the good of the community, not for the gratification of the individual. Such a church will be very much concerned with building up its members in obedience to the Lordship of Jesus; for to live under that Lordship is both the Christian's baptismal confession and his undying obligation. In the church where the Spirit is given freedom, the charismatic will not obtrude his gift, and the settled ministry will not fear it. Both strands need each other in the corporateness of the body of Christ; and both will, in the church where the Spirit is obeyed, resist the temptation of seceding from their sometimes awkward bedfellows. They will guard the unity which the Spirit gives, in the peace, joy and mutual service which are engendered by the same Spirit. Even when they stand together they are not complete. For the Church on earth can never be that. It was a Gnostic failing to imagine that the truly inspired man had the fulness of the divine Spirit in him *now*. Paul taught the Corinthians a better perspective. We never have the fulness of the Spirit *in ourselves alone*, but only as we are incorporate in that body, that temple in which the Spirit demonstrates the varied beauty of his harmony. And we never have the fulness of the Spirit *in this life alone*. For the Spirit does not give us his fulness in the world of time and sense. He is the first instalment of God's future. He is the guarantee of heaven. And life in the Church here and now is at best only a foreshadowing of the unity and service, the harmony and love, the final and complete reconciliation, the unending praise and worship, of heaven itself. This is no "pie in the sky when we die". It is the final climax of a reality we already enjoy if we are able to say from personal experience and commitment, "I believe in the Holy Spirit".

FOR FURTHER READING

The literature on this subject is immense, and I append only a sample. I have divided them into serious theological studies (marked with an asterisk, *) and books, paperback or otherwise, which are designed primarily for the general reader. In some instances I have put a few words of comment after the title for the guidance of those who may feel lost in the extensive and wide-ranging plethora of literature on the subject. Books which derive from Pentecostal or neo-Pentecostal sources, or are sympathetic to the charismatic movement are indicated thus †.

* C. G. Baeta, *Conflict in Mission* (S.C.M.)
* C. K. Barrett, *The Holy Spirit and the Gospel Tradition* (S.P.C.K.)
* K. Barth, "The Christian Life: Baptism as the Foundation of the Christian Life" in *Church Dogmatics* IV. 4 (Clark)
† Dennis Bennett, *The Holy Spirit and You* and *Nine o'Clock in the Morning* (Coverdale). Theologically unreliable, but exciting reading
*† Arnold Bittlinger, *Gifts and Graces* and *Gifts and Ministries* (Hodder). Thoughtful charismatic theological writing
* Raymond Brown, "The Paraclete in the Fourth Gospel", *New Testament Studies*, 1967, pp. 113–32, and *The Gospel according to John* (Anchor Bible)
* F. D. Bruner, *A Theology of the Holy Spirit* (Hodder) a major theological appraisal of Pentecostal claims, but lacking in empathy
* J. H. Charlesworth ed. *John and Qumran* (Chapman). See especially A. R. C. Leaney's article "The Johannine Paraclete and Qumran"
† Larry Christenson, *Speaking in Tongues* (Coverdale). Lutheran charismatic study

* J. G. Davies, *The Spirit, the Church and the Sacraments* (Faith Press) and "Pentecost and Glossolalia" in *Journal of Theological Studies*, 1952, p. 228–31

† Leslie Davison, *Pathway to Power* (Fountain Trust)

F. W. Dillistone, *The Holy Spirit in the Life of Today* (The Canterbury Press)

A. L. Drummond, *Edward Irving and His Circle* (Clarke)

*† J. D. G. Dunn, *Baptism in the Holy Spirit* (S.C.M.). Perhaps the most influential treatment of the Spirit in modern times, particularly concentrating on Pentecostal theology, its strengths and weaknesses. Also "Spirit and Fire Baptism" *Novum Testamentum*, 1972, pp. 81–92. "Spirit Baptism and Pentecostalism" *Scottish Journal of Theology*, 1970, p. 397ff. "2 Corinthians 3: 17 — The Lord is the Spirit" in *Journal of Theological Studies*, 1970, p. 309ff—an unconvincing article. "John 6—A Eucharistic Discourse?" in *New Testament Studies*, 1970, p. 328ff — strongly anti-sacramental

† S. Durasoff, *Bright Wind of the Spirit* (Hodder). An indifferent documentary of modern Pentecostalism

C. L. d'Epinay, *Haven of the Masses* (Lutterworth). A study of Pentecostalism in Chile by a sociologist

J. E. Fison, *The Blessing of the Holy Spirit* (Longman)

* Ernst Fuchs, *Christus und der Geist bei Paulus* (Leipzig)

* R. H. Fuller, "Tongues in the New Testament" *American Church Quarterly*, 1963, p. 162ff

† J. Goldingay, *The Church and the Gifts of the Spirit* (Grove Books). A brief but careful and balanced interpretation of 1 Corinthians 12–14

* R. H. Gundry, "Ecstatic Utterance (NEB)" in *Journal of Theological Studies*, 1966, pp. 299–307

* N. Q. Hamilton, "The Holy Spirit and Eschatology in Paul" in *Scottish Journal of Theology* Occasional Papers 6, 1957

† Michael Harper, *None Can Guess, As at the Beginning*, and *Spiritual Warfare* (Hodder). Descriptive of contemporary neo-Pentecostalism

* G. S. Hendry, *The Holy Spirit in Christian Theology*. Highly suggestive

* D. Hill, *Greek Words and Hebrew Meanings* (C.U.P.)

* L. Hodgson, *The Doctrine of the Trinity* (Nisbet)

† A. A. Hoekema, *What about Tongue Speaking?* (Eerdmans)

*† W. J. Hollenweger, *The Pentecostals*. A massive, critical and sympathetic consideration of classical Pentecostalism

† H. Horton, *The Baptism in the Holy Spirit* and *The Gifts of the Spirit* (Victory Press)

* J. H. E. Hull, *The Holy Spirit in the Acts of the Apostles* (Lutterworth)
* W. James, *The Varieties of Religious Experience* (Longmans)
* Nils Johansson, "1 Corinthians 13 and 1 Corinthians 14", *New Testament Studies*, 1964, pp. 383–92
* E. Käsemann, *Essays on New Testament Themes* (S.C.M.)
* L. E. Keck, "The Spirit and the Dove" in *New Testament Studies*, 1971, pp. 41–68
* R. A. Knox, *Enthusiasm* (O.U.P.)
* Hans Kung, "The charismatic structure of the Church" in *The Church and Ecumenism*
* Kirsopp Lake, *Beginnings of Christianity* 5, Notes 9 and 10 (pp. 96–121)
  G. W. H. Lampe, Two notable articles on the Holy Spirit in The Interpreter's Dictionary of the Bible (Abingdon Press) and in Hastings' Dictionary of the Bible (revised edition, Clark). Also * *The Seal of the Spirit* (Longmans), *"The Holy Spirit in the Writings of St. Luke" (in *Studies in the Gospels* ed. Nineham, Blackwell) and * *St. Luke and the Church at Jerusalem* (Athlone Press)
* E. Lombard, *De la Glossolalie chèz les premiers chrétiens et des phenomenes similaires: Etude d'exégèse et de psychologie* (Bridel, Paris)
* R. C. Moberly, *Atonement and Personality* (Murray)
  C. F. D. Moule, I have been greatly helped by two of his unpublished papers, *The Gift of the Spirit to the Church* and *The Holy Spirit in the Church*. *Christ and Spirit in the New Testament*, studies in honour of C. F. D. Moule (ed. Lindars and Smalley, Cambridge) is a mine of useful material
† W. Nee, *The Normal Christian Life* (Victory Press)
* L. Newbigin, *The Household of God* (S.C.M.) A seminal work showing the strengths and weaknesses of Catholic, Protestant and Pentecostal conceptions of the Church
* J. E. L. Oulton, *Holy Communion and Holy Spirit* (S.P.C.K.)
* E. M. Pattison, "Behavioural Science Research on the Nature of Glossolalia" in *Journal of the American Scientific Affiliation*, 1968, p. 73ff
† Graham Pulkingham, *Gathered for Power* (Hodder). The story of a church reborn
* H. Wheeler Robinson, *The Christian Experience of the Holy Spirit* (Nisbet). A classic from 45 years ago
  Dorothy Sayers, *The Mind of the Maker* (Methuen). Original and creative work
† Sam Shoemaker, *With the Holy Spirit and with Fire* (Harper)

* W. R. Schoemaker, "The use of RUACH in the Old Testament and of PNEUMA in the New Testament" in *Journal for Biblical Literature*, 1904

*† E. Schweizer, *Spirit of God* (Black), being an abbreviation of his article *Pneuma* in the *Theologisches Wörterbuch zum Neuen Testament* (ed. G. Kittel) and *Church Order in the New Testament* (SCM). Both of these works are invaluable

* E. F. Scott, *The Spirit in the New Testament* (Hodder)

† J. L. Sherill, *They Speak with Other Tongues* (Hodder)

* S. Smalley, "Spiritual Gifts and 1 Corinthians 12–16" in *Journal for Biblical Literature*, 1968, pp. 427–33. "Spirit, Kingdom and Prayer in Luke–Acts" in *Novum Testamentum*, 1973, pp. 59–72

* N. H. Snaith, *The Distinctive Ideas of the Old Testament* (Epworth)

J. R. W. Stott, *The Baptism and Fullness of the Holy Spirit* (IVF). A careful biblical dissuasive from the charismatic movement

* B. H. Streeter, *The Spirit* (Macmillan)

* J. P. M. Sweet, " 'A Sign for Unbelievers': Paul's attitude to Glossolalia" in *Journal for Theological Studies*, 1966, pp. 240–57. A significant study of a very difficult passage

* H. B. Swete, *The Holy Spirit in the New Testament* (Macmillan). Old, but invaluable and cool examination of the N.T. material

* Bengt Sundkler, *Bantu Prophets in South Africa* (O.U.P.)

J. V. Taylor, *The Go-Between God* (SCM) Superb, imaginative, poetic, but not adequately enough based in Scripture

* L. S. Thornton, *The Doctrine of the Holy Spirit* (Epworth)

*† Simon Tugwell, *Did you receive the Spirit?* Able Catholic charismatic work, which however evades the basic issue of baptism in the Spirit

† D. C. K. Watson, *One in the Spirit* (Hodder). Perhaps the most balanced short and positive evaluation of the charismatic movement

Douglas Webster, *Pentecostalism and Speaking in Tongues* (Highway Press)

† John Wesley, *Journal* (Epworth)

† D. Wilkerson, *The Cross and the Switchblade* (Hodder)

* E. W. Winstanley, *The Spirit in the New Testament* (C.U.P.)

* J. E. Yates, *The Spirit and the Kingdom* (S.P.C.K.)

* A Report of the Special Committee on *The Work of the Holy Spirit* to the United Presbyterian Church in the U.S.A.,

1970. A most careful evaluation of current neo-Pente-
costalism
*† *Statement of the Theological Basis of the Catholic Charismatic
Renewal*, ed. Fr. Kilian McDonnell, 1973
The Church Quarterly, April 1971 (various articles)